Laura Corn

101 Nights of Grrrreat Sex

Secret

Seductions for

Fun Loving

Couples

PARK AVENUE PUBLISHERS

Published by:
Park Avenue Publishers, Inc
Oklahoma City, Oklahoma

Printed in the United States of America

ISBN 1-56865-494-4

DISCLAIMER
PLEASE READ BEFORE PROCEEDING

This book is sold with the understanding that it is intended solely for the use of informed, consenting monogamous adults, tried, true, trusting and tested, who want to add a full year of dash and flash to their love life. The author is not a medical doctor or therapist. She has, however, studied this subject intensely for the past five years and is the author of a previous best selling book in this genre. Almost every recipe in this book has been recommended by doctors and leading sexual therapists.

The reader is cautioned that following the suggestions and scenarios contained herein is strictly voluntary and at the readers risk and discretion. Also, while the positions and products mentioned in the book are safe and satisfying for the majority of adult women and men, every individual is unique and you should not employ any position or product which is not suitable to your physical or sexual limitations.

Neither the author, publisher or distributor endorses any specific product or assumes any product liability for any product mentioned in this book. The choices and responsibility for any consequences which may result from the use of any product or following any suggestion or scenario herein belong to the reader.

The author and Park Avenue Publishers, Inc. shall have neither liability nor responsibility to any person or entity with regard to any loses or damage caused or alleged to be caused, either directly or indirectly, by the information contained in this book.

If you do not wish to be bound by the above understanding, you may return the book intact to Park Avenue Publishers, Inc., PO Box 20010, Oklahoma City, OK 73156, for a full refund of the purchase price of the book.

Cover Design Concept by Ron Larson

ACKNOWLEDGEMENTS

I am deeply indebted to a host of people who made this book possible. I have been especially fortunate to have so many wonderful teachers, friends and business associates. To each of them, I extend my heartfelt gratitude:

First and foremost, to the women and men in radio all across this continent, the brightest, funniest, hardest working people in creation, who provided the forum and granted me the audience which made my first book, "237 Intimate Questions Every Woman Should Ask A Man", a best-seller while enabling me to gather the knowledge and material for "101 Nights of Grrreat Sex."

To Joann Rossi, my friend, counselor, and confidante, whose contribution to both the concept and content of the book is priceless and whom I cannot thank enough for her loyalty, patience and dedication.

To Marty Bishop, DJ extraordinaire, whose fertile imagination and flair permeates this book and for whom I cannot find words eloquent enough to express my gratitude for his inestimable assistance and contribution.

To Bill Wright, my forever friend and shepherd, for his continuing support, faith and love through all the ups and downs. You love unconditionally and motivate me to achieve the impossible. No one has had more positive influence on me in my life.

To Michael Hutchinson, friend and mentor for his encouragement, for championing this project and for his advice and guidance into the wonderful world of direct response.

To J.P. my best friend in the whole wide world. Thank you for sharing this journey with me. Your love, encouragement and understanding inspires me everyday.

And last, but not least I am grateful to Larry Paregis, Tim Daze, Paul Nugas, Tracy & Donald Sonck, Kimberly Bennett, Marcella Gallagher, Bill Stamps, John & Cass Corn, Linda Seto, Jay Corn, Casandria & Dorothy Moore, and Terry.

And, to all the people who bought my books, responded to me on the air, stood in line for hours for a personal word with me, endured my probing interviews and opened up their hearts, minds and souls to provide me with the most essential ingredient in this book; their desires, needs and experiences.

Finally, a personal tribute to the aforementioned radio personalities. Gals and guys, I love you all and wish I could personally repeat my thanks to each of you for your invaluable contribution. Your numbers are legion and, again I apologize for inadvertent omissions and misspellings. If I have goofed, please let me know so I can get it right next time. Thank you so much:

Jeff 'n Jer and Tommy, Kidd Kraddick, Brother Wease, Cindy & Charlie, Johnathon Brandmeier, Buz, Carol Harmon, Tim & Mark & Mike, Mark & Brian & Rosemary & Frank Murphy, Don & Mike & Rob, Mancow & Irma, Jim & Scott & Bob & Chris & Pepper, John Boy & Billy & Randy & Leigh Melvin, Bob Sayer & Dean, Erin Heart, Mary Marlow & Scott, Connie Powell, Scott & Todd & Naomi, Lamont & Tonelli, Bob & Tom & Dean, Randy Miller & Kimberly Ray, Ron & Ron & Denise, Steve & D.C. & Courtney, Eddie Fingers, Bob Berri & Jimmy the Weasel, Jeff, Mark, & Cat, Max, Tanna, & Moffit, Bob, Madison, Jason & Lisa, Kato & Dave, Bubba the Love Sponge, Charlie & Ty, Shelly, Dana, Kim Petersen & Mike Rose, Troy & Rocky & Danger Boy, Kent & Allen & Leonard & Renee & Jennifer, Mike & Tyler, Chris & Beth & Kevin, Bobby & Footy, Peter Tilden & Tracy, Alex Bennet, Matt & Dave & Kathy & Merlin, Lewis & Floorwax, Rob Johnson, Lex & Teri, Dave Ryan & Pat Ebert, Kent & Allen, Paul Barsky, Alex B & Mary Ellen, Lisa & Mike Butz & Donna, Brother Jake, Jazz McCay, Matt, Jimmy & Kim, Jesse, & Gene & Dave, Jeff Chambers, Jeff & Flash, Manson & Sheehan, Kevin Baker, Sheri & Bob, Tommy & Rumble, Nicki Reed, Future Bob, Opie and Anthony, G.G.Young, Max & Tanna, Moffit, Scott & Erica, Jason, Lanigan, Webster & Malone, Bob Rivers, Spike, & Downtown Joe, Rick & Leah, J.D. B.J. & Jeff, Mike & John, Russ, Bo, & Dirty Jim, Johnny and Corey, Jerry Williams, Steve, Bill & The Coach, Christopher & Kerrigan, Joe & Stan, McGee & Beck, The Freakin Brothers, Kerry & Bill, T.J. & Jer, Mark Shannon & Ron Spensor, Dirk & Tom, Darla, Rick, & Scott, Andy & Scott, John Patrick & Cat Thomas, Chris & Steve, Don Kelly, Mark Spears & Mercedes, Hal Abrams, Allen & Karen, Pete & Dave, Mike Pentek, Eddie & Jobo, Robin & Bob, Lee Rogers, Stevens & Pruett, Brian Shannon, Danny and Rhoda Douglas, Carol Arnold, Paul & Phil, Fred, John & Richard, Gary & Erin, Susie, Dom Testa, Coach & T.K. Skywalker, Gary Burbank & Mike McConnel, Joe Elliott, Dave Otto, Dave Sposito & Ken, Mike Thomas & Steve Rouse, Samantha & Hollywood Hamilton, Jim Murphy, Tyler, Fisher & Todd & Erin & Guy & Julie, Marc Anthony, Bo & Bamma, John McCormick, Tim Spencer, Bev Hart, Dan Weber, Terri Evans, Pat McMurry, John & Scott, Bucky Barker, Coffy & the Jammer, Matty in the Morning, Andy Barber, Pete McMurry, Barry Beck, Rick Moffit, Dr. Drex, Terry DiMonte, Jack Diamond & Burt, Jim Kerr, Skip & Ben, Bob Boz Bell, Jeff Walker, Willie Rich, Ben Baldwin, Larry & Willie, Paul & Phil, Greg And Bill, Susie Waud & Mark The Shark, Spike & Bryon, John Lyle & Steve Hahn, Chris & Fred, Jeff Styles, Dave & The Fatman, Chris & Woody, Bob And Steve, Those Guys In The Morning, Joe Nugent, Kevin & Pete, M.C. Mitch & Rob, Ted & Marla, Phil Tower, Ted & Tom, Gina Miles, Daniels & Webster, Bax & O'Brien, Rex & Tim Parker, John & Dan & Clide, Kerry & Bill, Tommy Tucker, Ben Smith, Max Stewert, Phil & Brent, Keith & the Bearman, Billy, Super Dave, & Jack, Jeff & Phil, Sam Giles, Rob Reinhart, Fanny Koeffer, Dana, Rick & Suds, Beth & Bill, Ross, Pete DeGraff, Franky C, Howie & Fizz, Jeff Slater, Ross Brittan, Dave Kirby, Dave Abbott, Lee Fowler, Buck & Peg, Greg Holt & Muddman, Mike Miller, Doug & Mike, Rick Tower, Myrna Lamb, Gary Thompson, Picozzi & The Horn, Ed, Lisa & Dr. Drai, Art Sears, Rick Moffat, & Ben & Jim & Baxter, MoJo & Buckethead, Big Dave, Bill Carroll & Mike Cartalano, Chris & Rebecca, The Duke & Beth, Jerry Hart, Byrd, Mark & Lopez, Bruce Bond, John Swanson & Kathy Hart, T.C. & Dave, Much Music - Bill Welychka & Natalie Richard, Carolyn Von Vlaardingen, Art Sears, Carol & Paul Mott, Cindi Henderson, Frank Foley, Larry Norton, Darien Mckee & Colleen, Danny & the Barber, Gary Stone, Nancy Shock, Marc Razz, Ethan Carey, Larry & Lou, Steve Hansel, Johnny Danger, Ric Walker & Brad Kopeland, Gator, Josie Vogel, Dean, Roger & Joey, Mary Marlow, Scott Taylor, Larry & Willie, Nasty Man, Clay & Janice, Dave Welsh, Steve & Johnny, Katherine John, Tony Nesbitt, Sue McGarvin, Mark Benson, Randy Miller & Kimberly, Rick Lawerence, & Brad & Jim Bone, Tim & Darren, Stew Williams, Joe Mattison, Jennifer Sexton, Kevin & The Blade, Phil & Billy, Steve Ryan, Bob & Madison, Kato & Tom, Tim & Darreen, Mel & Frank, Billy Kidd & Phil, Larry & Lou, Billy & Jack, Paul Turner, Dirk Rowley, Bill & Norman, Ben Davis, Mike Spears, Steve Downs, Susan & Scott, Chris & Rebecca, Simon Will, and Thanks Again !

TABLE OF CONTENTS

1. "I THINK I MADE HIS BACK FEEL BETTER"
Her Eyes Only

2. KING OF HEARTS
His Eyes Only

3. UP AGAINST THE WALL
His Eyes Only

4. BURIED TREASURE
Her Eyes Only

5. THE VELVET TONGUE
Her Eyes Only

6. OBSTACLE COURSE
His Eyes Only

7. DANGEROUS WHEN WET
His Eyes Only

8. THAT WILL BE THREE HUNDRED DOLLARS, PLEASE
Her Eyes Only

9. UNDER THE HOOD, COWBOY
His Eyes Only

10. LINGERIE PARFAIT
Her Eyes Only

11. ANGEL WITH A LARIAT
Her Eyes Only

12. SOMEBODY STOP ME!
His Eyes Only

13. BEAT AROUND THE BUSH
Her Eyes Only

14. FIRE DOWN BELOW
His Eyes Only

15. THE LAURA CORN CHALLENGE
Her Eyes Only

16. THE GEE! STROKE
His Eyes Only

17. TOOL TIME
His Eyes Only

18. THE THRILL OF THE CHASE
Her Eyes Only

19. SCHWING!
Her Eyes Only

20. DOWN AND DIRTY
Her Eyes Only

21. WILD CARD
Her Eyes Only

22. MR. LUCKY
His Eyes Only

23. THE SECRET DESSERT
Her Eyes Only

24. HONEY BREASTS AND CREAMY THIGHS
His Eyes Only

25. FINGER LICKIN' GOOD
His Eyes Only

26. YIELD TO TEMPTATION
His Eyes Only

27. TAKEN BY SURPRISE
His Eyes Only

28. A QUIET ECSTASY
Her Eyes Only

29. JONI'S BUTTERFLY
His Eyes Only

30. NOT FOR BEGINNERS
Her Eyes Only

31. THE ONE HOUR ORGASM
Her Eyes Only

32. WAVES OF DESIRE
His Eyes Only

33. IT'S NOT ON THE MENU
Her Eyes Only

34. DREAMY LIPS
Her Eyes Only

35. PLEASE FEED THE BEAR!
Her Eyes Only

36. HUMMMMMM!
Her Eyes Only

37. PRIMAL MAGIC
His Eyes Only

38. THE EROTIC EQUATION
Her Eyes Only

39. WHERE NOBODY KNOWS YOUR NAME
His Eyes Only

40. MATING CALL
His Eyes Only

41. SIXTY MINUTE MAN
His Eyes Only

42. TITILLATION
His Eyes Only

43. LEAVE IT TO BEAVER
Her Eyes Only

44. HALFTIME SHENANIGANS
Her Eyes Only

45. SLAVETIME!
His Eyes Only

46. LE FEMME FATALE
Her Eyes Only

47. MIRROR, MIRROR
Her Eyes Only

48. A SUDDEN GLIMPSE OF LACE
Her Eyes Only

49. NIGHT MOVES
Her Eyes Only

50. SUBLIMINAL SEDUCER
His Eyes Only

51. RADIO PURR-DUCER
His Eyes Only

52. MORNING GLORY
His Eyes Only

53. ON TOP OF SUGAR MOUNTAIN
Her Eyes Only

54. SLIP AND SLIDE
His Eyes Only

55. SWEET SURRENDER
Her Eyes Only

56. THE PERFECT TOUCH
Her Eyes Only

57. TICKLED PINK
His Eyes Only

58. THE SENSUOUS SQUEEZE
Her Eyes Only

59. DELICIOUS DETOUR
Her Eyes Only

60. TRICKS OF THE TONGUE
His Eyes Only

61. SEVEN SINFUL FLAVORS
Her Eyes Only

62. THE SPECIALITY OF THE HOUSE
Her Eyes Only

63. THE PIZZA MAN ALWAYS RINGS TWICE
His Eyes Only

64. CHEMISTRY CLASS
His Eyes Only

65. WINNING HAND
His Eyes Only

66. THE FRENCH CONNECTION
His Eyes Only

67. TENDER OUTLAW
His Eyes Only

68. PUSS 'N BOOTS
Her Eyes Only

69. THE CAT TECHNIQUE
His Eyes Only

70. WET AND WILD
His Eyes Only

71. RED LIGHT DISTRICT
Her Eyes Only

72. CYBORGASM
Her Eyes Only

73. DOUBLE THE PLEASURE
Her Eyes Only

74. BODY TEASE
Her Eyes Only

75. THE KISS OF LEATHER
His Eyes Only

76. EPICUREAN DELIGHT
His Eyes Only

77. WILD CARD
His Eyes Only

78. MUSTANG SALLY
Her Eyes Only

79. MERCY!
His Eyes Only

80. SEX IN A SHOE BOX
His Eyes Only

81. THE PLEASURE PRINCIPLE
Her Eyes Only

82. WINDOW OF OPPORTUNITY
Her Eyes Only

83. DEN OF INIQUITY
Her Eyes Only

84. EROTIC IMPULSE
His Eyes Only

85. HOT LUNCH
Her Eyes Only

86. FOR EVERY MAN WHO LOVES TO KISS
His Eyes Only

87. OUTRAGEOUS FOREPLAY
Her Eyes Only

88. PANDORA'S BOX
Her Eyes Only

89. DOCTOR YES
His Eyes Only

90. SPECIAL DELIVERY
His Eyes Only

91. THE BIG SCORE
His Eyes Only

92. HIGH RENT RENDEZVOUS
His Eyes Only

93. POINT OF NO RETURN
His Eyes Only

94. STEAM HEAT
His Eyes Only

95. THE SEXUAL LEXICON
Her Eyes Only

96. JUST FOR THE FUN OF IT
Her Eyes Only

97. THREE THUMBS UP!
Her Eyes Only

98. STANDING OVATION
His Eyes Only

99. BARELY LEGAL
His Eyes Only

100. GATES OF HEAVEN
Her Eyes Only

101. THE LAST SEDUCTION
For Both of You

INTRODUCTION TO *GRRREAT* SEX!

*I*s your sex life perfect?

Are you totally thrilled, aroused, and satisfied after every erotic encounter? Is your life behind the bedroom door absolutely, completely, overwhelmingly fulfilling?

Then put this book down!!

Somebody else needs it more than you.

Most of us, in fact, find it all too easy to let *life* get in the way of love. Jobs and bills and chores and kids all conspire to push intimacy to the bottom of our list of priorities. If we can make any private time at all for each other, it's only when we're tired and distracted. The same old moves, the same old positions, and after a while sex gets, well —

Boring. Booooorr-ring.

In survey after survey, ho-hum sex is the number one complaint of couples across the country. And it doesn't have to be that way.

Because this book guarantees grrreat sex. 101 nights of it, just like the title says!

That's every week, twice a week, for one full year. Now, I know that's a lot to ask from one little book! But I promise you that it works. Here's how —

Every week, you and your partner flip through it, discussing the titles that catch your eye. This can be a real blast — it's a little like window-shopping for sex! Each of you then tears a page from the book, and in that one special moment, you've made a serious commitment to each other. You've created a new kind of bond between yourselves.

By removing a page right in front of you, your lover has just given a promise that, no matter what, *you are going to be seduced* in a fresh, exciting, original, and highly erotic manner. Sometime during the week, *your sensual pleasure* will be the only focus. You, of course, are making the same promise in return.

Each seduction contains written out step by delicious, detailed step instructions. Some of them are simple, and fast, and fun — "quickies" designed to startle and delight your lover. If you've ever felt like sex was getting too darned predictable, just wait'll you get to Seduction Number... well, I think I'll keep that a secret for now, too.

On the other hand, some of these scenarios require a bit of planning. You might spend hours setting it up just right, and the end result will be absolutely unforgettable. There is nothing in the world quite so thrilling as the thought that someone went to a whole lot of effort to make you feel special. And best of all — *you get all the credit!* Remember, these recipes for love are a secret, and your bedmate will never know which ideas came from this book...and which were fueled by your own steamy and slightly naughty imagination.

You'll eventually notice some common threads linking these seductions, and here's one of the most important — almost all of them ask you do something to *tease your lover*. Often it's just a hint; the tiniest little clue left lying about early in the week to tantalize your bedmate, to remind your partner of the surprise in store. Now, if you find a seduction that's not exactly your cup of tea, feel free to change it. I'll bet you can come up with something that suits you even better! But please — please! — *keep that element of anticipation*. It's the heart and soul of this book. That sense of expectancy is more than just spice in the sauce. It's what elevates sex from mundane to magnificent. It transforms intercourse from an athletic event into one of the mysteries of the universe. It makes you feel like a kid again!

And speaking of kids — I know what you're thinking. They might be the light of your life and your hope for the future...but the little devils can certainly put a damper on the ol' libido, can't they? Well, for every parent who tells me they couldn't use this book because there's just not enough time — *and no privacy, for crying out loud!* — I have three things to say.

First, intimacy is more than just fun and games. It heals us and sustains us and renews our deepest feelings for each other — *make it a priority*. Besides, you've got almost a week to pull this off!

Second, isn't it important to teach by example? Show your children that playfulness and sensuality is an important part of a loving, adult relationship. If your kids see Mom and Dad laughing and touching and writing love-notes and chasing each other around the house for a kiss, then that's the kind of grown-ups they'll learn to be...and the world will be a better place for it.

And third, if you really are pressed for time and can only follow through on, say, just one seduction each week — then this book will last you *two* whole years. What a deal!

And believe me, whether you have kids or not, once you make this a weekly practice, you'll *find* the time to carry it out. You'll come to covet these special moments together. That's because these seductions were created to give each of you *exactly what you're looking for —* that is, if you're anything like the thousands of people I've talked to over the years!

On hundreds of radio shows across the country, and all during the time I was preparing my first book, *237 Intimate Questions Every Woman Should Ask A Man*, I heard what men and women want in the bedroom. We want to know how to turn our mates on. We want them to know what turns *us* on. We'd like more variety...more foreplay...more surprises...more interest...new tricks...and once in a while, somebody *else* should do all the work! And that's what gave me the idea for this book:

Fifty seductions written for *his eyes only*, spelling out exactly how to get her attention, how to make her laugh, how to make her want you — and how to bring her to new heights of passion. Fifty seductions written for *her eyes only*, filled with clever and fun ways to spark his interest, each with an unusual twist or *advanced sexual technique* designed to fan that spark into a white-hot flame. And finally, one very special seduction to be read by both of you. Number 101 is a sort of graduation exercise for my newest Masters of The Erotic Arts — save this one for last!

And from start to finish, every single one of them is designed to make your mate feel like a million bucks. No halfhearted measures in this book! Every week, when it's your turn to turn on, you'll flirt and tease. You'll arouse. You'll build anticipation. You'll use new techniques. Just think of the fun you'll have when you bring your lover to a huge, gigantic, bedshaking, weak-at-the-knees, leave-'em-gasping, ohmigodimcomingrightnow ORGASM!!! And isn't it nice to know that you're guaranteed the same treatment in return?

There's more to *101 Nights Of Grrreat Sex* than, well, great sex. There's a wealth of wisdom and knowledge packed in here, too. On the page opposite each seduction you'll find terrific and useful sexual advice culled from fifty-four of the best-selling books in the field. In fact, almost every recipe in here has been recommended by doctors and therapists who are recognized as experts in human sexuality.

Most of these seductions also include something I like to call *frostings*...special bedroom skills that can bring you closer to your sexual peak and keep you there longer. And you can use them to drive your sweetie absolutely crazy!

But instead of simply explaining new techniques, this book incorporates them into each fun, erotic episode. This is not like some new diet, where you're expected to simply change your lifestyle overnight. *Here, you'll learn by doing* — slowly, gradually, month-by-month. And because you're doing it often — every week, remember, for a whole year — you'll actually turn interesting, exhilarating, unpredictable sex into a *habit*, and not just a special event.

I must confess that many of the ideas in this book are not originally mine. They were dreamed up by ordinary people from all over the country — regular folks who use these techniques to bring sexual excitement back into a mature relationship. I can't close this introduction without a word of thanks for their contribution to the book.

There are too many to list, and I don't even know all their names, but I'm sure they'll recognize their little tricks scattered throughout these pages! They managed to ride through the flood of phone calls we get on the radio and tell us the secrets to long term happiness in a relationship. They shared with us their knack for keeping sex fun and interesting months, years, and even decades into a partnership. They taught us about the importance of *comfort* — both in and out of our clothes.

And they helped me develop the formula for this book. The anticipation of an erotic encounter, plus the surprises you spring on your love, plus the excitement of the seduction itself, plus the thrill of trying new things with your lover — it all adds up to truly *Great Sex*. Don't just read about it. Do it! And thank me later.

— Laura Corn
Santa Monica, California
January 1995

Now — some final notes before you start your big adventure —

Hygiene. It's critical! I can't tell you how many men and women have told me they've lost interest in sex because their partner has some personal grooming flaws. Think of it this way — as you go through this book, your love is going to kiss and nibble and lick and suck various parts of you, a *lot!* You're going to do the same. Neither of you wants any, um, unpleasant surprises, and you sure don't want to give a reason not to do it again! Fresh breath, clean teeth, shampooed hair, and scrubbed skin — it's the uniform you put on *before* the game of love.

Money. Most of these seductions cost nothing at all. But for those that do, I've included little icons on the title pages to give you an idea of what to expect.

No $ at all means it's free, or under ten dollars.

$ means 10 to 25 dollars.
$$ means 30 to 60 dollars.
$$$ means 65 to 100 dollars.
☆   means over a hundred dollars.

Yes, there are even a couple that cost a lot — if your budget permits, the sky's the limit. And yes, I think you *should* plan one or two seductions every year where you pull out all the stops! Anniversaries, Birthdays, Valentine's Day, etc...What you're buying are memories that will last a lifetime.

The rest of the icons. The car means you're going somewhere. The sun means you need nice weather. The fork-and-spoon indicates a meal is involved.

Props. Lots of these seductions encourage you to buy extra little items to dress up the event. Most are inexpensive and easy to find, and to help you locate any that aren't available in your town, I've included a list of mail-order catalogues in the back of the book. Don't just ignore these special ingredients! It's extra touches like these that convince your sweetheart you really mean it. If you can't find what I've suggested, *substitute*. Use your imagination. It really is the effort that counts.

How to do it. Set aside one evening per week to look through the book. Sunday night is a good idea...you're relaxed, and you've got almost a whole week to plan the details of your seduction. Both of you get to pick one page, and then tear it out of the book. There's no turning back now! Your partner saw you do it, and is now expecting you to follow through. And of course, you'll be getting an erotic surprise sometime this week, too. Delicious idea, isn't it? The days will fly by!

Getting seduced. It may take a lot of nerve for your love to try some of these recipes, especially the ones that call for, um, bold behavior. So play along! Be encouraging. You will *not* regret it.

The Law. Hey, nothing in here is illegal. I think.

Laura Corn, I just CAN'T do that! *Yes, you can.* Sooner or later, especially if you're a shy person, chances are you'll come across a seduction that seems too wild or too extravagant or simply too much for you. I say — just do it! *Do it do it do it!* Others have already, so please give it a try. Your partner might be thrilled. You might learn to love something new. And if you can't, well, at least don't give up on your promise to your mate. Pull out another seduction...or make up one of your own! The important thing is to make your partner's pleasure a top priority at least once a week.

Did I mention GRRREAT sex? That is, of course, only if you finish this introduction, grab your partner, and start tearing out pages. Go on — start right now. I'm done.

You, on the other hand, are just beginning. It's a one-year course in the ancient art of seduction, and when you're done, you'll have one tattered, empty book cover....

And a lot of *grrreat* memories.

Enjoy!

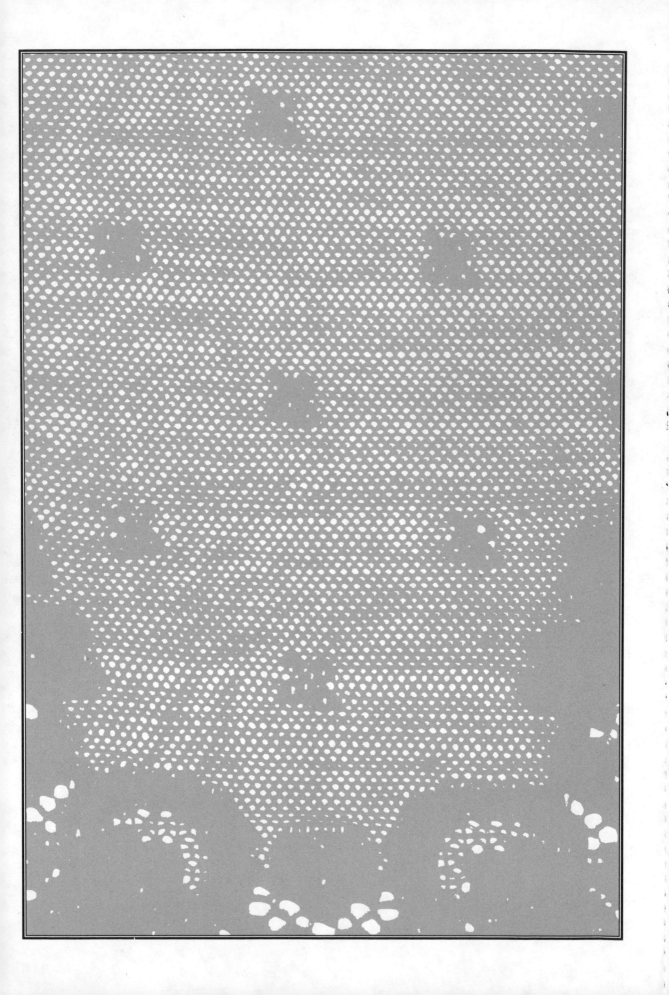

N.º

1

"I THINK I MADE HIS BACK FEEL BETTER"

For *Her* Eyes Only

THE HITE REPORT
Shere Hite

We have the power to make our own orgasms, if we want. You can get control of your own stimulation by moving against the other person, or by stimulating yourself directly in the same way as you do during masturbation. Although this suggestion may sound strange at first, it is important to be able to masturbate with another person, because it will give you power over your own orgasms. There is no reason why making your own orgasms should not be as beautiful or as deeply shared as any other form of sex with another person - perhaps even more so. The taboo against touching yourself says essentially that you should not use your own body for your own pleasure, that your body is not your own to enjoy. But we have a right to our own bodies. Controlling your own stimulation symbolizes owning your own body and is a very important step toward freedom.

COSMOPOLITAN
THE NICE GIRL'S GUIDE TO SENSATIONAL SEX
Nancy Kalish

Pursue your own pleasure. A woman who can be counted on to help achieve her own orgasm is always a highly rated lover. Many surveys have found that, far from ignoring their partners' pleasure, most men are so focused on it that they can't enjoy themselves unless they're sure their lovers are too. Perhaps that's because a man never feels more sexy, more powerful, more turned on than when he knows he's turning you on.

QUOTABLE SEX
Carole McKenzie

"I think I made his back feel better."
— *Marilyn Monroe*
after a private meeting with JFK

*H*ow did you learn to arouse yourself?

Over seventy-five percent of all women, including me, admit to discovering masturbation the same way. We become sexually stimulated by simply rubbing up against something — a pillow, perhaps a big stuffed toy, but usually nothing more than our bedsheets.

You and your lover are going to add this technique to your sexual repertoire, and along the way, he's going to discover that you've become every man's erotic ideal. Here's how....

Undress him and ask him to lay face down on the bed. Stand where he can watch while you peel down to bra and panties, then climb on top. Mmm, isn't it nice to straddle the powerful muscles in a man's back? Tension melts away as you massage warm oil into his skin. Then ask him —

Do you want to help make me come? Then I need you to stay very, very still....

Pull off your lingerie. He'll love the velvet touch of your bare breasts as you stretch out across his back. Slide your hands down his arms; braid your fingers into his own. Keep moving, keep touching. Make love to his back. Rock your hips in slow, small circles, pressing your *mons* directly against his tailbone. You're looking for a certain spot, a place that's *just right* for your clitoris to snuggle into to. You'll know it when you find it!

Now you can stoke your own fire. Let your aching clit set the pace as it rubs against his oil-soaked skin, up and down and around. When you find that special place, that *groove* — then start moving faster. He can't see you, so let your fantasies run wild. And let him know what's happening...whisper in his ear that you're getting close, and closer. Pinch his nipples, suck his neck. Hold him tight! Let him feel every twitch of your orgasm.

After all, you've become the bedmate men dream of — a woman who can get all the foreplay she wants...

All by herself!

— *Ingredients* —

1 Very Still Man / 1 Bottle of Oil / 1 Very Active Woman

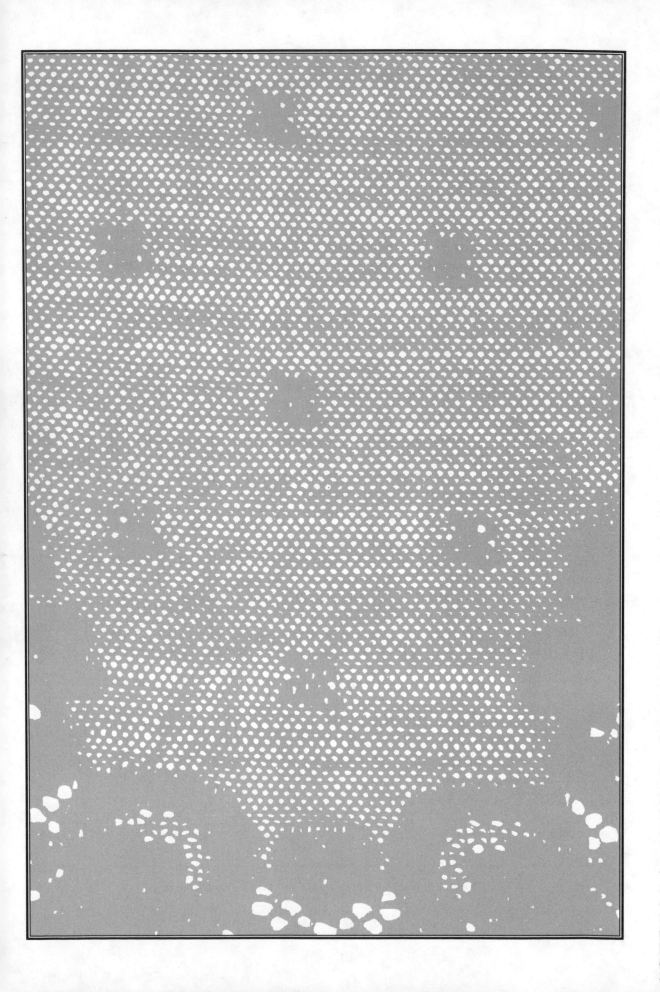

N.º

2

KING OF HEARTS

For *His* Eyes Only

HOT MONOGAMY
Dr. Patricia Love & Jo Robinson

For maximum effect, romance involves an element of surprise. We rarely get surprises as adults. As children we had surprise birthday parties, surprise holiday presents, surprise events orchestrated by adults. Life was full of surprises. Not so in adulthood. This makes it all the more meaningful to be pleasantly surprised—especially by one who loves you.

SOULMATES
Thomas Moore

Again, one finds seduction an important theme in the soul's progress.

To live an erotic life is to follow the bouncing ball, to allow oneself to be distracted and enticed by something playful and childlike, or, to be more precise, by life itself in its playful mode. Our habitual seriousness can prevent us from seeing, and certainly appreciating, the erotic lures that come our way every day. Our medically minded seriousness about sex can also prevent us from glimpsing the cure of our sexual maladies and opportunities for expanding our sexuality. We may take it all too seriously, with too much adult knowledge and sophistication. Sex can sometimes be an invitation to the soul to come out and play.

*O*kay, this is going to require a *lot* of preparation. But do it well, and you'll give your sweetheart an adventure she'll talk about for years to come. It's an erotic treasure hunt, a chase through a set of clues and on to a Grand Prize — a night of passion with you!

It starts one lazy Saturday afternoon when you hand her a copy of the newspaper.

Somewhere in this paper is a message just for you. See you later...

Wow! What an intriguing thing to say. As you head out the door, the last thing you'll see will be her jaw dropping in surprise. Naturally, she'll tear the paper apart until she comes across your ad in the classified section under the Personals heading.

"SUSAN!" (or whatever her name is — a pet name is especially good here) *"THIS IS IT! Go to 3438 N. Main right away. Dress sharp. I love you."*

The address is a favorite flower shop, and when she arrives, the florist has a present waiting for her. It's a rose — or a dozen, if your budget permits! — and another clue. *"Next stop: Victoria's Secret at the mall. Ask for the manager. And hurry!"*

Man, this is getting better with every passing minute! The staff at the lingerie shop is expecting her, and since they helped you pick it out, they'll all be grinning when she gets her next gift. There's another note on the box — *"Don't open this yet! Just come to the Doubletree Hotel on Broadway and ask for Mr. Peter Longfellow. There's one more surprise waiting for you there...."*

Mister, uh, *Longfellow* is you, of course, waiting in your love nest with her overnight essentials already packed. When the desk clerk rings to tell you she's on the way up, light the candles, turn up the music, and crack the champagne.

She'll walk through that door with her libido already set to Full Steam Ahead. You've given her a half a day of clues to decipher; fun clues and exciting clues and clues brimming with anticipation. And gifts! Her special package from Victoria's Secret contains an elegant, sensuous black teddy, which she will be more than happy to model for you. Now, can you imagine what she's got for you in return?

Peter, you haven't got a clue!

Ingredients
---

1 Classified Ad / 1 Florist / 1 Lingerie Store / 1 Hotel Room

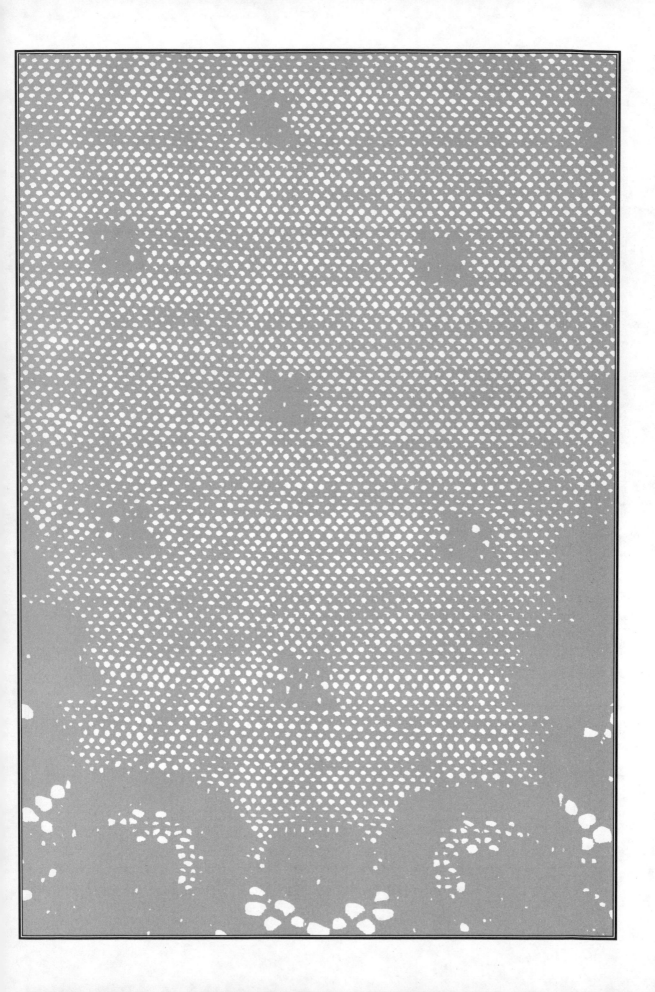

N.o

3

UP AGAINST THE WALL

For *His* Eyes Only

$

HOT AND BOTHERED
Wendy Dennis

The average length of time it takes for a woman to reach orgasm is anywhere from ten to thirty minutes, although thirty to forty-five minutes is not unusual, and it can take up to an hour.

The female orgasm typically lasts from six to ten seconds, although the rolling, mega-intense ones can go on for fifteen.

WINDOW OF LOVE
Dr. Lasse Hessel

Standing up Doggy Style: A position which many women describe as the best for achieving orgasm.

1. The whole of the vagina is stimulated but mainly the front wall. The man can vary the stimulation to excite the G-point to its maximum by not pushing his penis too high up into the vagina.

2. The clitoris is not stimulated directly but the woman can touch it herself.

3. There is maximum stimulation of the glans.

4. This again is a good position for pregnancy since the penis is in the closest position to the cervix.

5. Both the woman and the man have their hands free to caress.

*H*ere's a seduction that starts by making her crazy — and ends by making her wild! On Monday, move one of your kitchen chairs into the bedroom and place it up against the wall. Don't say a word. Just leave it.

She might move it back, so on Tuesday, return it to the bedroom with a note that says, "Don't Touch!" On the seat, place a pair of her sexiest shoes, the ones she wears when she really wants to look hot, *and a beautifully wrapped gift.* Well, well... now you've got her attention!

Wednesday, add a pair of stockings and a garter belt. The next night, a skirt; the night after, a blouse. By now she's *dying* to know what you've got planned, but you're keeping mum.

Saturday, ask her to put it all on. She probably thinks you're taking her out, here's the real story — you're going to be having fun with her *G-spot,* and the chair is going to help you do it! There are two special positions, according to researchers, that are ideal for stimulating that enchanted place. And *you,* you lucky boy, get to do the stimulating...*with your penis!*

Ask her to sit. Hike up her skirt; open her thighs as you move in for a kiss. Have fun with your foreplay! There's no rush tonight. But after you've aroused her...after you've tasted her, and fondled her, and stroked her...tell her it's time to reveal the secret of the chair. Invite her to stand and face it, legs apart but straight, waist bent, and hands on the seat for support. Ooh, how enticing! There she is, wide open with *nothing on under her skirt.* Slip inside, and ride slow and easy while the steam starts to build.

Now have her kneel on the seat, arms braced on the back of the chair. In this position, the head of your penis is riding across her G-spot with every stroke! Don't let her clit get lonely — reach around and tease it. Lean forward to cup her breasts; roll her nipples in your fingers. Let her feel your hot breath and warm mouth on her neck, but most of all — keep pumping, hard and fast. Please don't stop! That magic button deep inside will be aching with desire, burning with anticipation. Ultimately, it will be driving her to an intense and very powerful climax.

And you owe it all to a humble chair. Of course, every time you have company and someone sits in it, she'll break into giggles.

Gee!

Ingredients

1 Kitchen Chair / 1 Sexy Outfit / 1 Giftwrapped Surprise / 1 Grrreat Dinner

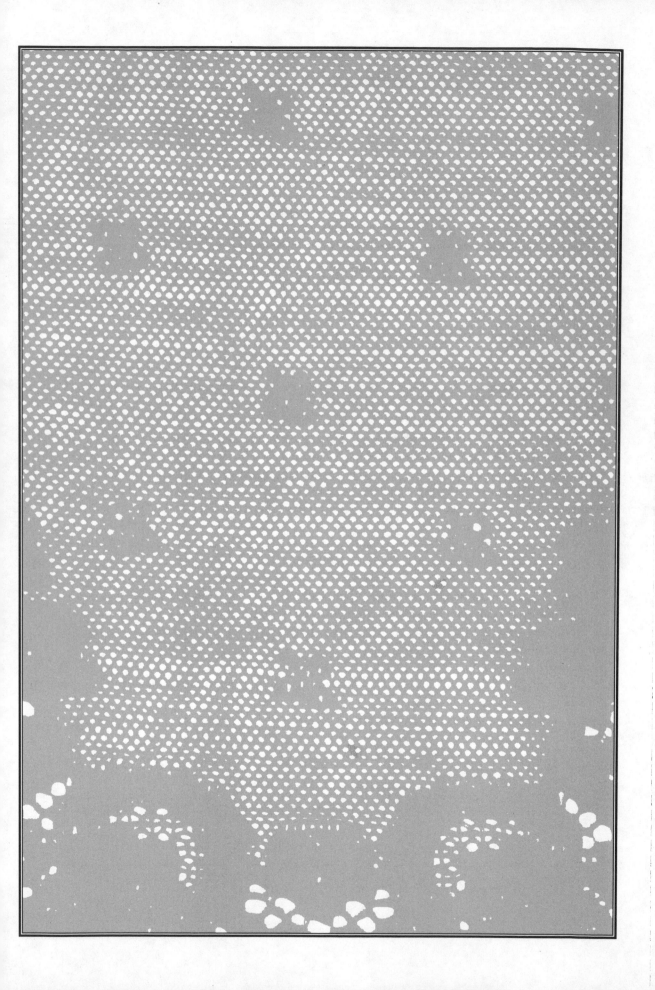

N°

4

BURIED TREASURE

For *Her* Eyes Only

$

SECRETS OF SEDUCTION
Brenda Venus

Has your lovemaking fallen into a routine? Do you experiment and take each other to new heights of creativity and fun - or has your love life become very predictable?

Romance is much like playing a game. It has elements of surprise, intrigue, fun, teasing, and breaking the rules.

Romance is about creating an illusion out of the mundane. This is the basis of all miracles - taking the ordinary and transforming it.

To be impressive, you must use your own particular talent to its fullest.

LIGHT HIS FIRE
Ellen Kreidman

Planning a surprise for your mate is one very direct way to show that you really care and to create a memory at the same time. The one receiving the surprise only gets to enjoy it while it lasts or as a memory, but you'll have the added pleasure of planning and executing the entire event.

Do something unpredictable, spontaneous, and different. Don't worry that you're "not the type" - everyone has the ability to be creative and exciting. It just takes time, energy, and the willingness to try something different.

*H*ere's a seduction that puts a whole new spin on a great old party game. It's an erotic treasure hunt, and *you* are the Grand Prize!

It'll take some preparation to pull this off, but once everything's in place your true love will have a lot of laughs, a lot of smiles, and one big climax in store for him.

One afternoon this week, hide in your bathroom and yell for your sweetie — *Honey, I need a couple of paper towels from the kitchen. Would you mind bringing them to me?* Something really unusual catches his eye as he heads over to the roll. It's a message, written in enormous red letters on the first two sheets.

"You are now on a Treasure Hunt. First stop — the mailbox."

Oh boy! You've got his attention now! In the mailbox he'll find an envelope containing two movie tickets...or if your budget permits, a couple of concert passes! There's also a note — *"Better check the oil. Not under the hood, but in the back seat."* Huh??

Your mysterious clue is made clear when he goes to the car and finds a bottle of massage oil, with yet another note attached. *"If you want to NAIL me, you need the right TOOLS."* That's easy! He'll open his toolbox where he'll find a small bottle of your favorite fragrance. More instructions —

"All those channels and there's SOMETHING on." Well, he's off to the TV set, which has been neatly draped with a large silk scarf. It also has a card — *"Last stop, the fridge. I'm hungry."* And in the refrigerator is a box with your picnic supplies. Chocolates, fruit, champagne and glasses, whatever appeals to you. The box bears another message — *"I miss you and I'm waiting for you. Bring everything."*

After all this extended teasing, he'll be in the bedroom as fast as his feet will carry him! And he won't be disappointed. There you are, stretched out on the bed in your sheerest lingerie and slyest grin. Now the real fun starts! I'll bet he knows just what to do with his accumulated treasures, except, perhaps, for the scarf.

That's to use as a blindfold, of course, in your next party game.

It's called *Pin The Tail!*

Ingredients

Massage Oil / Special Tickets / Fragrance / Silk Scarf
Hors d'Oeuvres and Champagne / Lots of Note Paper and Ink!

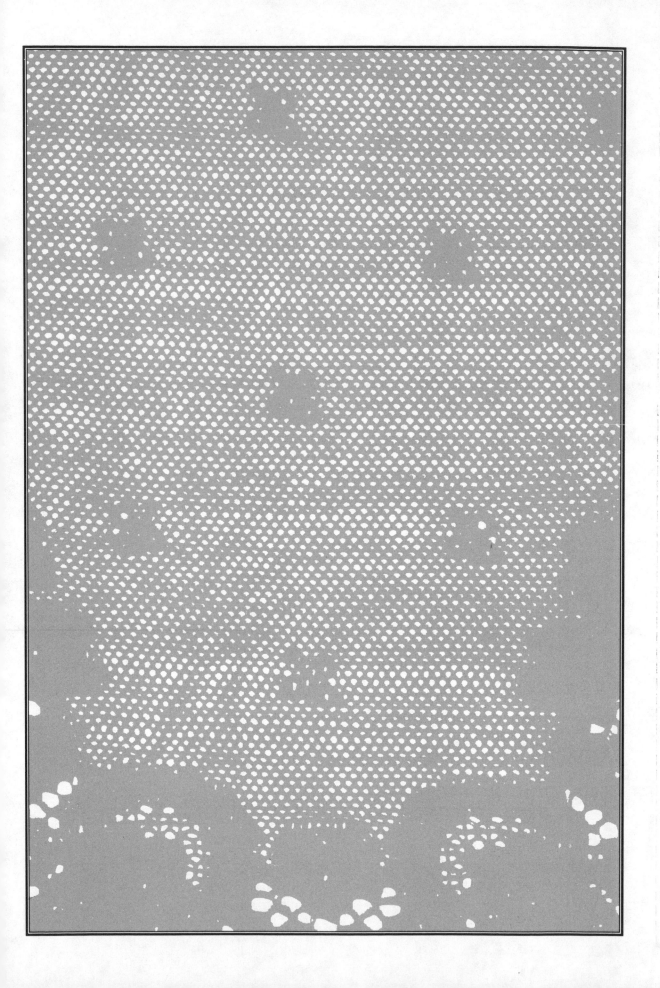

Nº

5

THE VELVET TONGUE

For *Her* Eyes Only

HOT AND BOTHERED
Wendy Dennis

Pepper Schwartz and Philip Blumstein also found, in American Couples (1983), "Heterosexual men who receive oral sex," wrote the authors, "are happier with their sex lives and with their relationships in general." What's more, several men I interviewed got all misty-eyed remembering the best blowjobs they'd ever received, even if they'd been performed twenty years earlier.

SINGLE WILD SEXY AND SAFE
Graham Masterton

To stimulate him toward climax, you may need to rub his penis with your hand as well as lick and suck him with your mouth. Keep up a rhythmical rubbing, gentle but strong. Don't keep stopping and starting, or changing your grip, or altering rhythms. Think how you like your clitoris to be stimulated consistently and persistently. Sexual climaxes are built up slowly and gradually, without constant distraction. And don't give up if he seems to be taking a long time to climax. Just keep at it and enjoy it.

If men don't seem to be as interested in foreplay as we'd like — maybe it's because no one ever taught them how incredibly great it is. This is a problem you're going to rectify this week....

He knows you pulled this page out of the book. Now ask him to stop by the store for some herbal tea...and some honey. If he points out that you already have tea in the house, smile sweetly and tell him you want some *different* tea — and he'll go get it if he wants a big surprise. *A surprise? Oh boy!*

Begin your seduction with a taste of your sweetened brew and a deep kiss. Explore the inside of his mouth with your tongue; run it across his teeth and his lips. Lightly lick his eyelids and lashes, then trail your tongue across his cheek and around his ear. Mmm, don't you just love nibbling a man's neck? Circle the outside of his nipples, then — a quick swallow to warm your mouth! — suck them quite hard. Pull them into your mouth, and as they stiffen, don't be afraid to bite.

Work your way down his belly, using the liquid to keep your mouth moist and your breath hot against his skin. Tickle his belly-button. Fill it up and lap up the juices! And when you get to his penis, completely soak it in warm, honey-flavored liquid; lick it — top to bottom, front to back. Pull his scrotum into your mouth, and let your tongue trace the outline of his testicles. He's been hot before, but your liquid fire is searing his senses and melting his passion. Before he comes....

Take a big sip, press your lips to his and let the sweet, sticky concoction flow into his mouth. Tell him not to swallow yet! Press your own nipple against his mouth. Ooh! Now you know the magic of the velvet tongue, too. Warm up your cup — you'll both want to continue your gentle, slow tongue-bath into the evening. Work your way, literally, from head to toes.

You might catch him in the kitchen a little more often now. (He *can* boil water, can't he?) And what's that song he's humming?

Tea for two, and two for tea,
Me for you , and you for me....

Ingredients
---

1 Pot of Tea, or any Hot Beverage of Your Choice / 1 Naked Man
1 Soft Wet Tongue / 1 Shower — Hey, this is sticky!

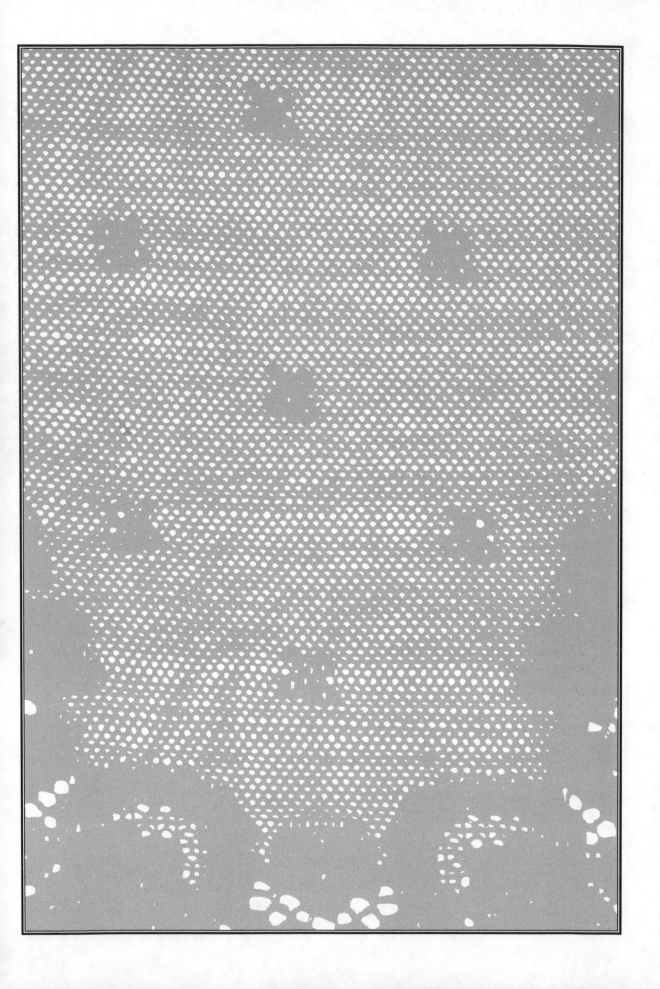

Nº

6

OBSTACLE COURSE

For *His* Eyes Only

THE NEW JOY OF SEX
Alex Comfort, M.D., D.SC.

Bed is the place to play all games you have ever wanted to play, at the adult level - if adults could become less self-conscious about such 'immature' needs we should have fewer deeply anxious and committed fetishists creating a sense of community to enable them to do their thing without feelings isolated.

Play is one function of sexual elaboration - playfulness is a part of love which could well be the major contribution of the Aquarian revolution to human happiness.

THE WONDERFUL LITTLE SEX BOOK
William Ashoka Ross

Do you remember the time you had that perfect orgasm? The one you and your partner still reminisce about? The golden screw? Everyone who's ever had it always wants to re-experience it. And when we can't, we feel frustrated because none of our efforts work, and we, of course, feel that should work?

Some people think that's why it doesn't happen anymore - because we're trying to repeat, to copy, to imitate. If, instead of trying to recapture the past, we could be open to the brand new, to all the newness and freshness and awe that life has to offer, who knows what wonderful experiences might come out way?

*T*he very first lesson we learn in life is that we always want most what we can't have. From toys and treats to cars and girls — and cars *with* girls! — it's the yearning and anticipation that makes a man's rewards the sweetest.

Okay, so you finally got the girl. Now great sex isn't a question of *if* but of when. *Grrreat Sex,* though — now that requires some effort! Here's how to turn your next seduction into a challenge.

First thing in the morning, leave one of your old ties where she won't be able to miss it — over a doorknob, or draped over her rear-view mirror. Pinned to it is a note:

Bring me to bed tonight. You're going to need me.

Oooh, baby! Now you've got her thinking. And after a whole day of high hopes and erotic expectations, you won't let her down. When she gets to the bedroom, explain the plan. She is to tie your hands behind your back and let you try to jump her. She can't assist you in any way except by unbuttoning her blouse and unzipping her jeans. You can instruct her to stand, sit, lay down, or move parts of her body, but that's it. The rest is up to your imagination   and teeth!

She will *thoroughly* enjoy your dilemma. You both may have to stop from time to time to get over a laughing fit. But once you're past shirt and pants, things take a decidedly more sensuous turn. Pulling her bra free means burying your face between her breasts. Tugging her panties down with your teeth puts your mouth *right there....* Don't miss an opportunity to kiss and nuzzle and lick and bite anything you might come across.

And don't think she'll miss her opportunity to take advantage of you! A big strong man, slightly helpless and restrained...wow. That's a compelling fantasy for most women; take it from me.

All that effort and delayed gratification will have your pulse pounding and your erection throbbing. But what are you going to do with it? Can you get it in without using your hands? Can you convince her to do it for you? Mmm, I dunno — you're on your own from here.

But I do know that you'll never again be able to tell your friends you're *all tied up* while keeping a straight face!

------------------------ *Ingredients* ------------------------

1 Woman with a Sense of Humor / 1 Man with Good Teeth / 1 Tie

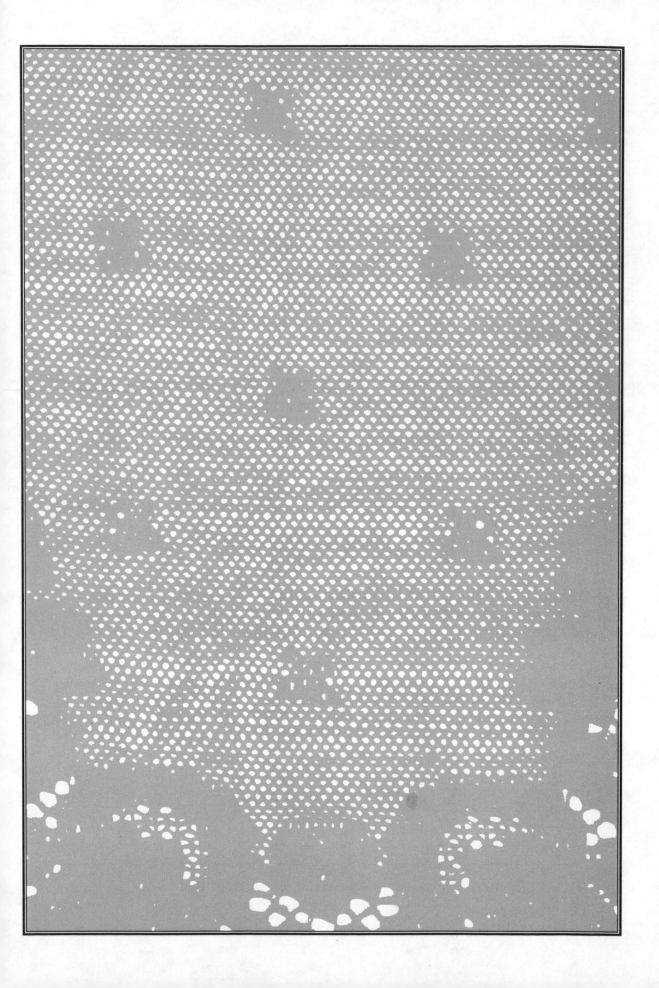

№ 7

DANGEROUS WHEN WET

For *His* Eyes Only

THE GOOD VIBRATIONS GUIDE TO SEX
Cathy Winks and Anne Semans

MUTUAL MASTURBATION

Watching him masturbate is just incredibly sexy because I can see what he's feeling in ways that I can't when I'm involved. It's so clear that he is intensely inside himself and his desire. It makes me jealous in this really neat way. I could swallow him whole, I think. Masturbating in front of him is great because I really enjoy my reactions- how wet I get, my sounds, my smell, how freely I can move - and I know that I am completely turning him on.

SINGLE WILD SEXY AND SAFE
Graham Masterton

Finally-while talking to all of the women who contributed to these chapters-I conducted a survey on their favorite methods of masturbation, and drew up a Top Ten of popular masturbatory techniques:

1. Light clitoral stroking

2. Clitoral stroking plus stroking or pulling of vaginal lips.

3. Rhythmical squeezing of thighs together, plus some light clitoral stroking.

4. Vaginal insertion of dildo or vibrator, plus some light clitoral stroking.

5. Playing of shower on clitoral and vaginal area, plus clitoral stroking.

6. Breast and nipple stimulation, plus some clitoral stroking

7. Anal insertion of dildo or vibrator, plus massage of clitoris and vulva.

8. Double insertion of dildoes or vibrators (vagina and anal)

9. Sliding silk scarf backward and forward between lips of vulva

10. Vaginal insertion of any phallic object (hair-brush handle, carrot, cucumber, shampoo bottle, soda bottle, pastry pin- even, in one case, a huge sausage, liberally lubricated with KY)

*T*he greatest orgasms happen when we try something *new* — something that startles us and surprises us and drives us way over our sexual speed limits. Tonight, you're going to give your lover one of those landmark orgasms.

Tonight, you're going to push her right over the edge.

Start by turning your bathroom into a palace of pleasure for your mistress. Candlelight, scented bath oil, mounds of big fluffy towels — and *her* favorite music on the stereo. Lead her to the tub and help her in; sit on the edge and spend lots of time washing and caressing her. Her mind will relax as her skin comes alive; she'll probably assume that this royal treatment is the whole seduction — *Ahhh, but she'll be wrong.*

Don't rinse her off yet. Simply start to drain the tub and tell her you want to try something new. Ask her to slide down toward the spigot...and have her spread her legs under the faucet, feet up on the wall. Adjust the flow of water carefully — not too hot! Not too hard! — and have her slip that most sensitive, private part right under the flow. Tease her with your hand; slide your fingers into those delicious, sensitive folds of flesh, and finally open her lips wide to the coursing water.

She'll be excited and more than a little surprised — surprised that you know this trick (although many women do!), shocked that she is essentially *masturbating* right in front of her lover—

And now you're going to blow her away.

Pile up some of those big towels in the tub as a cushion for her head and shoulders — *and your knees!* Slip off your robe, straddle her in the tub and kneel right above her face...but *don't let her take you in her mouth.* Instead, stroke yourself. Make yourself hard. Show her — up close and very personal — just how you like to be touched.

Chances are she's never watched a man play with himself like this before. She's never had quite this much warm, gushing, constant stimulation to her swollen clitoris before. The combination will send her out of control, beyond her usual limits, and headed for one of the greatest orgasms of her life — one that *you* gave her, and one she'll never forget.

———————— *Ingredients* ————————

Two Candles / Silky Bath Oil / Lots of Towels / One Spotless Bathtub
(And in the future...expect a higher water bill!)

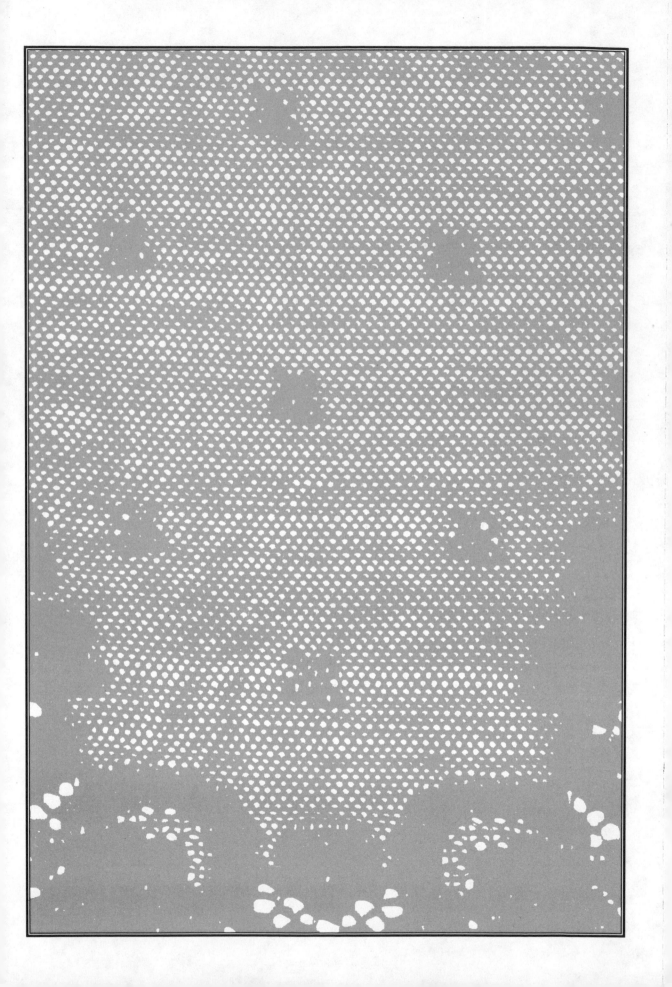

Nº 8
———————————

THAT WILL BE THREE HUNDRED DOLLARS, PLEASE

For *Her* Eyes Only

HOT MONOGAMY
Dr. Patricia Love & Jo Robinson

The Sharper Image, a company that specializes in electronics and high-tech gadgets, recently test-marketed two items of lingerie: a black lace hose and garter combination and a black lace body stocking. These two items alone added $1.5 million in "male" order sales. This sales figure doesn't surprise me. In one survey a thousand men were asked what turned them on most: dirty talk, X-rated videos, pornography, female masturbation, sexy lingerie, or "other." Of the men survey, 92 percent said they were most turned on by sexy lingerie. In an interesting footnote, 73 percent of these men said they relied on stimulation such as this to sustain their interest in a long-term relationship. In essence, a man who asks his partner to wear a lace teddy to bed may be saying to her, "Please help me be monogamous."

THE NEW JOY OF SEX
Alex Comfort, M.D.

We have said this before, but we repeat: sex is the most important sort of adult play. If you can't relax here you never will. Don't be scared of psychodrama. It works far better in bed than in an encounter group - be the Sultan and his favorite concubine, the burglar and the maiden, even a dog and a currant bun, anything you fancy for the hell of it. Take off your shell along with your clothes.

*O*n talk shows and in interviews around the country, I've heard this confession a thousand times or more. Both men and women harbor a powerful fantasy of no-holds-barred, no-strings-attached, anonymous and forbidden sex. It's a secret fascination with the high-class call girl, and this week — she's *you!*

Rent a motel room on the morning of your seduction. Put the key in an envelope, along with a note for him to meet you there at a certain time, and drop it off to him at work. Seal it with a kiss in your most luscious lipstick.

The room should be set up with glowing candles and a bucket of chilled champagne. Now for your makeover — wear a wig of a color and style different from your own hair. Changing yourself as much as possible will add a lot to the surprise! When he knocks on the door, greet him in a sexy black teddy with stockings and garter, your raciest high heels and a new fragrance of perfume.

Introduce yourself by another name, and while you saunter over to pour him some bubbly, ask him *what he wants* and *how he wants it.* Tease him and flirt with him, but make it clear you have only one thing on your mind. You're going to *get him off* like he's never had it before. Don't forget to name your price! Three hundred dollars seems fair, and you do take checks.

Guide him over to the bed. Slide your hands sensuously over his body as you undress him. Whisper that you find him *irresistible.* He's making you totally hot, and you just can't wait to take him in your mouth...like...*this....*

Begin with long, slow licks, as if you were eating an ice cream cone. Mmmmm! Go wild! Throw yourself into your performance, assured that you have an extremely appreciative audience.

Keep playing your role until the door shuts behind him, then get ready for your next "date." It's dinner with him, as your old sweet self! Be sure and offer to pick up the check. After all, you've picked up a little extra spending money lately.

"Honey, I'm thinking about taking on some part-time work...."

Ingredients

1 Motel Room / 1 Wig / 1 Daring Outfit / 1 Bottle of Champagne

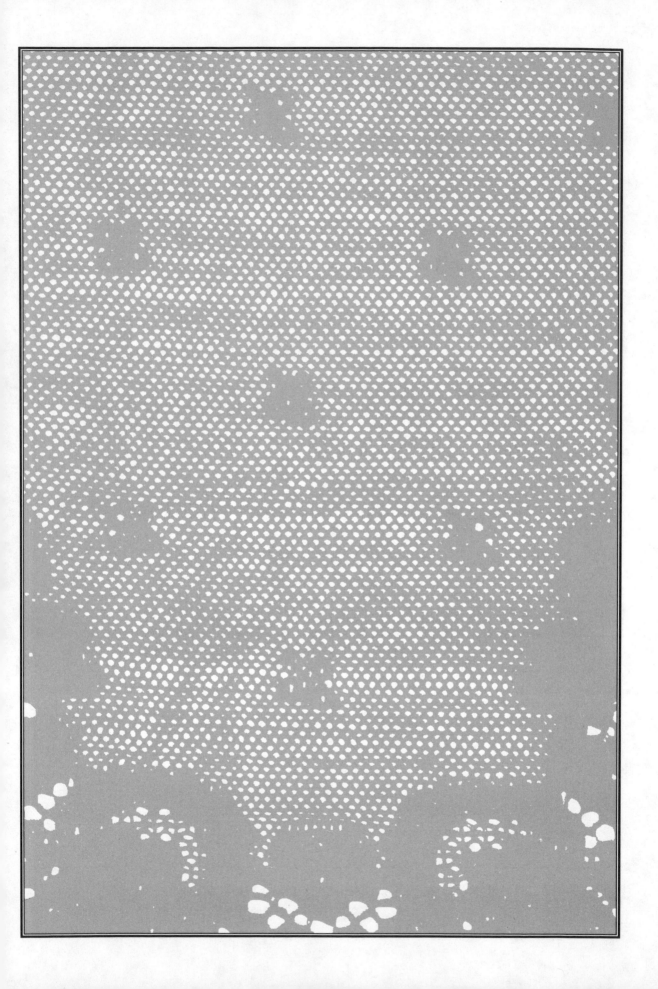

N^o *9*

UNDER THE HOOD, COWBOY

For *His* Eyes Only

THE ART OF EXTENDED ORGASM
Kathryn Roberts, M.A

Most of the time most women find the best spot on the clitoris to be between two o'clock and three o'clock. So you just want to rub consistently right in that spot...forever and ever and ever. Some women find just the opposite side in the same place between nine and ten o'clock very pleasurable. But, I would say about eighty per cent are going to find it between two and three o'clock

THE MAN'S GOURMET SEX BOOK
Peggy and Evan Burke

How well do you understand the most potent erogenous zone of her body, her clitoris? If you know nothing else about her sexuality, you should know all there is to know about this center of her pleasure. You should understand that it resembles in many ways the male penis, that it grows erect and sensitive under stimulation, and though it does not ejaculate, as does the penis, its nerves are the ones controlling and responsible for her orgasms.

ESO
Alan P. Brauer, M.D. and Dona J. Brauer

Many women complain that their men don't experiment enough with different kinds of strokes. Or that the experimenting happens too fast, the man moving from one stroke to another before the woman has had time to relax with it and see how it feels.

A woman loves the feeling that surges through her when the clitoris is touched *just right*. If you don't know exactly how she likes it stroked...don't feel bad. *No one* knows the best way to touch it. No one but her — and tonight she's going to teach it to you.

When your foreplay brings your mouth in contact with her lips...her *other* lips...pay special attention to the clit. It's a shy little devil, but you're going to coax it out to play. Touch it with your tongue, get it wet with your saliva, and then — pull away.

Coat your fingers liberally with astroglide and rub them across her lips; pull them gently apart. Imagine the face of a small clock before you, with the clitoris at twelve o'clock. Where on that clock does she want to be touched? Where do you stroke for maximum effect? Surveys tell us that more women touch themselves at *two o'clock* than any other position...but take your time getting there. Start at the top — right above the clitoris — and brush against her with fast, short, circular strokes. Move around to ten or eleven — does she respond more, or less?

Keep her wet. Dip your fingertips into her vagina; draw a trail of her juices up to the clock and rub it all over. Her clitoris will change as her arousal reaches new heights. It swells; it gets harder, and finally it makes its presence known when it climbs out from under the clitoral hood. The hood — a small piece of skin that protects all those nerve endings — will pull back, leaving that magic button exposed. Be careful! Too rough a touch, too much pressure, and her sexual revelry will be spoiled. But if you discover what really works *under the hood,* you'll be giving her a gift no other man ever has — an orgasm as good as her own.

So ask for help. Place her hand on yours. *Please, show me....*

Follow her lead. Memorize her every move. Does she rub fast? Does she press hard? Perhaps it's too sensitive; does she stroke the clitoris itself, or squeeze up against the base? Watch for signs she's approaching her climax...and see if she sustains her rapture by stopping short, changing tempo, then starting up again. Most important of all, learn *exactly* what she does when she finally erupts. That last move, that final, intense touch — or *no touch at all* — will make all the difference in the world.

In sex, as in golf, follow-through is everything.

Ingredients

1 Man with a Slow Hand / 1 Lover with an Easy Touch / Lubricant

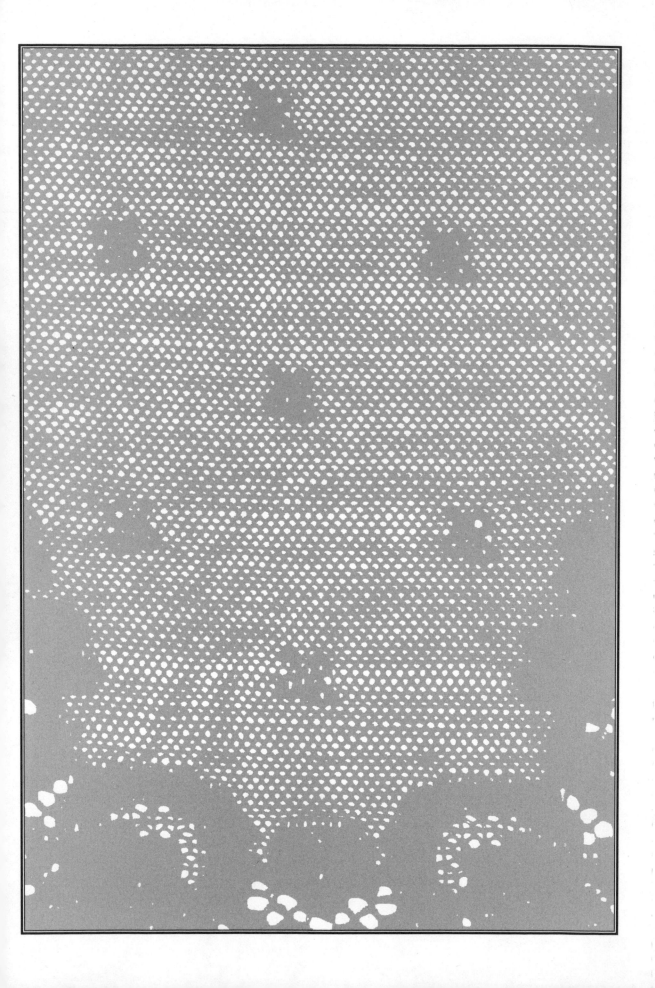

N.º **10**

LINGERIE PARFAIT

For *Her* Eyes Only

$

SEX IS LIKE A HOT FUDGE SUNDAE
Pauline Falstrom, Ph.D.

There is nothing more erotic than a visual presentation of sexuality done well—lighting perfect, clothing suggestive, and the couple excited about one another. Taking pictures of each other can be a lot of fun. It gives you an opportunity to try on all those things you bought at Frederick's, Nordstroms, or even K-Mart. The old items from your hiding place, or the small items purchased at the thrift shop now can come into play.

You can put on wild, outrageous make-up, dangling earrings that your mother told you never to wear, and perfumes you received as a gift.

HOT MONOGAMY
Dr. Patricia Love and Jo Robinson

This sales figure doesn't surprise me. In one survey a thousand men were asked what turned them on most: dirt talk, x-rated videos, pornography, female masturbations, sexy lingerie, or "other." Of the men surveyed, 92% said they were most turned on by sexy lingerie. In an interesting footnote, 73% of these men said they relied on stimulation such as this to sustain their interest in a long-term relationship. In essence, a man who asks his partner to wear a lace teddy to bed may be saying to her, "Please help me be monogamous."

THE LITTLE BLACK BOOK OF ANSWERS
Laura Corn

I asked 5,000 men:
If you could choose only one style of lingerie for a woman to wear for an entire week—
what would it be?

The top three answers in order are:

1. Basic Black. Men love black.
   Garter belt, stockings and high heels in ebony!

2. A see thru teddy — in reddy!

3. The minimalist approach — A hot G-string and lacy bra.

*A*sk any man and he'll tell you he only reads Playboy magazine for the articles. Uh-huh. Let's face it, a whole multi-billion-dollar industry exists because *men like pictures,* and you, you are going to turn that fact to your advantage!

Get a copy of Playboy (or have a friend pick one up) and leave it, neatly giftwrapped, for your sweetie to find. When he opens it he'll find a note attached with the words, "Please study." Well! He's sure to be grateful and surprised — but also a little perplexed. Clear up the mystery when you see him next by explaining that you hope he learned something from it. You've always wanted to be a centerfold, see, but you just could never be comfortable with another photographer. And with that, you hand him a Polaroid camera.

Lead him to your "studio," where you've laid out a selection of seductive clothing. Swimsuits, sexy robes, revealing lingerie — let your imagination go. With the right attitude, *anything* you wear can be enticing. You would be astonished at the number of men who get turned on by the sight of a woman in a well-tailored suit... and of course yours has nothing underneath it!

Have fun with your props. Hats are wonderful for playing peek-a-boo! Scarves, jewelry, whatever you like will work for this ultimate game of dress-up. Or dress-*off,* as the case may be! Try to duplicate some of those professional shots in the magazine. Feeling brave? Then raise the rating from R to triple-X! Legs apart, or bottom held high; let him direct your photo session any way he likes. This is the time to indulge your most intoxicating daydreams. So tantalize him... touch yourself for the camera. And if it has a self-timer, then by all means, invite your shooter into the shot.

Finally, at last — at long, long last! — the fantasy he's treasured since adolescence is becoming reality. He's making love to a centerfold.

And one with no staples!

Ingredients

---

1 Polaroid Camera / 1 Copy of Playboy / 4 Rolls of Film / Sexy Lingerie / No Inhibitions At All

(Why Polaroid? No negatives, no duplicates! All the
souvenirs of your adventure stay right in your own hand)

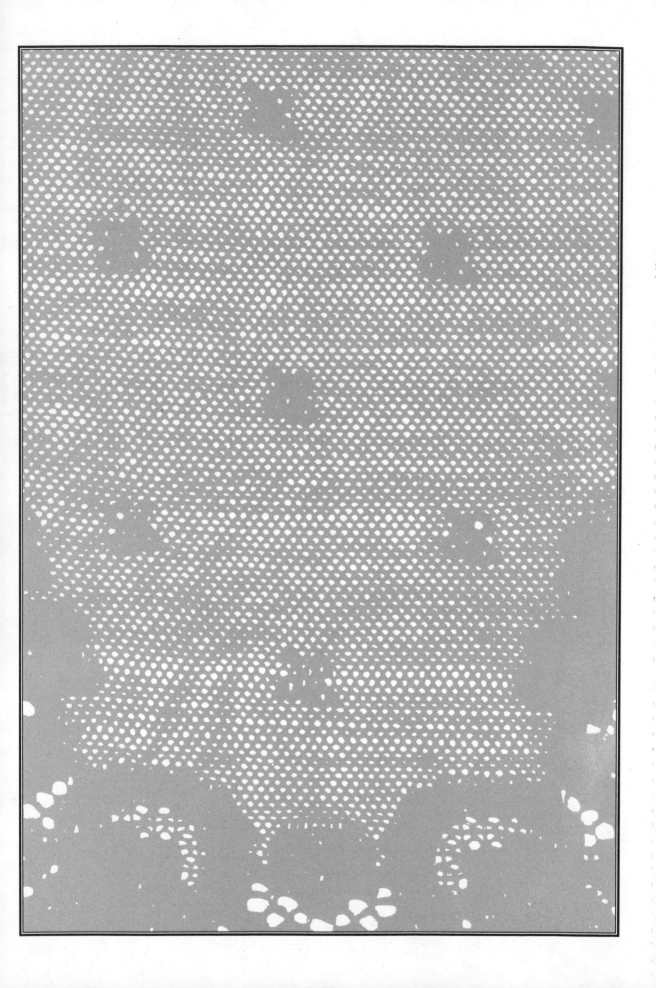

N.º

11

ANGEL WITH A LARIAT

For *Her* Eyes Only

THE NEW JOY OF SEX
Alex Comfort, M.D. D.SC.

The quickie is the equivalent of inspiration, and you should let it strike in lightning fashion, any time and almost anywhere, from bed in the middle of the night to halfway up a spiral stair: anywhere that you're suddenly alone and the inspiration is bilateral. Not that one or other won't sometimes specifically ask, but the inspirational quickie is mutual, and half the fun is that the preliminary communication is wordless between real lovers.

THE LOVING TOUCH
Dr. Andrew Stanway

There are many advantages to quickie sex. It shows how much you fancy one another on a purely physical basis. Romancing and subtle foreplay are all very well, but there are times when one or both partners need to be shown that they are wanted urgently.

A "quickie" can make sparks fly in any relationship. How about adding some spontaneous excitement to yours? This week, you're going to take your man completely by surprise.

Of course, before you can boink him, you've got to catch him, and that's where the real fun of this seduction lies. You're going to do it the old-fashioned Western way — with a *lariat*. And you're going to get him to make it for you!

Early in the week, tell him you need some rope for a special project you have in mind. Not too thick, and, oh, about ten feet long — *you won't mind picking some up for me, will you honey? You know how I hate those hardware stores. Please?*

When Saturday rolls around, ask him to make a *lasso* — and don't worry if his Boy Scout skills are a little rusty. A big knotted loop at the end of the line will do just fine. Once he works it out, thank him and take it from him...and then toss it over him!

Yee-ha! You just roped yourself a big stallion, and now you get to ride 'em, cowgirl! Drag him over to the stairs and make him sit.

"See this?" Lift your skirt. You have no panties.

"See this?" Show him a cake timer. Set it to five minutes.

"That's all the time we've got, cowboy!"

Climb on top, and straddle his face. Let him have a quick taste of your nectar — there's no more powerful aphrodisiac in the world, and I'll bet you can almost hear a *pop* as his penis instantly springs to full attention. Tug his trousers down; spread your legs and pull him into you. And when the timer sounds off — stop! Sorry, that's the rule today.

If an orgasm doesn't happen within that time limit, well, you can bet he'll be hot and bothered for the rest of the day. And you probably won't have to wait until evening for relief.

After all, there's no rule that says he can't rope *you* in, and reset the timer.

On your mark....Get set....Go! (And come!)

Ingredients

1 Cake Timer / 1 Lariat / 1 Hot Man / 300 Hot Seconds

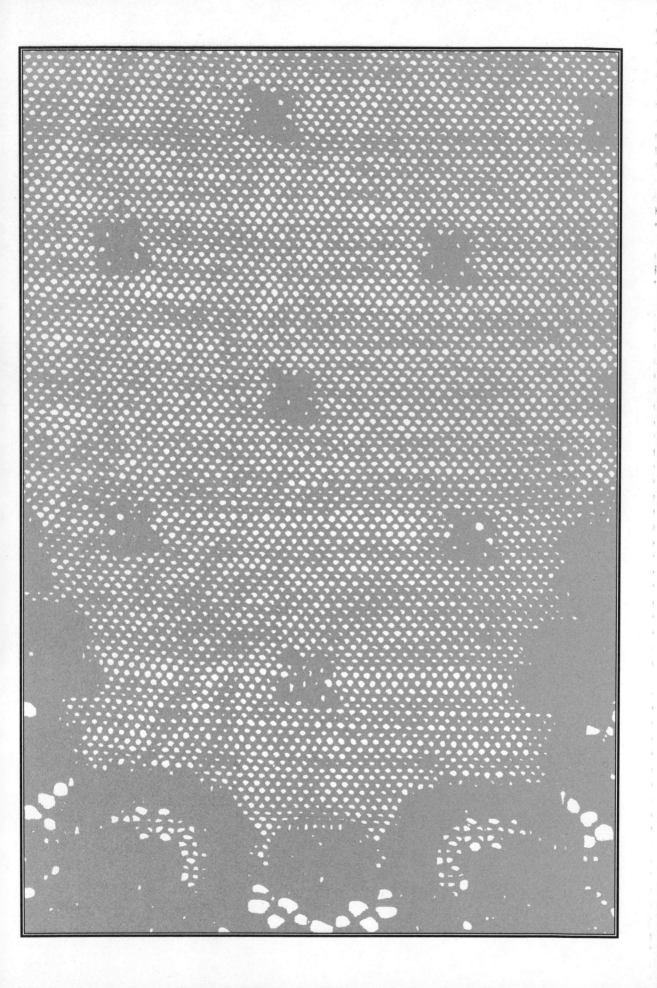

N.º

12

SOMEBODY STOP ME!

For *His* Eyes Only

$$

THE WONDERFUL LITTLE SEX BOOK
William Ashoka Ross

Sex and laughter go together. No one knows why. Good sex just naturally brings up bubbling laughter in you. Suddenly you laugh at existence, even at yourself. And it isn't even because anything is particularly funny. You don't laugh the way you would if you were watching a sitcom on TV. You laugh because life seems so simple, so easy. Worries you had only an hour ago are totally gone. All that weight you were carrying has totally disappeared. Isn't it amazing? If you revealed this to your local psychiatrist, he might never believe you - he might even think you were mad! Something like this happening just isn't logical, and yet, it happens all the time.

HOW TO MAKE LOVE ALL NIGHT
(and Drive a Woman Wild)
Barbara Keesling, Ph.D.

I tell men: Embrace your penis! Put out the welcome mat. Open a dialogue. Let it know it's a part of you and let it know you care. It's time to bring your penis in from the cold. The sooner you do, the sooner your sexuality will start to change. Now here's the best news. If you like your penis, your partner is going to like your penis. If you're proud of your penis, your partner is going to be proud of your penis. If you embrace your penis, your partner is going to embrace your penis. Sound Good? I thought it would.

*O*kay, it's going to cost you a little. But tonight you're going to recieve the *best oral sex you've ever had* — so read on —

Do you know the number one quality women say they look for in a man? It's a *grrreat* sense of humor! Here's an opportunity to show her yours, with just a little preparation. A few days before your date, hand your sweetie a sealed envelope and tell her not to open it until the night of the seduction. Shopping is next; you'll need some supplies.

When your special evening finally arrives, get dressed for your performance. First, put on a man's g-string. Over that goes bikini briefs, and finally a pair of outrageous boxer shorts. Cover it all with a robe, and invite her to bring her envelope into your little love nest. Ooh, baby, what a scene! The lights are low, the music's hot, and you've got every pillow you can find piled up for her to lounge on. Now samba across the room, a single rose between your teeth, a bowl of fresh, juicy grapes above your head. Remember, she's laughing *with* you, not at you....

Kneel before her and present her with the rose. Gently slip some grapes past her lips. She will simply *melt* when you massage her feet with scented oil. Rub it in, slowly and firmly, with special attention to each tiny toe. Whew! There's not a woman alive who wouldn't be in rapture by now.

It's showtime! Cue up a song on the stereo, one that makes you feel like dancing. No, not with her — *for* her, as her own private Chippendale dancer. Inside her envelope are dollar bills, twenty of them, for her to stuff into your underwear. Now go wild! Show her what a fun guy you are! Be as erotic as you can while you peel off the boxers and the briefs. She'll be cheering for more as you dash into the bathroom to change for the finale....

For your last dance, you seem to be bare, but she sees *something* glistening in the candlelight. You'll see a sparkle, too — in her eyes, when she discovers the beautiful bracelet around your swaying shaft. Think of it as a lure for her mouth   and don't stop your dance until she takes the bait. Tonight's talent show continues when she wraps her lips around you and blows the sweetest tune you've ever heard.

Keep in mind, the gift does NOT have to be expensive. And if it is, well, there's always extra cash to be earned on Star Search.

Ingredients

Baggy, brief, and very brief underwear, oil, grapes, and a rose
1 bracelet or watch (and it really is the thought that counts)

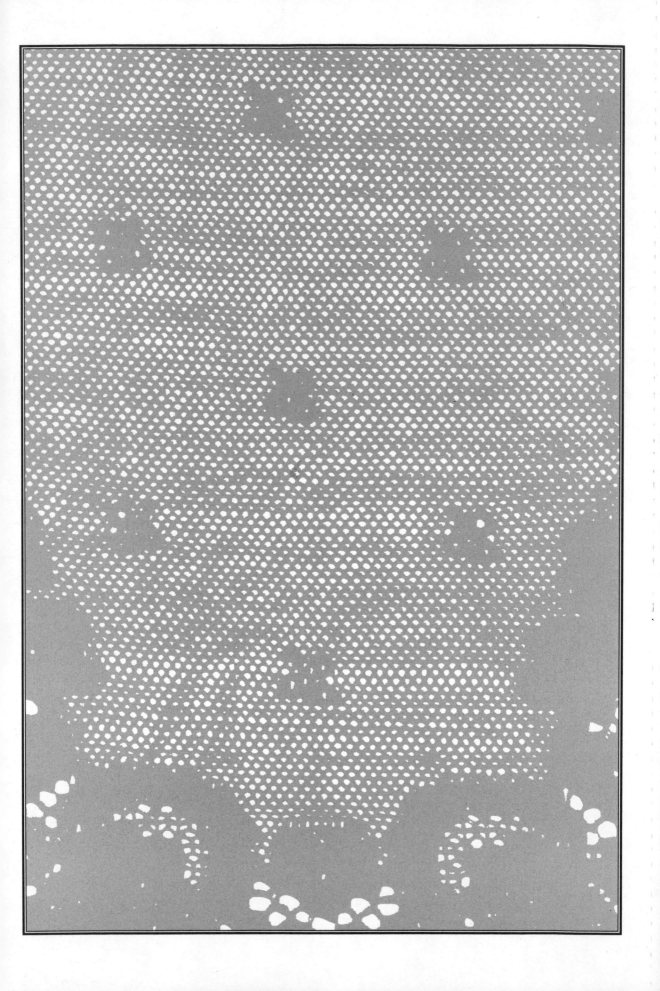

N⁰

13

BEAT AROUND THE BUSH

For *Her* Eyes Only

More men than you would believe thrive on a slight sense of danger. Men pick amazing places for sexual adventures. Some of the more trustworthy gentlemen I interviewed acknowledged that they had intercourse in-are you ready for these?- the Tomb of the Unknown Soldier, New York's Philharmonic Hall the week it opened, the ladies room of the Harvard Club, the choir loft of a church (I heard several variations on that one), underneath the bleachers at a rodeo, a band shell in a park on a rainy day and a department store window (the shades were closed) at night while the window was being decorated. The male animal seems to thrive on such nuttiness.

Remember those three important weapons that you should learn to wield effectively if you are going to keep the man you love in love with you:

      1. Imagination

      2. Sensitivity to his moods and desires.

      3. The courage to experiment with new sexual techniques, enticing situations and places.

*A*h, the great outdoors. All that sunshine and fresh air. It's invigorating. It's stimulating. And it's a *grrreat* place for sex! Of course, no venture into the wild is complete without a canteen. Find one and put it on the dashboard of his car with a note —

Let's go for a long walk. Someplace where we can study the birds.
And the bees.

Of course, you don't really need wilderness. A large park or preserve with lots of trees and hollows will do. If it's big enough to have walking trails, it's big enough to find a little privacy. The key is to dress for *easy access*. A long, flowing skirt and a loose button-up blouse is in order.

Once out on your hike, keep your eyes open for a concealed spot off the beaten path. The best places will probably be uphill — big rocks, overhangs and small crevasses will offer protection from prying eyes below. Throw out a blanket and enjoy the scenery. Commune with nature. If you don't see any wild animals right away, well, you'll just have to create one of your own. A few hot kisses and a few tight clinches will bring out the beast in him! Now, take advantage of your wardrobe.

Sit on his thighs and spread your skirt out wide. Invite him to slip his hands underneath. *Hmm, no underwear! Now this might turn out to be some picnic....* Your skirt covers his zipper, and as long as his hands are down there, ask him to open it. Once free, run your fingertips along the length of his timber. Stroke his erection *through* your dress. Draw the fabric across the taut skin of his firm flesh; wrap it up and squeeze it tight.

It's a powerfully erotic scene. He's being sexually serviced by a highly aroused woman, in a place where other people might come by, and if they did — *they wouldn't see a thing*. When you open a few buttons on your blouse, only he can look inside. When you slip him in and quickly, suddenly *sit* on his penis — your loose clothing covers all. As long as you stay on top you can literally make the earth move without being seen.

Now being heard is another matter. If your mate tends to bellow loudly when approaching climax, well — don't try this seduction during moose mating season!

Ingredients

1 Long, Voluminous Skirt / 1 Loose Button-Up Blouse / 1 Blanket / 1 Park or Forest
1 Canteen of Water and a Towel (For Cleanup Duty. No Bathrooms!)

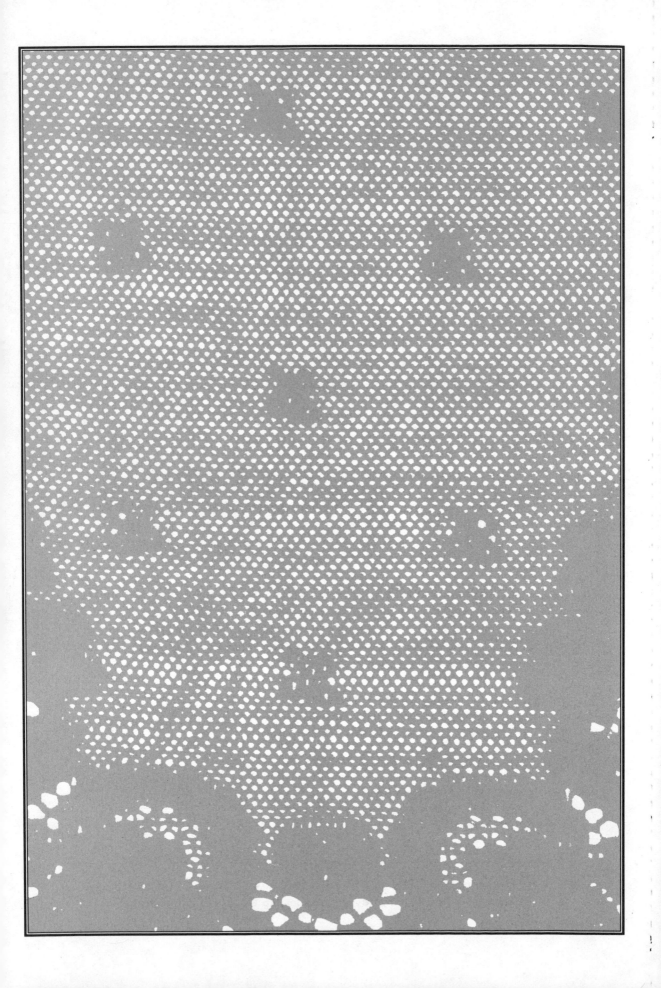

N^o *14*

FIRE DOWN BELOW

For *His* Eyes Only

TRICKS
Jay Wiseman

Nobody is sure of the reasons why spanking arouses some people (a very few even to the point of orgasm) and undoubtedly the reasons for this arousal vary from person to person. Some people speculate that the nerves that run to and from the genitals and maybe, in some as yet undiscovered manner, more closely linked in some people than in others. (This linkage could exist either in the peripheral nerves and/or within the brain itself, possibly the limbic area.) Thus, strong stimulation in one area (the buttocks) somehow "echoes" to the genitals.

DRIVE YOUR WOMAN WILD IN BED
Staci Keith

A lot of women reported sexual fantasies about being spanked or had actually engaged in spanking games during sex. Hitting is not spanking. The idea is to give her little spanks and bites and pinches where it's most tender. Tell her she's been naughty. Don't be grim about it - have fun.

*O*oooh! Here's a chance for you to discover if your darling has a hidden side that's just a wee bit...*kinky*....

The next time you're saying goodbye, give her your usual kiss. As she turns to go, though — swat her on the butt! *Hey, that's a great ass you got there, lady....*

She'll be startled and tickled, and delighted by all the attention you show over the next few days. Never pass up an opportunity to hug or touch her. Little does she know you're in training for Saturday's main event — when you're going to *wrestle!*

Of course, that doesn't mean you should lock her in a half-Nelson. But when the time is right, grab her in a big bear hug. Let her know how you missed her all week. As the evening wears on, get more physical with your affection. Do the dishes — then pop her with the dishtowel!

She should be feeling good and frisky by the time you move to the bedroom. Take your tussle to bed; try to pin her to the mat for a kiss. Is she flush with exertion... or is it arousal? As the carnal competition heats up, make your move. Straddle her back, facing her legs. Ahh, now you've got her where you want her! Tug her pants down; expose her bare bottom — and *spank her*. Oh, she'll squeal and squirm! But one good love smack will show her who's top dog in this battle of the sexes.

Now rub her cheeks. Play with them! She's certainly in no position to stop you. You've always admired her rear view, right? Then tell her — and swat her again! This time, as you knead the sting away, let your fingers trail down between her legs. No spanking here... only a soft touch as you probe the hot hidden secrets inside. Now again, lightly *pop* her bum with the palm of your hand, and then — back to your sensuous stroke. You're playing with fire, moving the heat back and forth between her thighs, and building the flame higher with every playful slap.

It won't be long before you can pass on paddling in favor of more, um, traditional forms of foreplay. But then again, she may not want you to stop. She might want to share.

And if she's a strong woman, close to your own size, well...you better *watch your butt,* mister!

Ingredients

A Light Touch / A Bare Butt

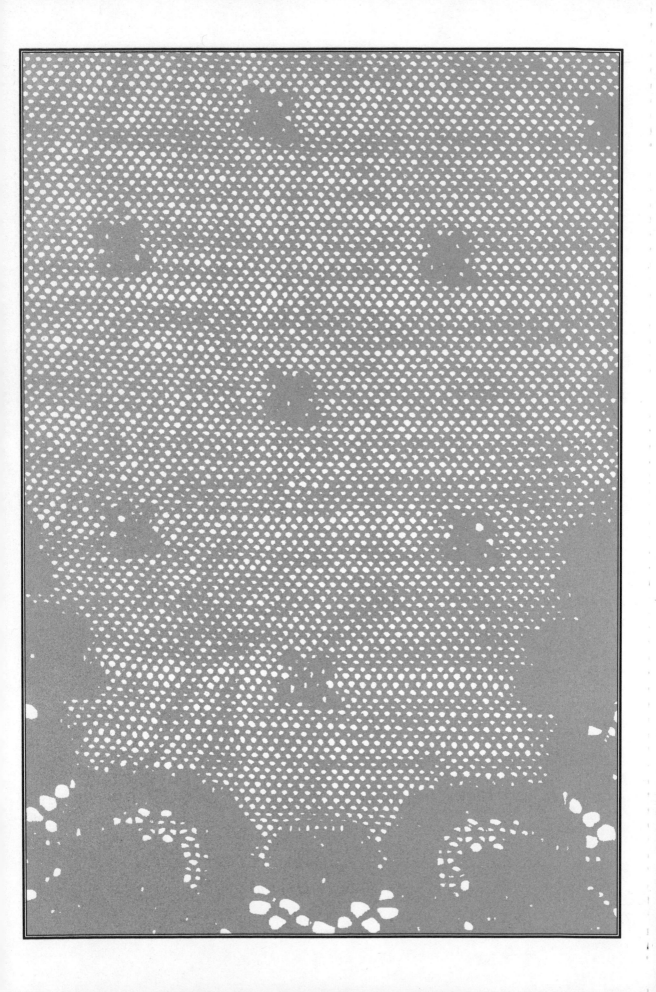

N<u>o.</u>

THE LAURA CORN CHALLENGE

For *Her* Eyes Only

WOMEN ON TOP
Nancy Friday

Because the taboo against female masturbation is so deeply embedded, let us think of ways of not losing the ground we've so recently won as expressed by the young women in this book. Our best defense is to make ourselves so consciously aware of what masturbation wins for women that we can't, won't unconsciously slip back:

1. Masturbation teaches us that we are sexual all by ourselves, separate from anyone, including mother.

2. Masturbation is an excellent exercise in learning to separate love and sex, a lesson especially important for women who confuse the two.

3. By teaching ourselves what excites us, we become more orgasmic and better sexual partners, responsible for our share, capable of giving pleasure, better able to give direction in what it is that excites us.

4. If we are to loathe to touch what lies between our legs, our revulsion spreads, leaving us eternally dissatisfied with the acceptability of the rest of our bodies.

5. Masturbation teaches us the difference between our clitoris, labia, urethra, and vagina.

6. Masturbation makes us far better candidates for contraceptive responsibility as well as for the sexual education of our children.

7. Last and most obvious, masturbation is one of life's greatest sources of sexual pleasure, thrilling in itself, a release from tension, a sweet sedative before sleep, a beauty treatment that leaves us glowing, our countenance more tranquil, our smile more mysterious. As one of the women put it, "Masturbation and fantasy is when I am most honest about myself."

Masturbation is a great teacher.

WHAT MEN REALLY WANT
Susan Crain Bakos

And many men ask: Why won't she masturbate for me?

"It really gets me going to watch a woman masturbate herself. That is one of the sexiest things a woman can do for a man. Yet few of the women I've been with are willing to do it. I had a lover who would look at me the whole time she rubbed circles around her clitoris. When her hips started grinding and her eyes got heavy, I almost came in my pants. That woman was hot," writes a chemical engineer.

*W*hy is it that men are such *voyeurs?* I've never met one who didn't privately relish the thought of watching a woman alone, secretly indulging her carnal nature. It's a powerful fantasy. Tonight, you're going to help him live out his most clandestine dream — and find one of your own.

Clear some space in your bedroom closet and position a chair inside so that its occupant will have a view of your bed. Set a mood — candlelight and music, a hint of your best perfume in the air. Lead him to his private seat and tell him it's very important that he stay completely quiet.

Shut the closet door *almost* all the way and leave the bedroom. Take a few minutes....Go make yourself a drink. When you come back, act like you're alone. *Think* like you're alone....

Undress. Sit on the edge of the bed and rub lotion on your arms, your shoulders, your neck. Snuggle back into your pillows and spread body oil across your breasts,....Play with them! Tug at your nipples; twist them and make them come alive. That wonderful, warm feeling will spread to your belly and on to your thighs; follow it with your fingers. You know where it leads.

Caress yourself. Slowly slide one finger into your folded flesh — and then another. Make them wet; make them slippery and then glide them in gentle circles around your clitoris. No one but you has ever known exactly how to touch it, how it feels best. Skirt the edge of orgasm until it's *unbearable,* until you can't stand another second of restraint and then...let go. Climax. Give into it totally! Remember, there's no one there to disturb your erotic dance of pleasure. No one, except that extremely horny, extremely erect man secretly hiding behind the door.

This, then, is the Challenge. Once you've mustered the cool courage it takes to abandon convention — once you've felt the liberation that comes with controlling your own sexuality — once you've discovered the power to *arouse your mate by arousing yourself* — you'll never look at relationships with men the same way again. You'll sport a fresh sense of confidence. You'll walk with a new spring in your step. You'll be a fully empowered woman, with a more mysterious smile, and it starts this week when you accept The Challenge.

--- *Ingredients* ---

1 Chair / 1 Room with a View / Candles, Fragrance, Music / One Confident Woman

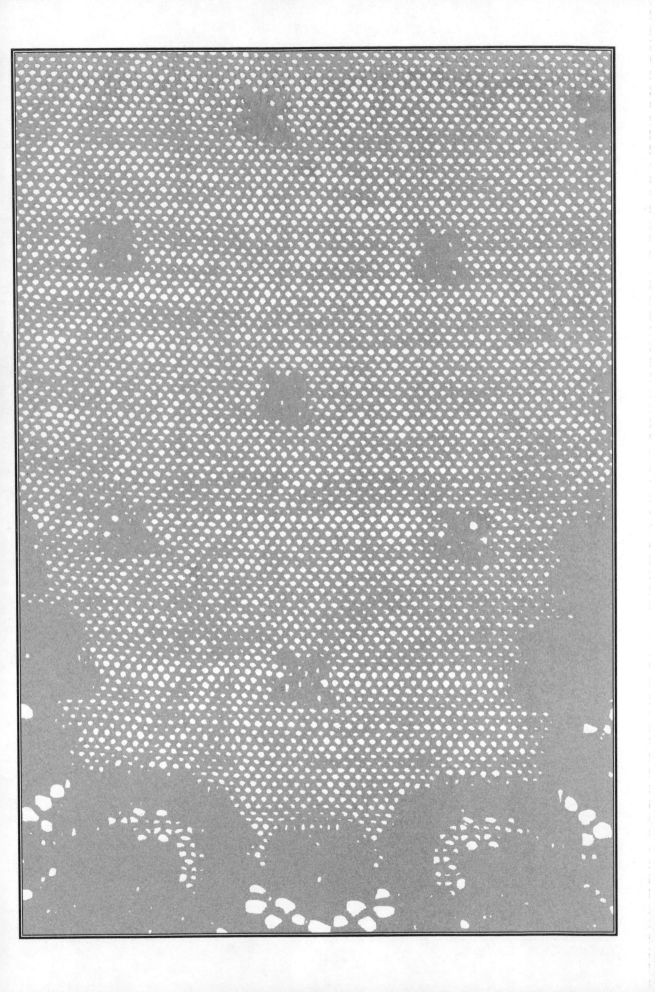

N.º **16**

THE GEE! STROKE

For *His* Eyes Only

$

THE G SPOT
Alice Kahn Ladas, Beverly Whipple, John D. Perry

Where exactly is the G spot located? The Grafenberg Spot lies directly behind the pubic bone within the front wall of the vagina. It is usually located about halfway between the back of the urethra (the tube through which you urinate) and near the neck of the bladder, where it connects with the urethra. The size and exact location vary. (Imagine a small clock inside the vagina with 12 o'clock pointing towards the nave. The majority of women will find the G spot located in the area between 11 and 1 o'clock) Unlike the clitoris, which protrudes from the surrounding tissue, it lies deep within the vaginal wall, and a firm pressure is often needed to contact the G spot in its unstimulated state.

If you have a partner with whom you feel comfortable, you may want to share the discovery of your G spot. You may find this easier if you are lying on your belly, legs apart and hips rotated slightly upwards. Have your partner insert two fingers (palm downs) and explore the front wall of your vagina (which will be closest to the bed) with a firm touch. Move your pelvis to facilitate contact with the G spot. Tell your partner what feels good. This position is also an excellent one for stimulation by the penis. If your partner inserts one or two fingers (palm up) into your vagina while you are lying on your back, the G spot can usually be felt by putting pressure against the top wall of the vagina, in an area about halfway between the back of the pubic bone and the end of the vagina where the cervix is located. Putting a second hand on top of the abdomen, just above the pubic hairline with a downward pressure, sometimes helps to stimulate the G spot.

HOT MONOGAMY
Dr. Patricia Love & Jo Robinson

You can incorporate G spot stimulation into your lovemaking rituals in a wide variety of ways. A woman may find it easier to reach orgasm if her partner stimulates her G spot and clitoris at the same time. ("When my boyfriend does that to me," confessed one young woman, "you have to scrape me off the ceiling.") Some women find that lovemaking becomes more pleasurable when the G spot is stimulated prior to intercourse, engorging the tissue and making it more responsive to pressure from the penis. A woman can intensify her orgasms by adding G spot stimulation as she reaches orgasm. Some people call this a blended orgasm because it combines sensations from both the vagina and the clitoris.

Finally, sexual athletes can experiment with using the G spot to produce a blended, extended orgasm, one that results in not just multiple but almost continuous orgasms. To create an extended orgasm, stimulate the clitoris until the woman reaches orgasm. Then, as her vagina begins to contract in orgasm, transfer your attention to the G spot. When the contractions subside and the clitoris loses its hypersensitivity, resume clitoral stimulation until she peaks once again. And so on. And so on.

*A*pogee means the very highest point in an orbit around the earth. This week, you're launching your true love straight into space with a technique that uses a *gee* of a different sort. No, it's not rocket science — it's *pocket rocket* science!

Get her curiosity aroused early in the week. Offer her an elegantly giftwrapped pair of g-string panties with a card that simply says, "Gee!" Don't explain, though, until your special evening rolls around — it's not her g-string you're interested in, but her *G spot,* and the advanced G-stroke technique.

And you've got such a nifty new tool to help you! It's the *G-spot stimulator,* and can be found in most adult stores. It's tiny, and so very, very friendly, but she might be a little startled at first, so start your hunt the old-fashioned way. Once she's thoroughly warmed up, slip a well-manicured finger into her. Mmm, doesn't that feel *good?* All that warm, soft, wet flesh inviting you inside....

Ask her to lay on her tummy, legs apart and hips slightly raised, as described opposite. Has it been awhile since you *fingered* her? Then take you're time — explore her vagina. Her G-spot may not be obvious at first, but as it gets stimulated, you may notice a pronounced swelling, a stiff spot, along the front wall. She'll notice, too; it's a tingle that is *not* the same as the one her clitoris gives her. And speaking of our little friend, let's not neglect it! If she rises to her knees, bottom in the air, you'll be able to stroke her clit while maintaining gentle pressure on the G-spot. And, of course, you have that incredibly erotic view....

Time for technology to lend a hand. Ask your sweetie to turn over and sit up, leaning back against her pillows, and slowly insert the stimulator. Start to thrust in and out, building up your rhythm. Listen to her body — it'll tell you if you're on track. Now get ready. She's about to have the orgasm of her life.

> *Five* ....Switch from G-spot to clitoris. Keep stimulating.
> *Four*.........Engines ignited. Switch back to G-stroke.
> *Three*.......Clitoris again. Rub faster. No turning back now.
> *Two* ....Add the G-stroke. Maintain C-stroke. Full throttle!
> *One* ....Rub faster. Kiss her goodbye! Ohhh, geeeeeeeee....
>
> *Blastoff*....and bon voyage!

Ingredients

1 G-String / 1 G-Spot / 1 Stimulator, adult stores or see Speciality Page
(Extra points! Learn the *blended extended orgasm,* opposite page)

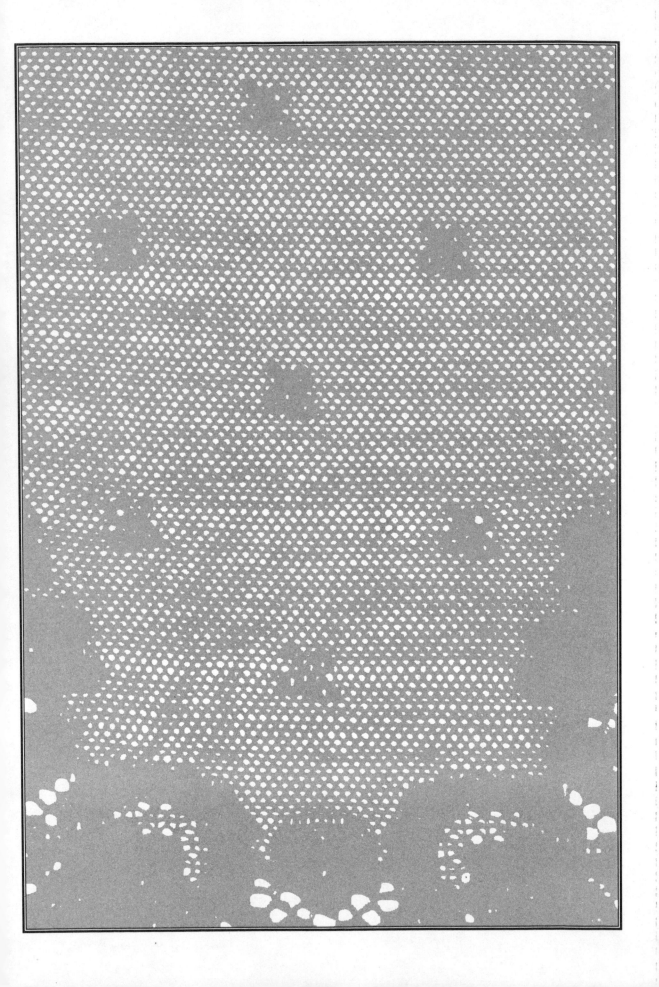

Nº

TOOL TIME

For *His* Eyes Only

$

WILD IN BED TOGETHER
Graham Masterton

When he's making love, a great lover thinks only about arousing the woman in his arms, by any means possible, and about how much she excites him in return. Concentration is what makes a great lovers' lovemaking electric and everybody else's lovemaking ordinary. From the moment that he brings her to a stunning and satisfying orgasm, a great lover gives her the impression that he thinks and cares only about making her feel special.

SECRETS OF SIZZLIN' SEX
Cricket Richmond & Ginny Valletti

Using a new, soft pediatric toothbrush, lightly stroke perineum up to the vaginal entrance then glide lightly around the opening. Now run the bristles away then back again. After getting sufficiently revved up, insert brush no further than an inch or two and gently swirl around. Sounds silly, you say? Don't give this idea the brush off til giving it a try.

Using a long-handled sable art brush, roll the bristles into a point before dipping tip in warm oil. Now "paint" a mini masterpiece on your hot little perineum canvas. Equally effective are cosmetic and narrow sponge brushes.

*M*ichealangelo may have been a genius, but he never dreamed up a seduction *this* enticing!

Well, at least as far as we know. Certainly it would have been hard for the guy to concentrate if he had the kind of subject you're going to be working with.

Start your seduction with a trip to an art supply store. Don't bother with the paint department — it's brushes you're after. Pick a variety, all with very soft bristles, and when you get home lay them neatly across your bathroom counter. Just leave them there for a day or two; let your sweetheart wonder what's up.

Then one night...especially after she's had a really rugged day...invite her to attend the *Grrreat Sex* School of Erotic Arts. Not as a student — she's going to be your model, and your canvas! A hot bath will unkink her muscles and soften her skin, and give you time to prepare your studio. Soft lights, some slow music, and a small bowl of warm massage oil are all you need.

Have her stretch out across the bed, and start your masterpiece. Begin with a dry brush softly stroking her face — cheeks, eyebrows, lips and nose. Work your way around her ears and down her neck. Now dip the brush in the heated oil, and draw a bold stripe straight down between her breasts to her tummy. Mmm, this is a delicious sensation! Sketch a design across her skin in sensuous, slick lotion. Write her name, and see if she can guess what it was!

Switch to a little brush, and swirl it around her nipples. Ooh — see how they glisten when they perk up? Very sexy....

Now for your smallest tool. Soak it in the oil and roll it into a fine point. Pull back the flesh around her clitoris, and caress it with warm, wet sable. At this point, the lubricant may get hotter *after* you apply it. Pick up your largest brush again and slooooowwwly drag it lengthwise past her clit. Let her feel every velvety strand of fur as it flutters by. Do it again, a little faster. *Flick it....*Can you make her come with only your brush and your skill?

If so, congratulations. You are truly one of the Old Masters. If not, well, you can always move into the, uh, Digital Age — and I'm not talking about *soft*ware, if you know what I mean!

Ingredients

Unscented Almond Oil, or Similar Massage Lotion
Several Soft Paintbrushes in Different Sizes

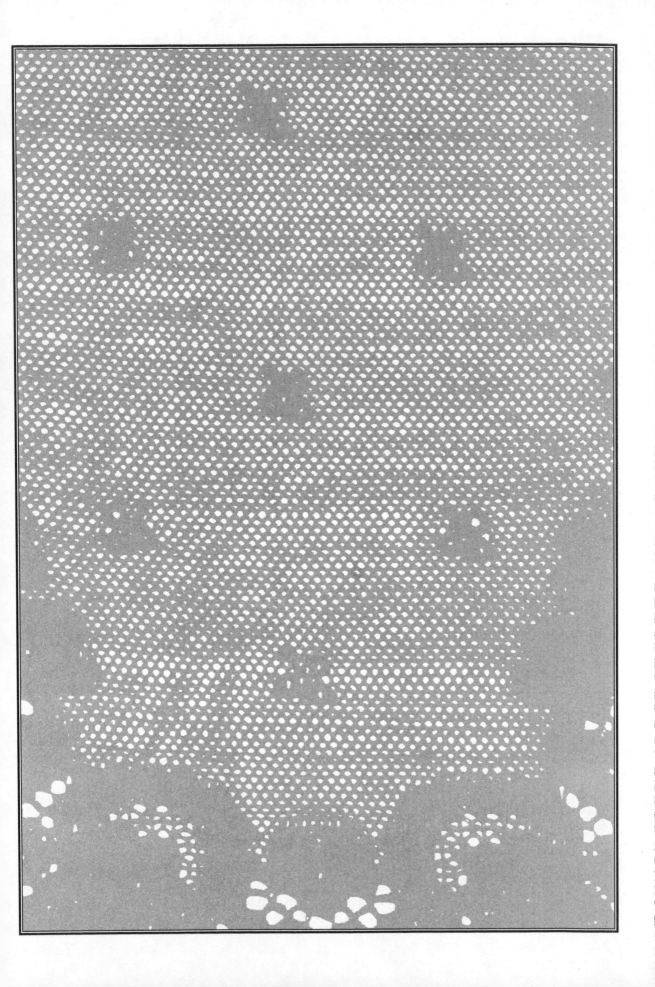

$N\!.^o$ 18

THE THRILL OF THE CHASE

For *Her* Eyes Only

HOT MONOGAMY
Dr. Patricia Love & Jo Robinson

Romance is playful and flirtatious. I asked a group of middle-aged men what said "romance" to them, and they all agreed that playfulness was one of the key ingredients:

Chris: When I think of romance, I think of coquettishness. A certain playfulness. I like to be teased. Seduced.

Patrick: There's kind of a creativity involved, too. There you are, plodding along, doing your thing, and your lover takes you away from all that. The surprise phone call. "Let's do something different." It's a relief. It's youthful. It's like being a colt, being filled with energy.

Jim: If a woman is playful, I don't care if she's one hundred and twenty. I'm going to get horny.

SECRETS OF SIZZLIN' SEX
Cricket Richmond & Ginny Valletti

Nothing's more inhibiting to unbridled sex than thinking someone will meander in and catch you bottoms up, bikini down. Privacy is essential to effective eroticism.

If you share your humble abode, securing privacy may seem the impossible dream. Whether contending with children, guests or roommates, there are ways to insure uninterrupted encounters. A little advance preparation can protect sexy seclusion in the midst of mayhem. Since everyone deserves time, place and space to let their clothes and guard down, let's lock in a workable solution.

*T*here's absolutely nothing a man enjoys more than the pursuit of a woman. The compulsion to chase and capture a mate is written right into his genetic code; it's what keeps his adrenaline pumping and his testosterone flowing. In one form or another, men rely on this impulse throughout their lives to drive them to excel — on the playing field, at work, or in the bedroom.

This week you're turning that instinct to your advantage by sending him on a quest — *for you!* Set your lure out early. Slip an envelope in his briefcase or pocket one morning as he heads out the door. He'll smile when he opens it and finds a pair of your prettiest panties. He'll be intrigued when he sees the note: *The trail starts at the garage door....Happy hunting!*

I hope he can get some work done — because he's going to spend the day thinking about *you!* His naughtiest suspicions will be confirmed as soon as he gets home; sure enough, there are your stockings, draped provocatively across the doorknob. Inside the house, he'll find your blouse, your bra, your skirt, and more — clearly marking a path to paradise! Think he'll be surprised when he opens the bedroom door and finds you wearing only a towel and teasing him to catch you?

As he comes through the doorway, bombard him with pillows. Keep a pillow in your hand to playfully bat him away when he tries to grab your towel. Play cat-and-mouse until he pauses to catch his breath — then get up and run! Make him chase you again until he finally manages to capture his sweet prize.

There is, however, one last obstacle for him to get through. When he pulls the towel off of you, he'll find your body covered tightly with Saran Wrap!

Ohhh no! Here's a man who has a hard time unwrapping sandwiches, forced to pull off yards of plastic before he can savor his victory. Don't skip this step, though — three parts arousal and one part frustration makes a *grrreat* recipe for seduction. And don't let go of your pillow just yet. You'll need it in case he turns out to be a smart-aleck as he peels the film away.

If he says *"Hmm, leftovers again, honey?"* —

Hit him! And run like crazy!

Ingredients

1 Scattered Outfit / 1 Towel / Several Pillows / Plastic Wrap

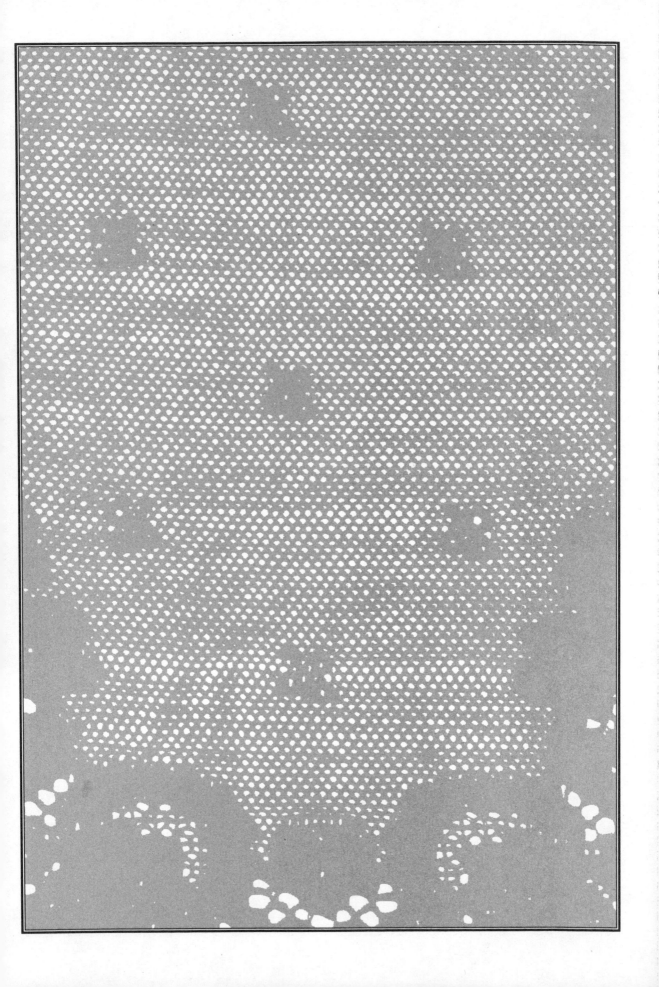

N.º *19*

SCHWING!

For *Her* Eyes Only

SINGLE WILD SEXY AND SAFE
Graham Masterton

Perhaps the most famous use of visual stimuli was Sharon Stone's quick flaunting of her pantielessness in the movie Basic Instinct. I'm not suggesting for a moment that you walk around with no panties, opening your legs to every sexy man you meet, but you can use this and other visual teasers to keep your *own* man's sexual interest at a very high pitch.

The "no panties" trick is one of the best. Actually, you don't even have to show your beau that you're not wearing any panties. All you have to do is whisper to him, halfway through the evening, "I forget to put on my panties. " Then see what effect it has on him. Nobody else will be able to see whether you're wearing any panties or not, but your man will stick to you like Crazy Glue for the rest of the evening-just in case-and believe me, he won't be able to think about anything else.

SECRETS OF SEDUCTION
Sue Jordan

Sex is about having fun and taking risks, so don't be afraid to let go and be creative! After all, how long can you do the ol' in and out? Get rid of the ordinary. Relax and be willing to make a fool of yourself. I'm not talking whips, chains and handcuffs; if that's your flavor, it's your business. I'm talking about trying something new and inventive for a few passionate moments. put yourself in a state of inspiration. And remember, there's no such thing as can't.

*H*ow long has it been since you and your sweetheart played miniature golf? Remember how much fun it was! Today's special round has more to do with *tease* than tees, though, and while you won't improve his game — you sure might help him score!

After you pay for the game and collect your equipment, excuse yourself for just a second. Run to the ladies room, and when you come back, hand him his golf ball wrapped in your panties. Tell him you wanted to make the game a bit more...challenging.

Take your turn first. You've practiced with this same skirt in front of a mirror, so you know exactly how to bend and place your ball for the best view of the, uh, scenery. Take your shot, and then make him squirm — *now honey, you do know where the hole is, don't you?* A quick kiss, a brush of your fingers across his zipper, and you'll have his putter standing at attention!

Stroll over to the hole while he sets up his shot, and crouch down behind it with your knees just slightly apart. Remind him to pull his jaw off the ground — *and try to keep your eye on the ball, big guy.* Ri-i-i-ight...If he wins this first hole, shame on you!

You'll have a blast taunting him with every glimpse, every touch.

Ooh, they really keep it...well trimmed, wouldn't you say? Gosh, it feels really breezy out here today. Have you seen my panties? Gee, dear, you seem to be playing with some sort of...handicap....Is that a golf ball in your pocket, or are you just glad to see me?

On the way home, give him a longer peek under your skirt. Take his hand and trail his fingertips up your thigh. Hey, what's a game of golf without a trip to the nineteenth hole? Reach over and squeeze him — gently! — while he tries to concentrate on the road. *What kind of driver you got there, fella? Is that an eight-iron or is it a...a big, long nine-iron?*

If you're feeling brave, you can open up his, mmm...golf bag and find out. Think about that automatic ball-washer down at the driving range — any ideas? Oh, and as long as you're in traffic, be careful with your teeth. Don't want to end up in the rough!

FORE!

––––––––––––––––––– *Ingredients* –––––––––––––––––––

1 Miniature Golf Course / A Lot of Balls / 1 Short Skirt

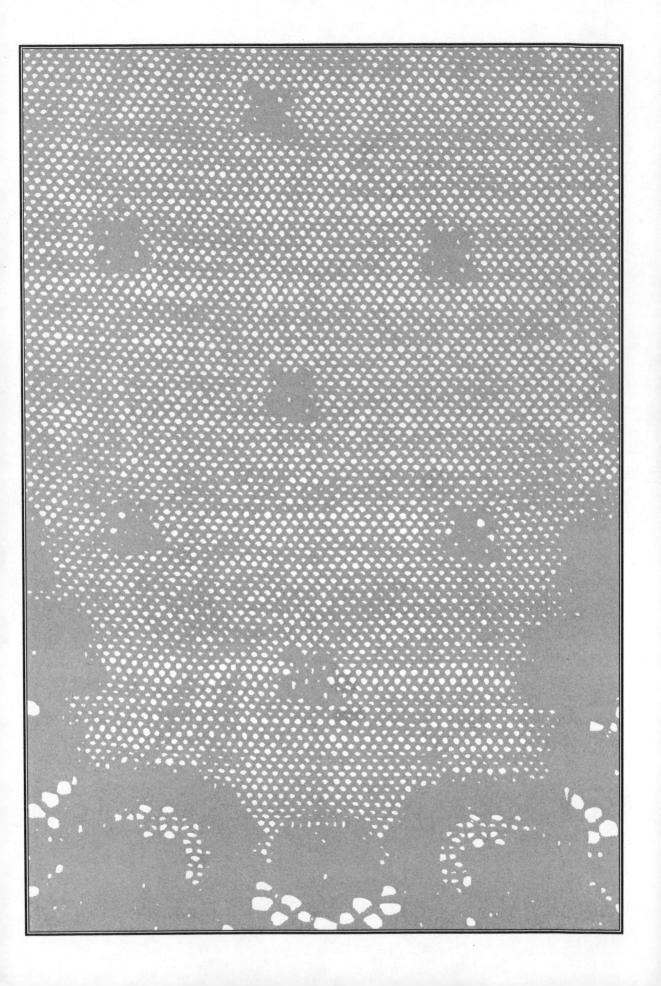

N? 20

DOWN AND DIRTY

For *Her* Eyes Only

IF IT FEELS GOOD
Joan Elizabeth Lloyd

Although background music may be the thing we think of first when we think about the sense of hearing, it isn't the only way that sound can be used to enhance lovemaking. Four-letter words, spoken at an auspicious moment, arouse many people. Cock, fuck, and cunt may sound grating in ordinary conversation, but in the heat of passion the phrase "I want to feel your big, hard prick inside of me," or "I love to suck your titties" can be just the stimulus needed to raise the level of sexual intensity one more notch. Try a sentence in the heat of passion and feel your partner's reaction.

THE SEXUALLY SATISFIED WOMAN
Dr. Ronnie Edell

Tease him with your voice. Your voice is a powerful instrument for seduction. Depending on what you say and how you say it, your voice can carry a potent message about your sexuality - and pack an erotic punch that leaves your lover speechless.

Your voice is the most versatile sex toy you can add to your collection. Play it for all it's worth! Use it to soothe, seduce, goad, challenge, control, or charmingly condescend and you'll keep your partner on his toes all the way through the final stages of this game. To keep the element of surprise in the tease, use your voice to convey the endless variety of your emotions: intense desire ("Kiss me, now!"); playful disapproval ("You call that a kiss?"); mischief ("Why are you so excited? Why is your penis so erect?"); sensuality ("Mmmm...that's the way I like it."); innocence ("I'd love to touch you there and make you feel really good, but I've never done that before. You'll have to show me how."); confidence ("Lick me here- and do it like you mean it.");

THE LITTLE BLACK BOOK OF ANSWERS
Laura Corn

I asked 5,000 men:
If a woman wanted to intensify your orgasm,
what words should she whisper in your ear right before?

The top three answers in order are:

1. I'm coming.

2. I Love you.

3. **** me harder!

*W*hy are men so fascinated by *bad girls?* A woman who's exceptionally secure in her sexuality, who clearly relishes hot, sweaty flesh-to-flesh contact, whose very attitude says, "Just do me" — this woman will never lack for attention.

Your own mate, of course, is a gentleman and respects you too much to even look at another woman, no matter how naughty her behavior. Right? *Right?* And no doubt he loves the fact that you're always a perfect lady. Still, there's a part of him — and I think you know what part — that would like to see you be like those other women. Just a little...a smidgen...a teensy bit...*nasty.*

This is the week you're going to do it! The best way to warm him up for it is to catch him in public — at his job, or with a group of friends — and whisper, so close that he feels your hot breath on his neck, *"You look really good today. And I have this incredible urge to fuck you."*

He will blush the deepest shade of crimson. *"I just touched myself, and guess what? My panties are all wet."* His pulse just went off the charts. *"Meet me at home. I want to see how many times I can make you come tonight."* Ohhhh, yes!

Don't be shy. Remember, you share a bed with this man — you're allowed to get down and dirty with him. You're *supposed* to get down and dirty! And just wait'll you see how aroused he gets when you do. As soon as he gets home, jump his bones. Tell him exactly what you want, in language any sailor would understand.

Oh God, I nearly came in the car on the way home. Can you feel how wet I am? Oooh, that's nice.... Stick your fingers in me oh! yes just like that. Ummmm... I don't know what got into me, but I just kept thinking about your cock all day. How it feels deep inside me. Oooh and your fingers on my clit... the way you get me off first before you fuck me. Oh, yeah keep your hand right there, ohh just a little harder...yes ...I think I'm going to come ohhhh, I'm coming....

His blood is now boiling. He might actually be speechless, but don't let that stop you from talking. Talking dirty — like the secretly nasty woman you are.

Good girls go to heaven.
Bad girls go *eeeeverywhere!*

Ingredients
---

1 Part Lady / 1 Part Slut!

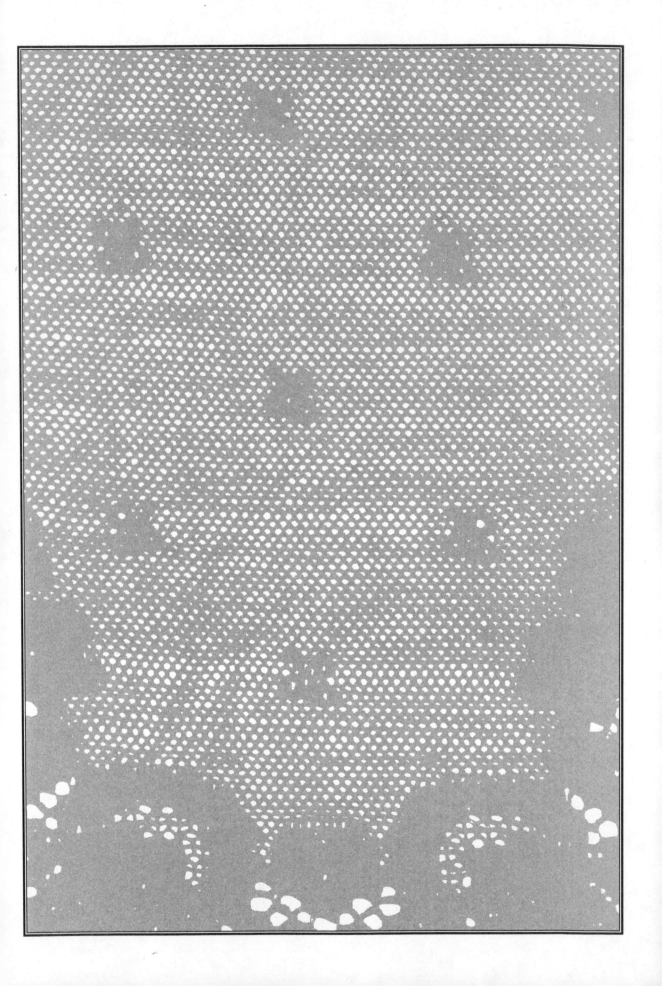

WILD CARD

For *Her* Eyes Only

RED HOT MONOGAMY
Patrick T. Hunt M.D.

Ladies, change your usual position, your cologne or perfume, your technique. Keep them off balance, never knowing what or where to expect love-making to happen.

Plan on having sex all over the house. Exotic locations like on the dining room table add a degree of excitement and naughtiness that your partner will love.

SECRETS OF SIZZLIN' SEX
Cricket Richmond & Ginny Valletti

Women erotically aware make room for a chair. They know it's used for more than sitting or plunking clothes on. Space permitting, a chaise lounge is an alluring accessory, since you can position yourself in a variety of pleasurable ways. A Victorian rocker or wicker chair with plump cushions and matching ottoman keeps you sitting pretty. A thick, overstuffed armchair or recliner can elevate eroticism. Almost any chair could be useful for amour and more. What's this, you'd love adding a neat seat but, there's no room? Suspend your derriere in an artsy, woven swing. Requiring no floor space, it can be slipped off the hook when swinging sessions are put to sleep.

*H*ooray for beds! We sleep in them, cuddle in them, laugh in them, make love in them. All in all, we probably spend too little time in them. But there's a lot of fun to be had *out* of bed, too, and that's the idea behind this week's seduction.

Drive home this point by making up a small sign that says "Off Limits" and tape it to your headboard while your favorite playmate is out of the house. (For a real chuckle, go to one of those novelty shops in the mall and get several "Police Line — Do Not Cross" banners. Wrap them all around your bed.)

Tease him through the day, and when you've got his temperature raised, explain the mystery of the Forbidden Zone in the bedroom. Your assignment for tonight is to make love *somewhere else...* some place or some piece of furniture you've never used before. My favorite — the stairs! If you've got them (and if they're padded and carpeted) they're a wonderful playground for consenting adults. Start near the bottom. He sits; you make magic with your mouth. Climb up over him so that you can kneel on a runner while straddling his face. It's not exactly going down when you're going *up,* is it? Climb higher still; let him stand and slip inside you from behind. Climb to the top, and sit on the landing; he'll know what to do.

Don't stop there. Keep moving! Use your imagination. Have you ever done it next to the kitchen sink? Under the dining room table? Mmm, I'll bet you've already discovered the joys of a washer on its spin cycle. Let that humming machine shake you out of your washday blues.

Move to the garage! Sure, it's his turf, which is precisely why he'll love it so much. Jump up on his workbench and ask him to show you his "drill press." And you've got a little *vise grip* you'd like to demonstrate. If you're feeling daring, keep the lights out and open the garage door.

Atop the sofa, in the entry hall, above a stereo speaker (with the bass turned way up!), on the patio — any place you've *never* made love should be the next place you make love.

And if you've had an itch to move the furniture around, well — you're looking right at a big, strong, happy man who will be willing to do anything you want so long as you *just... don't... stop!*

Ingredients

1 Sign or Banner / 1 House Full o' Love

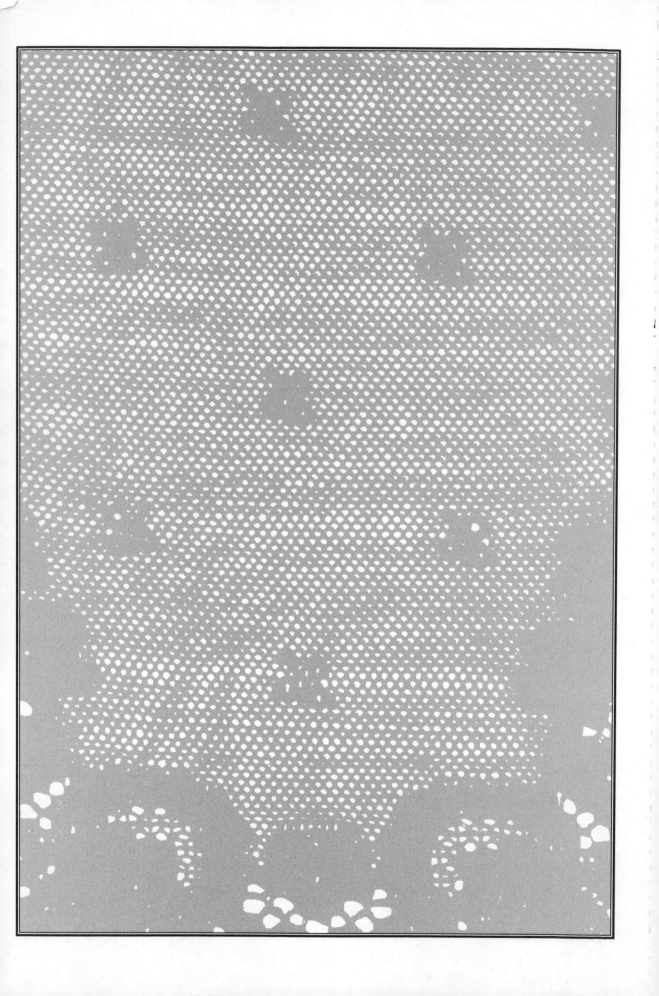

Nº **22**

MR. LUCKY

For *His* Eyes Only

s

GOOD VIBRATIONS GUIDE TO SEX
Cathy Winks and Anne Semans

Please allow us to set the record straight: A dildo is not a penis substitute any more than riding a bike is a substitute for taking a stroll. A dildo is an object which allows you to penetrate yourself or your partner in a marvelous variety of ways. Dildos are a logical, dare we say, natural response to the fact that while many of us enjoy having our vaginas or anuses filled, no two of us have exactly the same preferences in terms of the length, width and shape of the object filling us. Why should your experiences with penetrations be defined by the dimensions of your current partners' penises or fingers? Few of us limit our dining experiences to eating only whatever is in the refrigerator at home. Think of dildos as the takeout food of the sexual realm; they offer novelty, spice up your routine and teach you about the range of your appetites.

COME PLAY WITH ME
Joan Elizabeth Lloyd

We who buy sex toys are old, young, creative, and ordinary. We have great, active sex lives and play with our partner, or we are solitary users of sexual items and please only ourselves. We play frequently, or we bring out the toy bag only once or twice a year, when we're on vacation or on the rare occasion when we're feeling especially adventurous.

Are these products so exotic? Not really. Intriguing? Yes. And frequently, they lead to all sorts of activities you never thought you and your partner would be interested in trying.

Most people would have more fun in bed if they let go of all their inhibitions and just played.

Ooh, I get by with a little help from my friends...
— John Lennon and Paul McCartney

*T*his week, you are going to have a *ménage a trois.*

No, not with an extra person. The third party in this seduction is *Mr. Lucky,* and while he's not much for conversation...he has some really smooth moves!

He's a *dildo* — an artificial penis of any size, color, or style you choose. You'll have a blast shopping the adult stores to find him, but remember, you want to turn her on, not scare her to death! Nothing in the, er, elephant category. Now don't tell her exactly what you have in mind. Just say that tonight is going to be different from any other!

Start with a soft and sensitive massage from her neck to her toes. Tell her to close her eyes and relax, feeling only your smooth, tantalizing strokes. Spend a lot of time between her thighs, circling her most precious place with your fingers. When she's quite thoroughly aroused — when she's *wet and ready* — introduce her to Mr. Lucky.

He could use a little rubdown of his own. Coat him generously with Astroglide or one of the other premier sexual lubricants, which are water-based and guaranteed not to cause any adverse reaction on tender flesh. Start outside, gliding your little pal across her clitoris, warming him in the gentle folds of her flesh. Insert it only partially at first — then withdraw. More slow passes over her clit, and then in again, a little further this time.

Keep repeating this action from clitoral stimulation to insertion, going in deeper each time with slow, firm movements. Gradually speed up your motion, then slow down to a teasing pace again. Fast, slow, in and out; don't stop the process or break the spell.

When you're ready to enter her with your own erection, you'll find that she's been anxiously awaiting your arrival. Mr. Lucky's a lot of fun—

But YOU got the right one, baby! *Uh-huh!*

Ingredients

Massage Oil and Astroglide / 1 Dildo / 1 Strong Arm / 1 Easy Touch

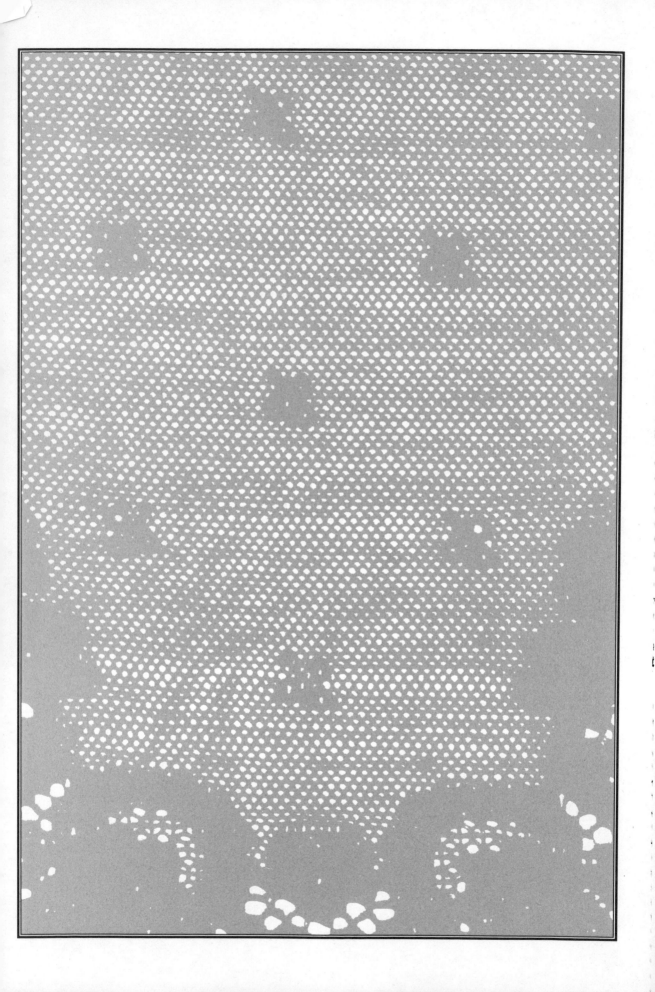

Nº

THE SECRET DESSERT

For *Her* Eyes Only

WHAT MEN REALLY WANT
Susan Crain Bakos

Sex in semipublic places is high on the male wish list. They want to do it on the balcony or patio, in bathrooms or closets at parties, in your childhood bed while visiting Mom and Dad. What's a close second to the fantasy of intercourse on a plane or train, a Forum readers' favorite? Having her perform fellatio while he's driving on an interstate highway. Partly he craves the visual thrill of watching her do something she wouldn't do without being coaxed. And partly the risk of getting caught arouses him.

SECRETS OF A MISTRESS
Rose Smith

A marital affair is like a classic movie. It's not something you want to indulge in everyday because that will make its magic average and ordinary. Instead, it's something you want to use now and again to turn the routine into something exciting and wonderful. One element many people who engage in extramarital affairs cite as enticing is the secrecy of meeting their lovers in hotel rooms and secluded restaurants. The marital affair offers you the chance to do the same, but without the dire consequences of an extramarital affair. What could be more arousing than a clandestine meeting with your spouse as your date? Both of you can steal a few moments to stop worrying about everyday hassles and enjoy being together as passionate lovers.

*M*en!! They can be such little kids sometimes, can't they? It seems like they never lose that foolhardy need to take chances, that compulsion to live on the edge. And they're never happier than when they can scare us with the risks they take! Clearly a testosterone-thing, don't you think?

It's time to turn the tables on the man in your life. This week, you're taking him on a wild ride. He's going to get the thrill of a lifetime, and you're going to get — chocolate! Sounds fair....

Send him a formal invitation to share a meal with you. Write it out exactly like this: *You're invited to come at dinner with me this Saturday at eight.*

AT dinner?? Did he read that right? Must be a typo. Now, the key to the success of this seduction is not the type of restaurant — but the type of restroom! Scout it out before you make reservations, because it must be an intimate room with *a lock on the front door.*

When you special evening arrives, insist on hors d'oeuvres and wine before your main course. You want his appetite — and his libido! — to be simmering. Go on, flirt with him. Reminisce about your hottest sexual experiences together. And once you're certain he has sex on his mind, jolt him. Lean in close and whisper that your *panties are getting wet.*

Take his hand and, after reminding him to pick his jaw up off the table, lead him to the back of the restaurant. You want to show him the, er, dessert tray. When you get to the restroom — smile wickedly. Pull him in with you, and lock the door.

Pounce on him at once! Greedily kiss his mouth. Lean back against the vanity and wrap one leg around his thigh. As the passion builds, pull your dress up and let him feel your moistness. Tug at his zipper; free his pride swelling under your fingers. Don't bother with removing your panties. Just pull the elastic aside to make room for his probing fingers — and his throbbing erection. Foreplay? That's another seduction. This one is about fast, hot, short, intense orgasm.

You should be able to make it back to your table in time for your entree. You're waiter probably didn't even notice your strange disappearance. He might get suspicious, however, if you both break out in peals of laughter when he asks if you're ready for dessert. *Gee — AGAIN?!*

Ingredients

1 Restaurant / 1 Locked Bathroom / 1 Hungry Man

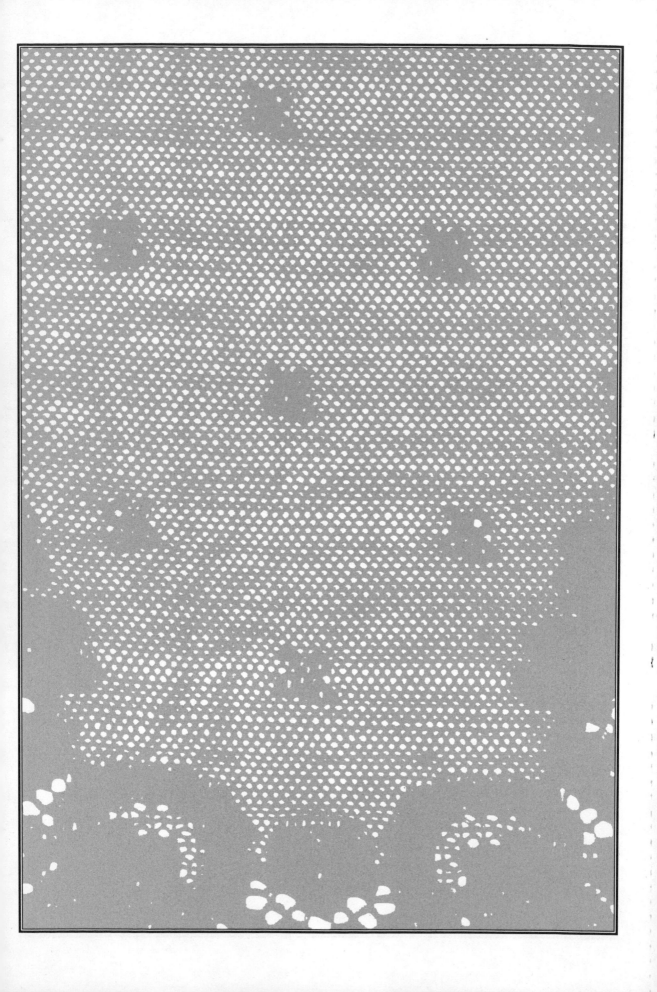

No. 24

HONEY BREASTS & CREAMY THIGHS

For *His* Eyes Only

HOW TO DRIVE YOUR WOMAN WILD IN BED
Graham Masterton

After you have stimulated the clitoris a little, part her outer lips with your tongue (not with your fingers) and probe inside her vulva so that you can open her inner lips. They may be open already, depending on what position she's lying in and how aroused she is, but now you can insert your stiffened tongue into her vagina, and relish the taste of those celebrated juices (although don't expect the sluice gates of the Hoover Dam to open, because even in the juiciest of women they won't).

At this point, after a little in-and-outing-with your tongue, you can carefully hold the outer lips of her vulva apart, which will have the effect of exposing her vagina and her clitoris much more prominently. Run your tongue tip back up to her clitoris and lick it softly and steadily and keep on licking it softly and steadily until you can sense that she is beginning to feel aroused. Whatever fancy tricks you do with your tongue and your fingers, it is the persistent rhythmic lapping of your tongue tip on her clitoris that will bring her to a climax, so make sure that you don't ignore it for too long.

*T*astes good already, hmm?

And not only does this seduction taste delicious to you, it *feels* delicious to her!

When she's out of the house one afternoon, lay some wax paper on your kitchen counter and leave a little clue about the treat you have in store for her. It's a big heart — drawn in whipped cream! Inside you can write your initials, or maybe "I Love You..." *or how about "eat me!!"*

Tonight, bring a can of whipped cream and a jar of honey to bed. Want to be a little creative? See if you can find a chef's hat or an apron... they won't stay on for long! Drape an old sheet or towel across the bed, and ask her to lay down — while you prepare dessert.

Start by dripping some honey on her nipples... let it drip, sticky and sweet, down the sides of her breasts. That's the easy part; the hard part is licking it all off without making a huge mess. Mmm, mmm, *good!*

It's time to move south.... Give the can of whipped cream a good shake and squirt a circle on her stomach. Draw a target around her bellybutton, and fill up your bullseye with honey. That's the easy part; the hard part is sucking it all out without sending her into fits of giggles. If she's ticklish — watch out!

There's one final selection on our dessert menu this evening, and I'll bet you already know what it is. (Ooh, I like the way you think!) Shake up the whipped cream again and squirt it between her thighs. Hungry? Then dive in and keep eating until it's all gone — and then maybe twenty or thirty minutes *after* it's gone.

That's the easy part; the hard part — well, you've got a hard part of your own by now... and I hope you saved some cream to put on it! After all, she's entitled to a little dessert of her own.

Bon appetit!

Ingredients

1 Jar of Honey / 1 Can of Whipped Cream / 1 Strong Tongue / A Whole Lot of Towels
And for tomorrow — 1 Diet Book!

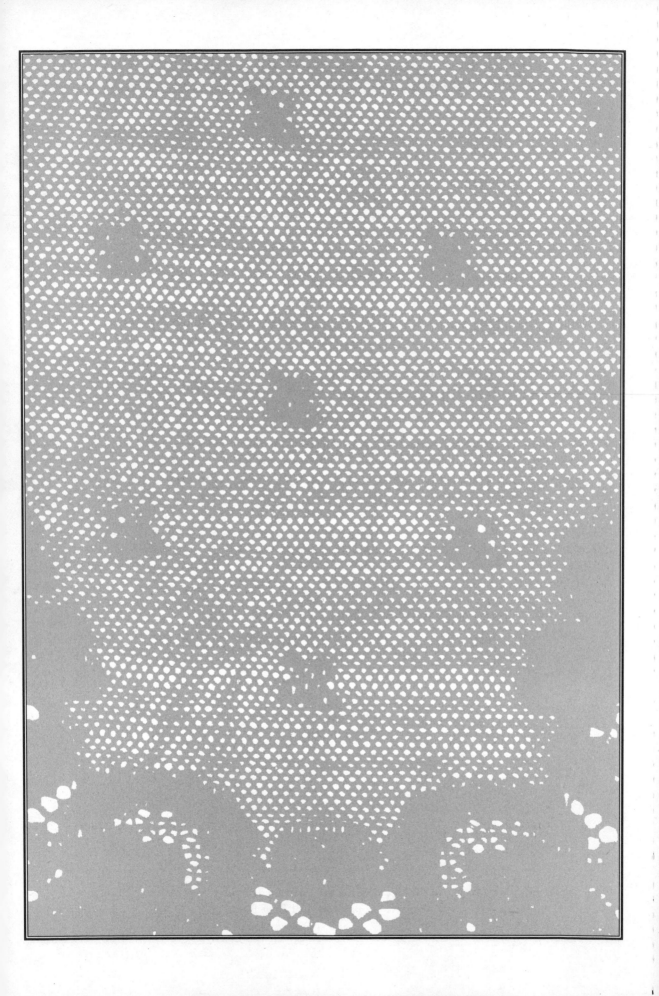

FINGER LICKIN' GOOD

For *His* Eyes Only

$

THE LOVE MUSCLE
Bryce Britton

Studies at the State University of New York show that people who enjoy food usually enjoy sex. It doesn't matter how much you eat, just how much you enjoy it. Food and sex have always been linked, since Aphrodite was the goddess of both love and crops.

THE NEW JOY OF SEX
Alex Comfort M.D. D.Sc..

The Wet Look - Another superskin releaser - it makes you tight and shiny. Some people like the real thing with real water - try showering in a clinging cotton shift: this both feels and looks sexy.

SECRETS OF SEDUCTION
Brenda Venus

It's no coincidence we use "appetite" and "hunger" for both sex and food.

In my experience, a man who can appreciate the delights of a delicious meal can best enjoy the delicacies of a scrumptious woman. A man who cares how his food tastes also cares about the quality of his lovemaking.

*T*his one starts as a VERY casual dinner date at home. Casual because you begin by eating messy food, and end by messing up your wardrobe!

Think your sweetheart will be intrigued when you tell her to wear jeans and a white t-shirt tonight? Good, let her wonder. The first reason is that your menu includes nothing but finger-food — barbecued ribs, fried chicken, corn on the cob, water-melon, whatever you can think of that makes a complete mess when you eat. And the other reason is your private little wet t-shirt contest, starting as soon as supper's over!

Begin your cleanup with a big, wet kiss. Mmm...you haven't lived until you slurped barbecue sauce off the face of a beautiful woman! Lead her to the bath, which you've stocked with piles of towels, beautiful flickering candles, and more wine if you like. Turn on the shower and adjust the temperature, but before she gets undressed, pull her under the streaming water with you. Smother her giggles with kisses as you tug at her clothing. Pull her shirt up, but not off; gently bite one nipple *through* her bra. Unzip her jeans and slowly work them down over her hips, but leave her panties in place.

As you lather her up — a liquid or gel soap works best here — scrub her *through* her soaked underclothes. The sensation of warm, slippery skin riding up against wet fabric is intensely erotic. As your hand glides over her *mons,* the rest of her slick, soapy panties will be sliding over her swelling lips and buttocks, caressing her most tender and sensitive flesh. Let your fingers slip underneath to brush against her nipples or her clitoris, but don't take off any clothing. Massage her *through it* — or under it, or gently pull it aside as your fingers and face explore her body. Kneel before her; stroke her. The steam, the sensuous spray, the stimulation of your glistening wet fingers will push her right to the edge of orgasm... and beyond.

If you end up on the floor of the shower...or the bathroom...remember those extra towels for comfort. Clothes may come off as the evening progresses, but at the end you should both be at least partially dressed.

The best part about sex in the shower? *No cleanup time!* Now, if only the dinner dishes could be so easy....

Ingredients

1 Messy Dinner / 1 Large Shower Stall / Liquid or Gel Shower Soap
Clothes you don't mind messing up! / Lots and *lots* of towels / Wine Candles

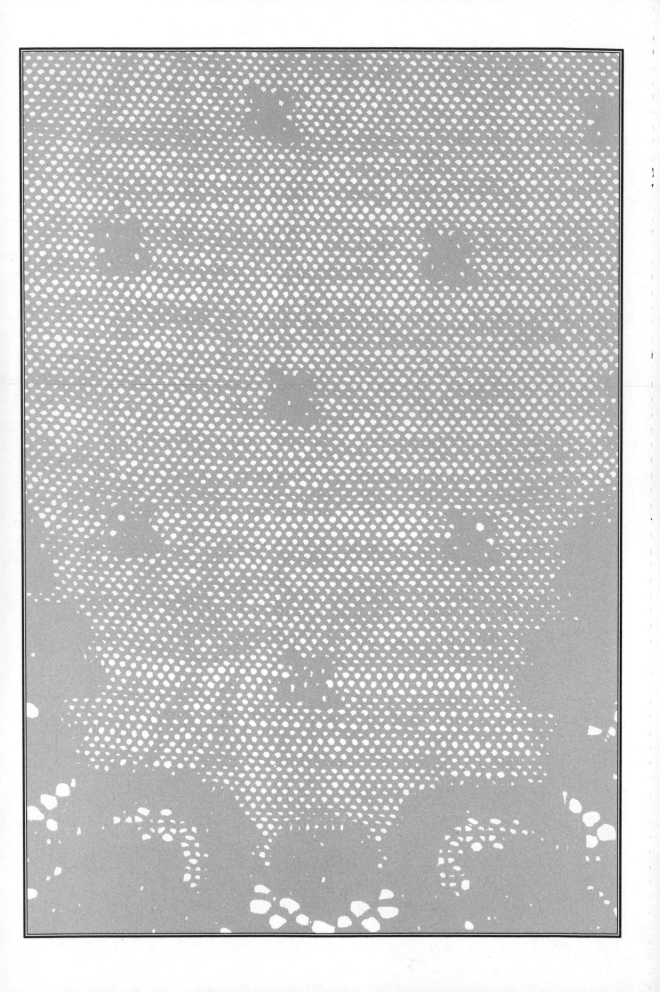

N.º

YIELD TO TEMPTATION

For *His* Eyes Only

THE LOVING TOUCH
Dr. Andrew Stanway

Playing games can be fun - especially when the aim of the game is to enjoy making love.

Secrecy Games - These are an extension of the 'talk' game. Having a secret between you that no one else understands can be a great turn-on. A common form of the game is that in which the woman is naked under her dress when going to a party or public place. The best way to play this is for her to tell her man just as they are going into the place so that he has no time or opportunity to do anything about it. The tease of this can be almost unbearable for both - and the woman can later, apparently accidentally, open her legs when sitting opposite him so that he gets a tantalizing glimpse of her thighs and vulva, yet no one else knows what is happening.

SECRETS OF SEDUCTION
Brenda Venus

Who you are as a man is who your are in bed. That's why life and sex flow into each other. To get, you have to give, and that includes passion. To please a lady you must be willing to go out on a limb. If you're afraid to take a risk, you'll miss all the fire a woman has to offer. So, let your heart and spirit soar!

Woman love men who have confidence. Nothing's more sexually exciting than a man with a feeling of certainty about himself; a man who knows how to move, how to dress, how and when to touch a woman. I'm not talking about "macho" or "cocky" - that's *pretending* to be a man. I mean the kind of man whose assuredness springs from the depths of his soul. He's genuinely positive; he doesn't pose or assume a phony attitude. He's as real as a tiger!

*W*arning! This is one of the most expensive seductions in the book! But as you'll see, it can pay off for years and years to come.

Tell your lady you'd like to take her out to dinner — an elegant dinner that will be full of surprises and some very special gifts. There is this one catch, though. She should dress nicely — her favorite suit, or a sharp jacket and skirt — but she is to wear *absolutely nothing underneath!*

She'll be burning with curiosity but *definitely* excited. And soon she'll be blushing, because you're going to convince her to give you a peek at her hidden treasures...*right in the restaurant!*

Be charming, but don't be afraid to beg! She'll check out the room to make sure no one is looking, and she'll wait until the waiter disappears, but then she'll let her blouse fall open *just so...*

At this point you'll smile and sigh deeply. Tell her how beautiful and erotic she is and that you think she deserves a reward. Reach into your pocket and pull out *one* striking gold earring.

And that's how the game is played! Next, convince her to let you touch her — That's right, you're going to slide your fingers into her blouse and stroke her breast in this public place, and *no one is going to catch on!* Lean close; grab her lapel as if you're examining the fabric, but let your hand slip inside the jacket, and *inside her blouse.* Gently brush the back of your hand across her nipple. Feel it stiffen as you roll it between your fingers (and watch her struggle to keep a straight face!). Oh yes, she's earned another reward. Time to bring forth the other earring.

The sheer delicious *naughtiness* of this public seduction may have you both pawing the ground and ready to skip dessert. There is, however, one final step — she has to earn the last piece of jewelry in your pocket, and by now she's figured out how. She'll squirm in her seat, she'll cross her legs, she'll tug at her skirt — and for at least one brief moment you'll catch a glimpse of Paradise. Don't be surprised if the new gold chain in your pocket isn't the only thing that's glistening in the candlelight! Once dinner — and your private show — is over, head for home.

And in the future, when she puts on her "special" jewelry, watch for a smile on her face. You may be about to see your little investment pay off again...and again...and again...and again....

— *Ingredients* —

Gold Earrings, 1 Pair / 1 Beautiful Gold Chain
1 Dark, Cozy Restaurant / A Lot of Charm!

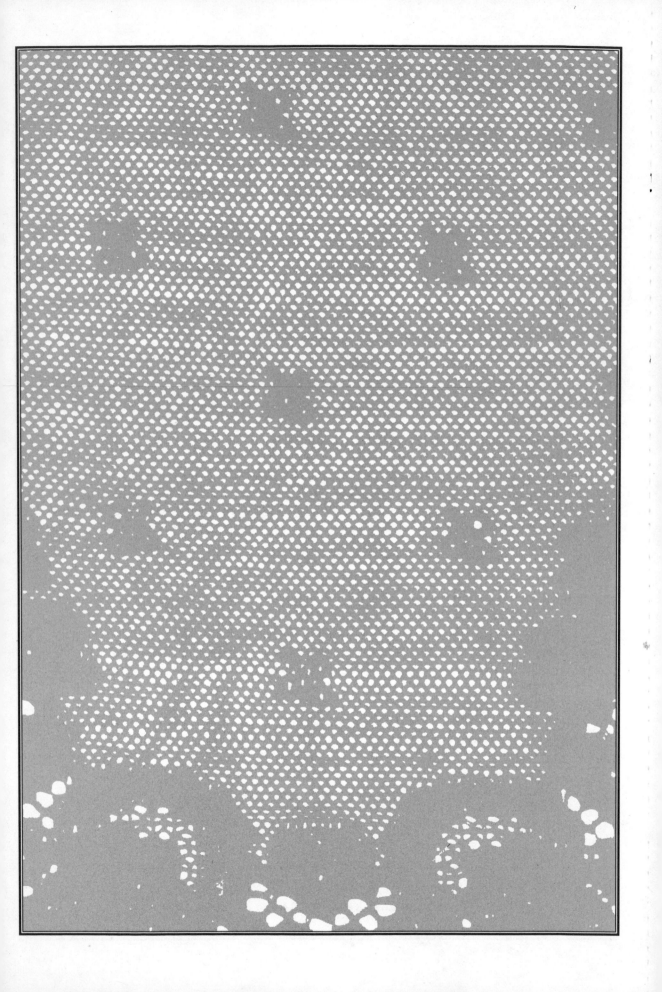

_No._ 27

TAKEN BY SURPRISE

For _His_ Eyes Only

IF IT FEELS GOOD
Joan Elizabeth Lloyd

Remember the scene in Flashdance where Jennifer Beals changes from her going-out clothes into a loose sweatshirt with a very wide neckline? Then she takes her bra off from under the shirt. For me, that was a very erotic scene, both because of what she wore and because of that wonderful "I want to fuck your brains out" look on Michael Nouri's face. If that's the look that you would like to see on your partner's face (and who wouldn't), try something similar.

COME PLAY WITH ME
Joan Elizabeth Lloyd

Ed and I have found a balance between comfortable, predictable sex, which is warm and very rewarding, and wild, fantasy-filled sex that's like fireworks and champagne. I guess it's like food. Fancy foreign food can be wonderful and different, but it will never take the place of good old beef stew. Both are wonderful and each has its place.

Play as frequently or as seldom as you wish. Find a game you enjoy or a toy that's fun to play with and savor those lovemaking sessions. But enjoy your other encounters, the soft, gentle, predictable ones, too. Whatever you do, share your pleasures, communicate, and continue to explore each other. Investigate the myriad sexual experiences open to sexual, sensual couples.

Remember: Sex is fun. Go for it.

A woman really appreciates a man with a grrreat sense of humor. Good sex is wonderful, but a good laugh...well, it's just essential to the health of a relationship.

Fortunately, you found this seduction — guaranteed to generate a lot of giggles *and* a lot of steam!

First, you've got some homework. Find a t-shirt and pants of hers that she won't wear any more — leggings work great. Get a similar outfit for yourself, and go to work. Use a big Magic Marker to draw dotted lines around the area where her nipples will be...yours too! Cut the seam of her pants open at the crotch.

When you bring her into the room, tell her you bought her an outfit that you'd like her to try on for you. She'll be intrigued and delighted, and when she sees what you've done — she'll be tickled pink! Your *creativity* and *effort* is what women like most, even more than the gift itself.

The sight of the two of you in clothes with your genitals exposed is silly and goofy...good for a big laugh. While you're still chuckling, explain to her that her outfit could use a little tailoring. Why, just a little cut *here* , and over *here*....

Trust me, she'll let you be a little more forward than her regular tailor. Use your scissors to cut on the dotted lines, freeing first one nipple and then the other. Gently pinch them and pull them through the holes in her shirt — she'll be startled by the sensation of being fully dressed at the same time that a warm mouth is nibbling her breast. She'll cut away the marked areas on your chest, and when she's ready to go for the zipper — *Uhhh, honey — I started without you....*

With that, you reveal that the crotch of your pants has already been cut away, and only held by a safety pin! Which she promptly removes, of course.

And that's as undressed as you need to be. Feel free to just play around. Soon enough a deep, wet kiss will turn your fashion show into a lovemaking session in which *only* your erogenous zones are revealed. The sound and feel of clothed bodies rubbing together will remind you of your high-school make-out sessions. If only these outfits had been in fashion then....*Holey Moley!*

Ingredients

1 Holey Outfit for a Man / 1 Holey Outfit for a Woman
Scissors — be careful! / A hole-lotta shakin' going on!

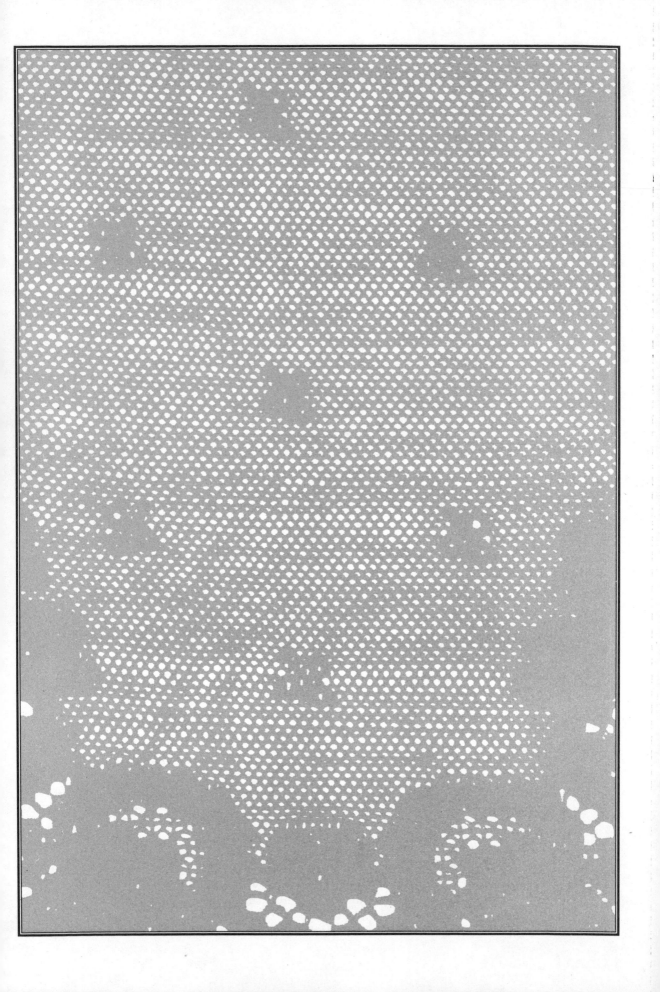

N° 28

A QUIET ECSTASY

For *Her* Eyes Only

SECRETS OF A MISTRESS
Rose Smith

Mistresses don't get headaches. At least not when they're in the throws of an exhilarating lust affair with someone else's man. The vivid picture of the other woman most of us are familiar with finds her stretched out sexily on a sensuous bed with satin sheets draping her hot, perfumed flesh. She's anxiously anticipating her "date's" familiar knock on the hotel room door. And when he does, she lets him know she's ready for a night of erotic lovemaking. When he takes her in his arms, no way is she going to utter those words, "Not tonight dear, I have a headache."

Schedule in Lovemaking? Nancy doesn't have a bewitching spell on Bob. She does, however, understand the importance of reserving quality time for love. One of the most significant reasons the other woman always seems so eager to make love in that hotel room once or twice a week is because: Another best kept secret...she schedules it in.

There's absolutely nothing wrong with lusting after your mate. Think about it from his point of view. When you want him to kiss you, you want your man to sweep you up in his arms and plant the most passionate smacker on you. If he reacted like he barely wanted to touch you and looked at you as if he's thinking, "All right, let's get this over with," you'd be disappointed. When you want love, knowing the person wants your love makes all the difference, doesn't it? Well, that's exactly the way most men feel. By showing your man you're in absolute lust with him, you're showing him you want him. Nothing is sexier to a man than that.

*Y*ou are getting sleepy, very sleepy. You can hardly keep your eyes open. This afternoon, when you hear the word "fragrance," you will have an uncontrollable urge to take a nap. Once in bed, you will not wake up no matter what I do to your body. You will neither stir nor speak, or the spell will be broken.

He may not be hypnotized — not yet, anyway — but he sure will be fascinated when he reads this note, left next to his breakfast plate Saturday morning! Don't be surprised if he rushes to get through with his weekend chores. Even a hard-core workaholic will be looking forward to this intriguing little snooze.

Later in the day, touch a few drops of perfume to your skin. Snuggle close and ask if he likes your new *fragrance*...then watch him yawn and head for the bedroom!

Give him a few minutes alone, and then enter the room. In complete silence, approach the bed. He is sound asleep — or pretending, anyway — so be gentle as you examine his body. You don't want to wake him as you explore with your softest caresses.

But otherwise, you now have the freedom to do anything you want! If there are certain things you're curious about, now is the time to discover them. And off in "dreamland," he'll be in an incredible state of anticipation, wondering where you are going to touch him and what you are going to do next!

Undress him. Study all the places that you want to touch. Brush your lips across his eyelids; kiss his neck, his nipples and belly, his thighs and toes. Try to find new erogenous zones; observe the way his skin reacts as you trail your fingertips across his warm flesh. Did you know that a man's perineum is nearly equivalent to a woman's g-spot? Lightly rub this area between scrotum and anus and you will send him into an erotic trance. Press your fingers deeper into it as you massage a rich cream into his rising manhood. Take all the time you need to observe his penis in it's various stages of arousal. If he's a good boy — if he follows the rules and *stays asleep* — stroke him until he comes, filling the palm of your hand with his steaming seed.

You're actually giving him two gifts this week, you know. First, you're handing him a truly *grrreat* climax. Second, he gets to fall asleep right after sex — without feeling the least bit guilty!

What more could a man ask for?

Ingredients

1 Quiet Room / 1 Quiet Man / 1 Provocative Note

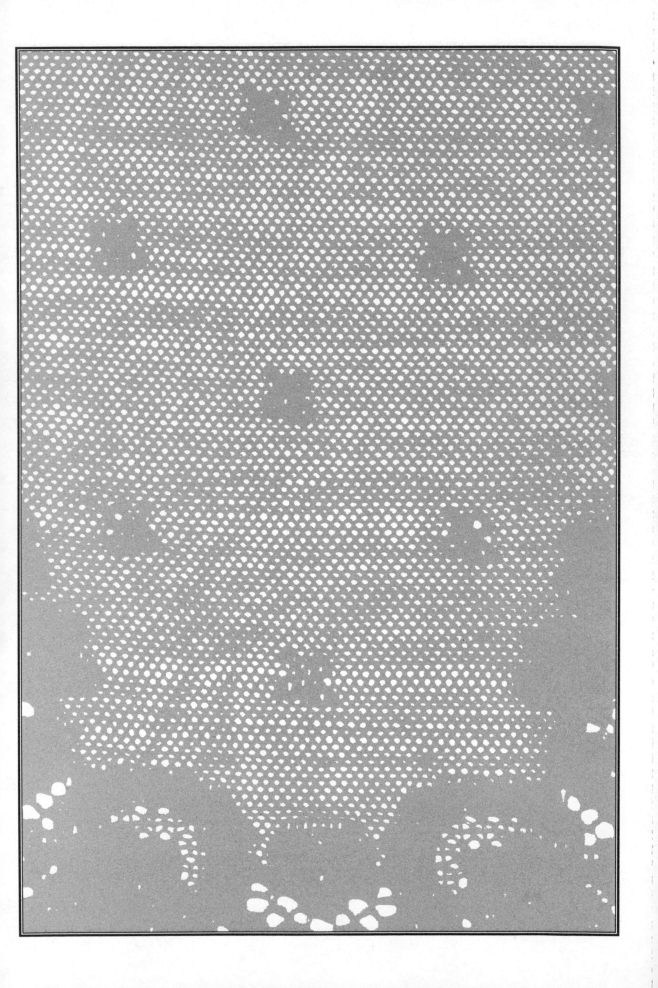

№ 29

JONI'S BUTTERFLY

For *His* Eyes Only

$

SINGLE WILD SEXY AND SAFE
Graham Masterton

The best selling sex toy ever is Joni's Butterfly (or variations of it). This is a butterfly-shaped vibrator of pink vinyl that a woman straps over her vulva with four elastic bands. It has a "clitoral stimulator," and "anal tantalizer," and four rows of stimulating nodules". All a woman has to do is switch it on and the butterfly will "fly and flutter its tantalizing vibrations throughout her vaginal area." The intensity of the vibrations can be controlled with a hand-held switch. The advertisement for Joni's Butterfly says: WARNING: Once strapped into position and activated there is no escape from the pleasurable sensations.

HOT MONOGAMY
Dr. Patricia & Jo Robinson

The so-called sex toys have zoomed in popularity in recent years. A 1978 Redbook survey of married women found that a mere 20 percent used some sort of "device" during lovemaking. In 1993 nearly 50 percent of the women who responded to a similar survey by Ladies' Home Journal acknowledged using erotic aids.

The appeal of vibrators is simple: When pressed against a woman's clitoris (not inserted in her vagina), they can produce a speedy orgasm. Many women who have difficulty climaxing experience their first orgasms with the help of a vibrator. Another reason for the popularity of vibrators is that they can be purchased without embarrassment from department stores, variety stores, and pharmacies.

In my view, using a vibrator does not have to make sex mechanical or impersonal, especially if the couple finds some way to maintain skin or eye contact. To provide a feeling of closeness, I recommend that couples who use vibrators snuggle close together, look into each other's eyes, or caress each other with their free hands.

*W*hat would you give to have the power to grant your lover an earth-shattering orgasm...on command? What *wouldn't* you give for the ability to bring her to the edge of ecstasy, and then *hold her there* for as long as you wanted?

Meet Joni's Butterfly — in concept, nothing more than a miniaturized vibrator. In practice, though...*wow!* It's molded to fit snugly against her *mons veneris*, centered right over her clitoris. Clearly, this is a sex toy that was designed by a woman! The controller, however, is attached by a length of wire so *you* can keep it in your hand — and therein lies the magic!

Build some anticipation first. Have it gift-wrapped (don't forget to install fresh batteries!) and present it to her at the start of your date, explaining that it's a very special gift and must only be opened at a very special time. She'll be burning with curiosity! And when the most intimate part of the night arrives — tell her it's time to take a ride on the Butterfly....

Help her put it on, or hold it snug against her clit. Cuddle up behind her in the spoon position, and then...start the machine. Slowly at first...let her get used to the incredible tingle coursing through her most intimate place. Then, when she's quite warmed up...*turn it off!* Nibble her neck, squeeze her breasts, let her feel your own arousal as you rub against her backside — but *make her wait* to get that delicious buzz again!

And then give it to her. Slow, then fast; off...then on. You're building her up for an explosion but using your remote control to keep it *just out of reach.* From behind, slide your hand between her legs and feel the wetness pouring from her. As she draws near to orgasm, let your thumb find it's way inside while your fingers press the Butterfly hard against her, increasing the power of the vibrations. Now enjoy the sensation as she *rides your hand* ; imagine how it will feel when it's your own swollen sex inside her. Finally, when she can stand no more teasing, when she pleads with you to let her come...slip in from behind. Turn the Butterfly up to overdrive — *oh, you'll feel it too!* — and let your passion push you both over the top.

Now, the next time you're both watching television with friends and they tell you they often argue over who gets the remote control, you can say you also have the same problem...*and then look at each other and laugh!*

Ingredients

One Joni's Butterfly (available at adult stores or see speciality shop page)

N.º

30

NOT FOR BEGINNERS

For *Her* Eyes Only

THE HITE REPORT ON MALE SEXUALITY
Shere Hite

"My wife frequently masturbates to orgasm when we are in bed. She says, 'Make and ice cream cone.' I cup her breast in both hands and suck her nipple. She has masturbated since age eight and habitually during our marriage. It is another happy way for us to be close. Sometimes she kisses my scrotum or sucks my penis after intercourse while masturbating. Occasionally I masturbate while she watches. It is intimacy."

A woman stimulating herself to orgasm is highly arousing to me. A woman's self-stimulation is also useful in several ways: it shows me exactly the type and speed of stimulation she likes; it generally produces stronger and more consistent orgasms for her; with each of us in charge of our activity.

THE HITE REPORT ON FEMALE SEXUALITY
Shere Hite

"Can a woman stimulate herself manually while she is with a man? In the same way that men said that women often don't give them the correct manual stimulation of their penis, isn't it difficult for one person to know just how to stimulate another? Although learning to do just that with a partner can be very loving and exciting, it is also very important for men and women to feel that they can stimulate themselves during sex with a partner. This can be an extremely intimate activity, while at the same time removing many frustrations and pressures from both the woman and man."

*S*o just how intimate are you with this man?

Are you close enough to *masturbate* while in his arms?

Now, now, don't panic. If you haven't done it before, the thought of flying solo with another person nearby can be a little intimidating, I know. But with true intimacy comes tremendous freedom. Not only does your soulmate want you to indulge in your full range of sexuality...*it will make him totally hot, too!*

Does he carry a briefcase or some kind of bag to work? Then that's where you should leave your gift for him this week. It's a giftwrapped copy of Penthouse, with a note: *Any good letters?*

On the evening of your seduction, ask him to bring his present to bed. Snuggle up next to him, and have him flip through the pages. The pictures may not do a lot for you — *then again, they might!* — but they sure will lift his, uh...spirits. Now ask him to start reading from the erotic letters section of the magazine.

Okay, some of the stories are dumb, but it doesn't really matter. Tonight you're creating a sensual fantasy of your own. Drape a leg over his; part your thighs. Let your fingers drift under the sheets, down past your tummy. At first he won't notice; your movements are small. But when at last he catches on....

He'll think he's fallen into one of the Penthouse letters. For a man, you see, there is simply nothing more erotic than a woman who freely indulges her own carnal nature. His pulse will race, but if he makes a move to take over, tell him — *No. Just watch.*

Ask him to hold you, or kiss you, or cup your breast, but *don't stop your own stroke.* Focus only on your clitoris; listen to it sing. Oh, his turn is coming, but not quite yet. When that outrageous, delicious, shamelessly sexual tension gets to be too much — give in. *Let him feel the thunder of your climax too....*

Wow. Scrumptious, wasn't it? Now — didn't you leave a highly aroused man laying around here somewhere? And the night is young! I'll bet you can inspire him to write a story of his own —

Dear Penthouse, I always thought your letters were made up, but then one night, my lover asked me to read some aloud....

— *Ingredients* —

1 Copy of Penthouse / 1 Itch to Scratch / (Optional: 1 Vibrator!)

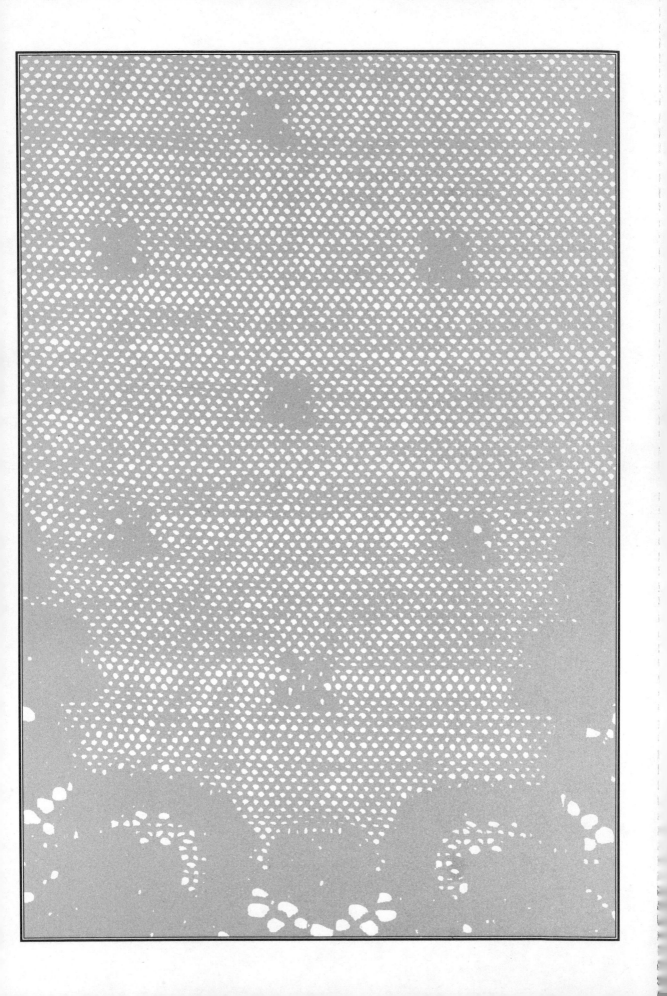

Nº

31

THE ONE HOUR ORGASM

For *Her* Eyes Only

ONE HOUR ORGASM
Dr. Bob Schwartz, Ph.D.

"Peaking" is a technique that is designed to increase your ability to feel. As you are rubbing yourself and begin to feel the sexual pressure or tumescence build up in you, stop rubbing or slow down, or change direction. Especially do this when you are on the verge of an orgasm. As tumescence builds, bring yourself as close to the upper side of that feeling as is possible without going over the top...then let yourself down by stopping, slowing down, changing to a lighter pressure, or changing the direction you are rubbing.

WOMEN ON TOP
Nancy Friday

The most popular theme of male fantasy also reverses reality. How burdensome and tiresome it is for men to always have to make the first move, be responsible, in charge, and how understandable that they should wish to flee from all this hard work and imagine women happily taking on all the sexual initiation, giving the men no choice but to lie back and be done to for a change.

It is equally burdensome and tiresome for some women to play passive little girl. It requires a great deal of effort and not much happiness if the role doesn't fit. Some women have always had the IN CHARGE fantasy and repressed knowledge of it. No longer.

237 INTIMATE QUESTIONS EVERY WOMAN SHOULD ASK A MAN
Laura Corn

Question 190:
How many times do you like to be brought to the brink of orgasm, before it actually happens?

*T*onight you'll be practicing a very advanced sexual technique. Courtesans have used it for centuries; whole books have been written about it. And once your lover feels its power, he'll be begging you to try it again.

Give him a call at work and ask, in your sultriest voice —

What makes you have your strongest and longest orgasm?

Is he surrounded by people on the job? Good! He'll be flustered and blushing when you lead him through his options, to which he has only to say yes or no.

Do you like it best when you come inside me, or when I suck you with my mouth? Would you like me on top or underneath? Does it get you hottest when you see me on all fours with my bottom sticking up in the air? Can you come home soon?

Take him by the hand and lead him to the bedroom. Undress him. Kiss and nibble and suck on each part as it's unveiled. But don't let him touch you! Tonight, you are in total control, and you have only one very important job for him.

He has to tell you when he's about to come. He has to tell you *before* he comes, and if he can't say it out loud, you need a signal — two sharp taps on your thigh. Make him promise!

Then start him on the road to his favorite orgasm. Was it intercourse? Then get him hard — use a lubricant, if you like — and mount him. Don't let him move, and don't let him touch you! He can only watch as you drop your hips against his, taking him inch by inch deeper inside. Ride! Have fun, and let him see you getting aroused. When he tells you he's about to come or gives you the signal — *stop all stimulation*. Tell him not yet....

If he's a little unhappy about missing his opportunity, just smile and tell him it'll happen — if he does what he's told. Then catch your breath and start again...and *again*, stop everything when he's on the brink. It's the sweetest kind of torture.

His torment comes to an end on the third go-round. This time you don't stop. This time you speed up your motion as he reaches his peak. Kiss him passionately as you hold him tight. Pinch his nipples, force him into the orgasm you've denied him for so very long. It will be absolutely explosive.

Good night, sweet prince....

Ingredients

1 Telephone / Lots of Control

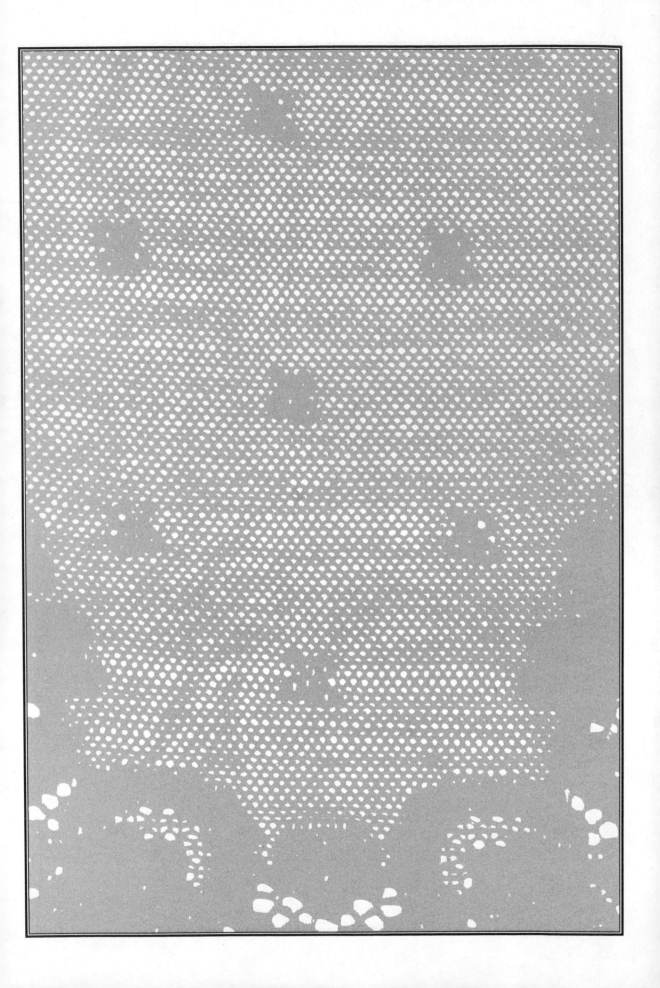

N.º

32

WAVES OF DESIRE

For *His* Eyes Only

§

MAKING LOVE A MAN'S GUIDE
Whit Barry

Women's objections to the accomplished lover are really aimed at how they perceive these accomplishments being used. What they don't like are men who display their sexual prowess as just that- a display of expertise rather than a means of bringing pleasure. "I don't what it is," one woman reported, "but I can be with a man who is doing all the right things, and instead of getting turned on, my reaction is to think I should be applauding. I feel like an audience he is trying to dazzle."

So do learn the techniques, but don't forget that the reason for learning them in the first place is to create with your partner a physical and emotional experience that will bring the two of you closer together. When one of you "performs," the result can only be distance. And that always leads to trouble.

Most important, remember that creating this experience does not begin with sexual gymnastics, no matter how accomplished. First, you need to create an atmosphere in which she feels cherished, cared for, appreciated, special. In this context your lovemaking skills become an expression of your feelings toward her and not a demonstration of your proficiency as a lover. It's a distinction that makes all the difference.

Aruba, Jamaica, ooh I wanna take ya,
Bermuda, Bahama, come on pretty mama
Key Largo, Montego, baby why don't we go?
— "Kokomo" The Beach Boys

*A*hh, there's nothing like a little R & R at a beachside resort to charge your batteries. Exotic music drifting through the evening air, waves crashing on the shore....It's incredibly romantic.

It can also be incredibly expensive. But if there's anything you should have learned about women by now, it's this — when it comes to romance, it really *is* the thought that counts.

So improvise! If Club Med is beyond your means, a handful of Club Med brochures surely aren't. Pick some up at a travel agency and leave them lying on the table. Tape one to your bathroom mirror. *Oh, I know we can't really afford it right now, but isn't it nice to dream about? I'd give it to you if I could, dear...*

Give her a few days to think about a tropical vacation, and then — *give her one*, in her own private luxury resort. It's your bathroom, but it never looked like this before. Candles of all shapes and sizes and colors cast a ruddy glow. Champagne and glasses are perched on a small table. There's soft music on the stereo — something classical to suit the classy tone of the evening. Towels are piled like sand dunes at the edge of the tub, which is capped with the sparkling white foam of a bubble bath.

Watch her expression as you crack open the door and invite her to peek inside. It's not just the elegance of the evening, it's the *effort you put into it* that touches her heart and brings a smile to her face. Now follow the winding path of candles, laid out on the floor and leading her to the bath.

Put out to sea with her. Tight squeeze? Sure — that's half the fun. Make a toast to her beauty. Kiss her...and decorate her face and body with the froth from your artificial surf. Your slick, soapy skin in such intimate contact is startlingly erotic. Soon your fun play turns to foreplay, and your caresses and strokes, your every move, will send waves splashing onto your terrycloth beach.

Daaaah-dum. What's this? *Daaaah-dum....*Could it be?! *Dah-dum dah-dum dah-dum dah-dum* look out! It's the Great White Shark! *Dahdumdahdumdahdumdahdum.* He's, um, rising from the depths, and he's got his eye — (he only has one eye) — on his next victim!

Ingredients

1 Tub with Bubble Bath / 1 Bottle of Champagne, with Glasses
Tons of Towels / A Case of Candles / A Box of Brochures

No.

IT'S NOT ON THE MENU

For *Her* Eyes Only

$$ 🍴 🚗

HOW TO MAKE LOVE TO THE SAME PERSON
FOR THE REST OF YOUR LIVES
Dagmar O'Conner

Probably all of us have fantasies about having sex in public. Certainly, the media have picked up on the popularity of this fantasy: The best remembered scene from the movie Shampoo depicts Julie Christi crawling under the table at a formal dinner party and, hidden by the tablecloth, attempting to have oral sex with Warren Beauty. Much of the titillation of this scene comes from the fact that it is a formal party; the idea would not have been half as exciting if they had been at a dark and sleazy nightclub.

THE NEW JOY OF SEX
Alex Comfort, MD.. D.Sc..

One of the most important uses of play is in expressing a healthy awareness of sexual equality. This involves letting both sexes take turns in controlling the game; sex is no longer what men do to women and women are supposed to enjoy. Sexual interaction is sometimes a loving fusion, sometimes a situation where each is a 'sex object' - maturity in sexual relationships involves balancing, rather than denying, the personal and the impersonal aspects of physical arousal. Both are essential and build-in to humans. For anyone who is short on either of these elements, play is the way to learn; men learn to stop domineering and trying to perform, women that they can take control in the give and take of the game rather than by nay-saying. If they achieve this, Man and Woman are one another's best friends in the very sparks they strike form one another.

*S*omewhere in every restaurant you can find one couple having the time of their life! This week, it's going to be the two of you. You'll drive him so wild, he won't notice what he's eating. You're taking him out to dinner, but tonight's main dish is *not on the menu!*

Many restaurants have booths, balconies or tables in separate rooms. You can choose whatever arrangement that will help you hide your naughty behavior. Insist on sitting right next to him so you can use one hand for eating — and the other for roaming.

Sit as close to him as you can, and begin your tease as soon as the waiter comes for your order. Squeeze his knee; glide your fingers over his inner thigh. Each time you are left alone, get a little more daring. Just make sure the tablecloth is long enough in front of you so others can't really see what is going on. This seduction isn't for their entertainment...only his!

Sometime during dinner, reach over to unzip his pants while continuing your meal. Keep up the conversation — well, your end of it, anyway — and, as nonchalantly as you can, *wrap your hand around his penis.* You don't think he'll choke on his food, do you? Better know the Heimlich Maneuver, just in case!

Call the waiter over for more bread and water — while keeping up your look of innocence and your sensuous stroke. When the waiter leaves, drop your napkin on the floor and bend down under the table to pick it up. On your way back up, slide your tongue over his exposed penis Mmm! Nobody on the restaurant staff ever got a tip *this* good!

Continue to talk about silly subjects through the entire dinner while sexually arousing him. When the waiter brings your check, be sure to tell him that the dinner was *grrreat.*

In fact, it was simply orgasmic!

Ingredients

Dinner at a Restaurant / 1 Secluded Table / 1 Tablecloth
A Good Sense of Humor / 1 Nosy Waiter / 1 Free Hand

N^o

34

DREAMY LIPS

For *Her* Eyes Only

SINGLE WILD SEXY AND SAFE
Graham Masterton

Oral Sex is such an important part of making yourself irresistible to the man you love that you love that you ought to make a point of thinking about doing it at least twice a week-and not just at bedtime, either, What about those times when he's just come out of the shower, and he's sitting around in his bathrobe, watching TV? What about in the middle of the night, when he's asleep? What about waking him, by sucking his cock? What about surprising him in the tub and giving him a licking? In terms of the sexual appreciation and affection that your spontaneous acts of oral sex will earn you from the man you love, you will be making one of the best investments of your life. And that's a promise.

HOT AND BOTHERED
Wendy Dennis

What do men want? No doubt about it, men love blow jobs. In the Hite Report on Male Sexuality, in 1981, Shere Hite found that almost all of the more than 7,000 men she polled were positively effusive about fellatio and gave it two thumbs up. "If I could find the woman who would suck me off in the morning to wake me up," one respondent told her, "I would lay my life in the mud at her feet."

"You've got an early wake-up call this week."

*T*hose are the words you'll inscribe on a card for your sweetie, and if he asks what you mean, tell him he'll just have to wait to find out. What he's going to find is *oral sex,* but delivered in a fashion that makes this all-too-rare treat intensely memorable.

Every man's had the altogether pleasant experience of waking up with a woody — and a pretty good idea of what to do with it! One morning this week, though, you're going to take him to a whole new level of arousal. He's going to wake up with your lips already wrapped around his tumescence. And oh, what dreams he'll be having until he does!

Early one morning, while he's still asleep, slip under the covers and take his sex into your mouth. Draw it all in, and enjoy the changes that come over it as it grows. At some point he'll start to stir, but don't assume he's completely awake. And don't ask to find out! Just keep cuddling with your lips, circling with your tongue. Suck forcefully while slowly drawing back, a technique called "Sucking a Mango" in Eastern erotic literature. Here's another favorite trick. Grasp his penis firmly and slide your hands from top to bottom. Stretch the foreskin tight to enhance it's sensitivity, and then apply your mouth. Nibble, ever so gently, along the coronal ridge — that rim of firm flesh just behind the head.

By now he's fully conscious, though he may think he's dreaming. Men never get as much oral stimulation as they want, and yet here you are, pleasuring him before he's even up — so to speak. This seduction is a "quickie," and may take only a few minutes, but it will have an impact on him all day long. And it just might have an impact on you — all night long!

The only trick to this seduction is waking up before he does without using an alarm. You may discover that it's not so difficult; lots of people find they can set their internal clock to wake themselves early. Of course, he has no idea what you're up to, so you've got a whole week to make it work. And you'll definitely want to make it work; remember —

The early bird gets the worm!

Ingredients
---

1 Sleepyhead / Some Sleepy Head

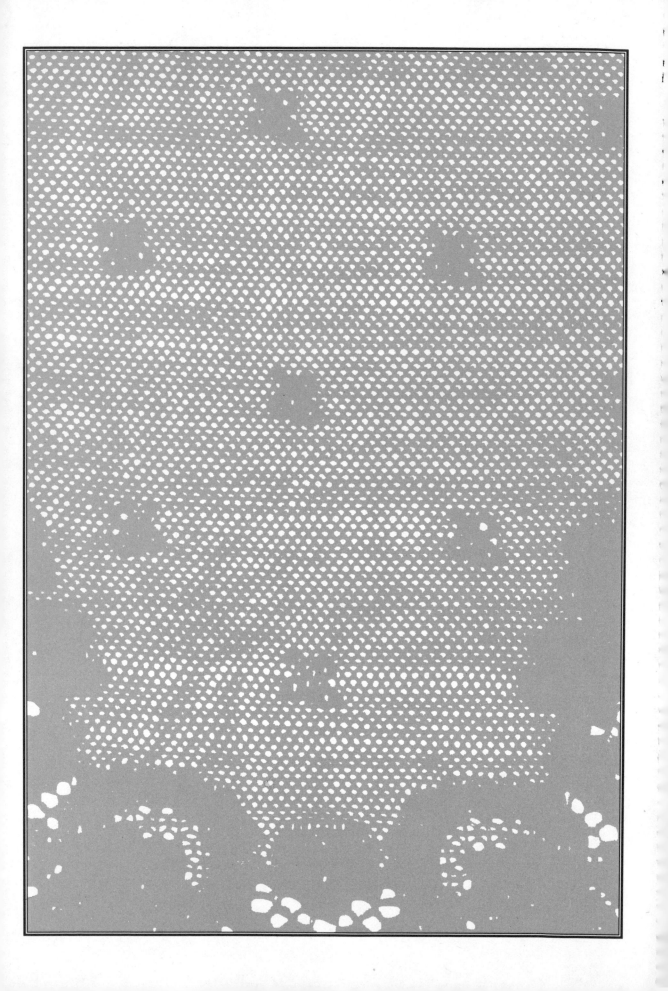

Nº **35**

PLEASE FEED THE BEAR!

For *Her* Eyes Only

203 WAYS TO DRIVE A MAN WILD IN BED
Olivia St. Claire

Most women don't like to have their head pushed and pulled while giving oral sex but this time try it as an exercise. Pretend your a Pez dispenser. Tease him with your tongue for a few minutes and then ask him to hold your head while you continue. Just go with it, most men like a certain rhythm and you'll discover what speed of manipulation your man prefers. By experimenting, you'll remember this is for his pleasure. Let him push and pull while you use the Hoover technique.

THE NEW MALE SEXUALITY
Bernie Zilbergeld, Ph.D.

Feeling, which refers to a willingness to allow sex to have many expressions and faces, reflecting and expressing different emotions. Sometimes it's a tender lovemaking; at other times, it's an almost brutal fuck, where the only feeling is unalloyed lust; at other times it's just light fun and games. On occasion, sex can even be the expression of angry feelings. Sometimes it's mainly for the pleasure of just one partner, sometimes for the other, sometimes for both. It may last only a minute or two, or it may go on for hours. Depending on the dominant feeling, on some occasions there may be soft moans and words of endearment, on others that may be screams and obscenities.

Couples who engage in this kind of variety are cutting a broad swath. They don't have to go elsewhere for a quickie, or more physical sex, or more loving sex, or anything else. They aren't left thinking that they could do, say, be, or feel something different with someone else. They can do, be, feel, and say whatever they want right where they are. Contrast this with the situation of many couples, where the mood and feelings in sex usually remain the same. It's always serious, always tender and loving, always lusty, or always fun and giggles.

Even fun and giggles get boring if that's all you ever get, and the same is true of lust.

*S*exual studies dating back to the Kama Sutra have described the erotic power of the *delayed orgasm*. By arousing a man to full erection and then withholding relief — by simply starting and stopping — you ensure that his climax, when it finally arrives, will be a heart-stopping, breathtaking experience.

Of course, there's not a man in the world will do this to himself voluntarily! Poor fellas, they're just so lacking in self-control. So it's up to you to take charge of his orgasm. You're the Peter Police, if you will, for one extremely tantalizing day.

Pick a day off, a morning when you can both sleep in a bit. When you awaken, kiss him while you gently cup your hands around his testicles. Make them feel cozy and loved. Get him hard. And then — *oops, it's time for a shower! Wanna join me?*

Bring him back to full mast in the shower. Lots of soap, lots of water, lots of rubbing, then — *oops! Outta time.* He will NOT be especially happy at this turn of events. But smile sweetly and swear to him that he will get what he needs, like the Grrreat Sex book says. It just can't be right now. And he can't do it himself. A twist of the shower knob to *cold* should convince him!

Sometime in the middle of the day, grab him and start over. Unzip his pants and expose him to your touch and tongue — and then STOP. Promise him the best orgasm of his life...*later.* Soon!

When you get back to bed that night, ask him if he's finally ready to let go. Tell him it's been torture for you, too, because you've just been dying to take him. It's time. And it's going to be explosive. The chemistry of bliss has been working in his blood as well as his brain, sharpening his senses and strumming his nerves. Copious amounts of love-juice have been stored away — under considerable pressure, I'm sure he'd say! — in anticipation of a release that keeps getting delayed. Until now, that is....

Jump him. Don't stop; don't even slow down. Use your hands and mouth and keep moving. *Let him grab your head* while he thrusts — that's part of a compelling, dark fantasy shared by all men, and in his whole life he's never had a more urgent, aching need to do it. This bear you've unleashed might even surprise you a bit, but don't worry. He may be more powerful than a locomotive —

But he's going to be faster than a speeding bullet!

Ingredients

1 Pound of Patience, Stretched Thin

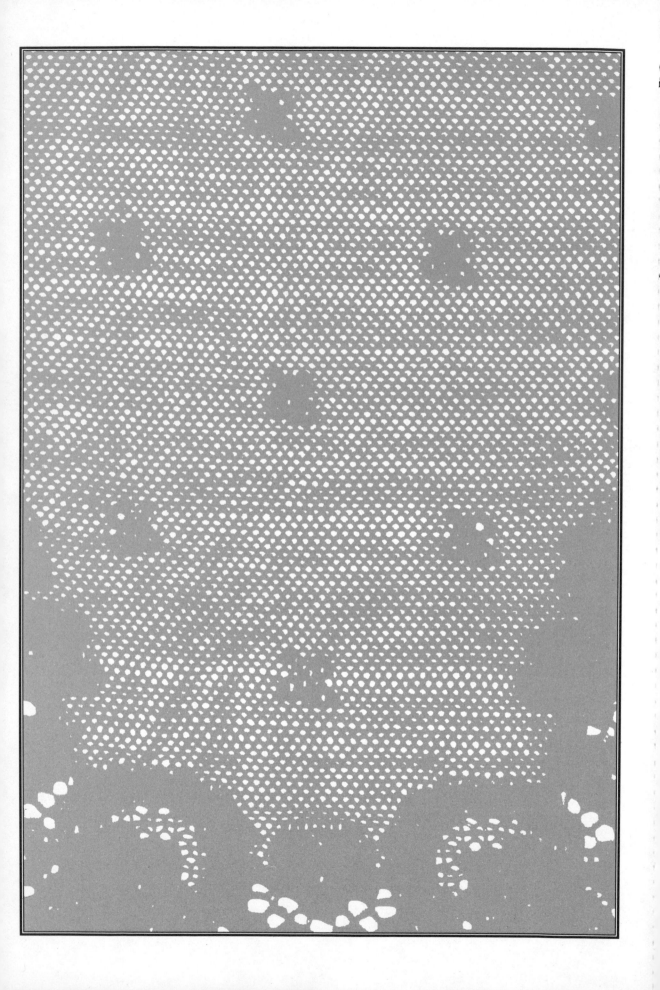

N.°

36

HUMMMMM!

For *Her* Eyes Only

$

THE GOOD VIBRATIONS GUIDE TO SEX
Cathy Winks and Anne Semans

The belief that masturbation and vibrators are just a temporary substitute until a real live body comes along is a prevalent one. As you read through this book we hope you're struck by the number of men and women who reject this notion by happily incorporating masturbation and sex toys into their partner sex play. Sometimes we just need to be reminded that it's worth taking a little risk now and then-remember mom telling you to share your toys? Take her advice - sharing your sex toys can add an exciting new dimension to your sex life. Chances are, if your partner knows something brings you that much pleasure, she or he will want in on the action. Seize the opportunity to expand your sexual repertoire, rather than confine it. Instead of assuming that your partner will be threatened or disinterested, take the time to find out how she or he feels. Vibrators may be just the thing to help you break out of a dull routine.

I love waking up in the morning with a jolting orgasm from my beloved vibrator. Better than a cup of coffee! Vibrators are the best kept secret of the twentieth century.

There are thousands of people out there plugging in and turning on, and it's not because they're dysfunctional, single, man-hating, sex-crazed, sex-starved, frustrated, preorgasmic or disappointed with a partner-it's ' because vibrators feel great. There are a million ways to have fun with a vibrator - you're limited only by your imagination.

SECRETS OF SIZZLIN' SEX
Cricket Richmond and Ginny Valletti

All kidding aside, if you have a Mr. Wonderful, your vibrator can add variety and verve to partnered playtimes. Presented in a light way, it's not difficult convincing your guy to befriend a surreal surrogate. In spite of many men's fear about being replaced by a machine, once properly introduced, they're delighted at the difference it makes in a relationship. For example, vibes 1) eliminate performance pressure, 2) almost always guarantee you'll reach orgasm and 3) feel fantastic on him, too.

Hummmmmmmmmmmmmmmmmmm!

If you own a vibrator — and sister, you should! — you know what a delicious sound that is. Play that note to a room full of people, and the men will immediately think of an electric shaver. The women, however, will try to hide a sly smile...or a deep blush.

It's time to share your secret joy with your favorite bedmate. Yes, I mean *share it* — because he can get a good buzz from a vibrator, too! Of course, the model you buy for him should NOT seem quite as phallic as most. No, you need to pick out a machine that looks like a tool, and a pretty heavy-duty one at that. No dorky penlight batteries for this bad boy! A real man uses a vibrator that sucks serious amperage right out of the wall.

Wrap it nicely and leave it on his dresser one day this week. No, he may not open it until the evening of your seduction. When he does, he'll assume it's for you. Uh-uh. Not tonight. This time, it's *his* turn to take a ride on the Electric Pony, starting face down....

Use it to work the kinks out of his neck. Rub a little lotion into his skin, then zap the tension from his shoulders. Dig into the muscles of his back. In minutes, he'll be Jell-O... well, most of him, anyway. Now head south —

Buzz the backs of his thighs, his buttocks. Have him spread his legs a bit, and...gently...slide the head of your little hummer down to his testicles. Hmm! That area between scrotum and anus is *much* more sensitive than most guys imagine!

Keep it up, so to speak, as you make love. The ultimate electric thrill puts you on top, straddling his penis and facing away from him. From this position you can press your toy right against the base of his shaft...and *right against your clitoris.* Each tiny pulse sends identical shock waves through your bodies. Your pleasure centers are now perfectly synchronized; your orgasms are riding on the very same wave. And your new third partner does all the work, taking you both along for a ride into ecstasy.

Remember, it's his gadget. But it sure is nice to have something to do while he's, uh, catching his breath!

She's givin' me good vibrations; she's givin' me excitations...
— "Good Vibrations" The Beach Boys, 1968

Ingredients

1 Big, Macho Vibrator, Giftwrapped / 1 Spare Set of Fuses!

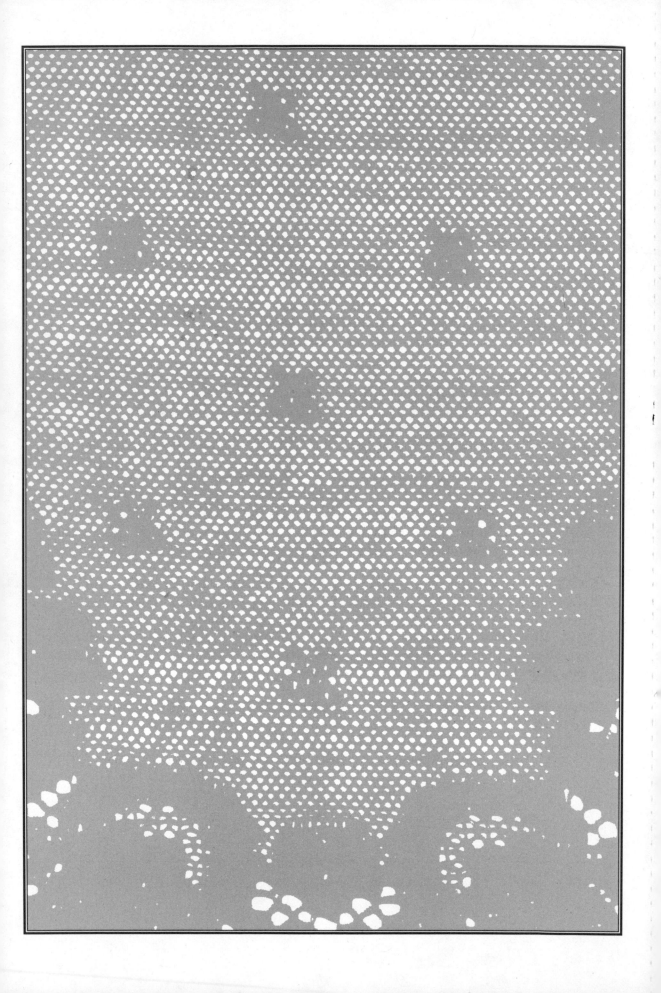

№ 37

PRIMAL MAGIC

For *His* Eyes Only

DRIVE HIM WILD
Graham Masterton

*Women need physical stimulation and
regular climaxes in order to be sexually satisfied

*They need affection, warmth, reassurance,
security, and a sense of masculine strength

*But they also need a sense of excitement-even a sense of sexual danger.
They need creative and colorful sex-the sex of fantasy and romance

Literally scores of women have told me about fantasies that closely resemble Marion's. In each case, they have been naked in front of dozens of purient eyes-either posing or masturbating or making love. It seems clear that many women have a strong element of exhibitionism in their sexual makeup, and that they are very aroused by the idea of showing themselves off sexually to an audience.

It's one of those fantasies that translates well into reality...one of those fantasies that are easily acted out and which can give your sex life a whole lot of extra excitement, with no emotional or physical risks.

*T*here's something about the great outdoors that makes men such...men! And though women may tease their guys about it, the truth is we *love* to see men in their natural element.

We don't, however, always share your need to commune with Mother Nature...so don't let her see you digging out the camping gear! She may suddenly have *other* plans if she thinks you're taking her on a trek into the wilderness. No, this is a seduction that works best when you take her completely by surprise....

And what a surprise it is. Your evening starts normally, but when bedtime draws near, take her by the hand and lead her outside into the night. Crisp air, a sprinkling of stars, that gentle hush that falls over the neighborhood in the evening...it's a perfect setting for *amore'*. And what a coincidence — there are those two sleeping bags conveniently hidden out there, zipped together and just waiting for two warm bodies.

Shoes off, then climb in. She'll be tickled at the idea of camping out right at home, and delighted that you planned it all for her, right down to drinks and snacks. Now wrap your arms around her and enjoy the view. Tell her how beautiful she is by moonlight. There's not woman on the planet who doesn't love to be held. And snuggled. And nibbled. As the heat builds in your cocoon — and in her — it's time to face your true challenge tonight...getting clothing *out* of a sleeping bag while you stay in!

Hey, so what if the neighbors are nearby? Even if they looked, they couldn't know that you're stark naked in there. They're probably spending another boring night watching the tube, but *you're getting laid* in a semi-public place! Scary? No, it's exhilarating — and highly arousing. Be forewarned, though. Once she discovers the secret thrill doing it where you might get caught, well...you could get jumped just about any old place!

If you don't have a yard, plan your seduction on a porch or by a big window with a view. You can still have the same *grrreat* night of sex, and she'll be much less tempted to indulge her newfound love of outdoor fun by grabbing your pants —

And running for the house!

Ingredients
---

2 sleeping bags that can zip together (borrowed, if necessary)
1 starry night / 1 tray of snacks / a *little* privacy

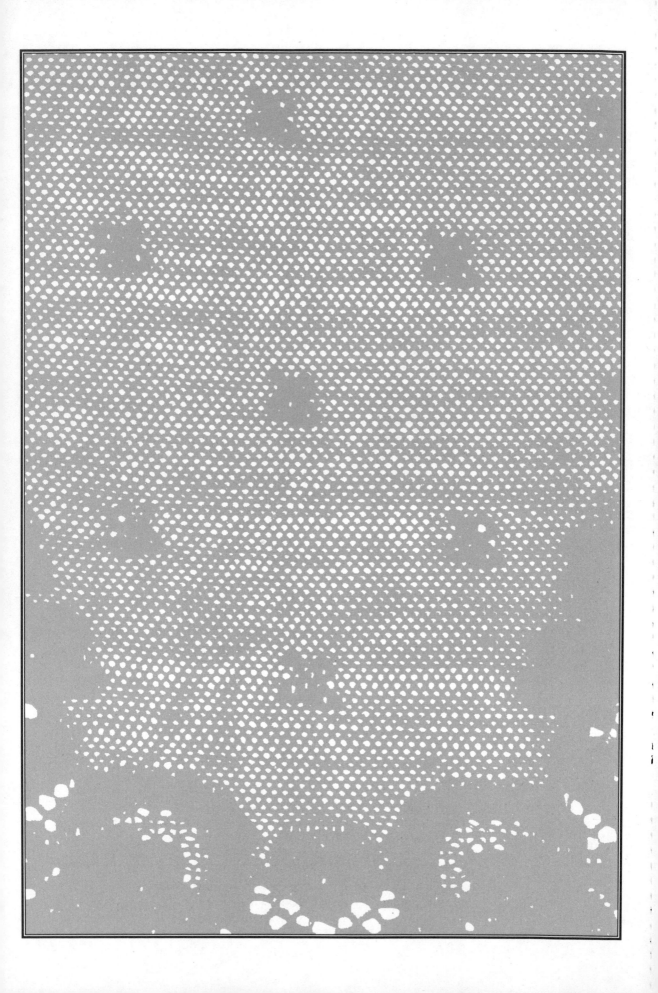

N°

38

THE EROTIC EQUATION

For *Her* Eyes Only

THE EROTIC IMPULSE
Edited by David Steinberg

THE FOUR CORNERSTONES OF EROTICISM
Jack Morin

Sexual arousal, whether it involves romance or pure lust, is highest when there is a tension between the attraction pulling us toward the partner, and one or more barriers standing in the way. The formula for hot sex is ATTRACTION + OBSTACLES = EXCITEMENT. The obstacles necessary for high excitement may be external or internal, conscious or unconscious. They can arouse us whenever something makes it difficult to get together. Or the chemistry between something makes it difficult to get together. Or the chemistry between the partners can bring its own obstacles into the encounter. Overcoming barriers is a testament to the strength of the attraction.

WOMEN ON TOP
Nancy Friday

When we deny our fantasies, we no longer have access to that wonderful interior world that is the essence of our unique sexuality. Which is, of course, the intent of the sex haters, who will stop at nothing, quoting scripture and verse to locate that sensitive area in each of us. Beware of them, my friends, for they are skilled in the selling of guilt. Your mind belongs to you alone. Your fantasies, like the dreams you dream at night, are born out of your own private history, your first years of life as well as what happened yesterday. If they can damn us for our fantasies, they can jail us for the acts we commit in our dreams.

The intent of my friend's rude remarks about my books on sexuality is that I should stop writing them out of shame. In your life, not everyone will embrace your sexuality. Remember envy, especially between women over matters sexual; do not buy their shame and give up your sexuality so that they can rest more easily.

*S*ex should be anything but boring. When passion starts to give way to routine, I always turn to the Erotic Equation, described on the opposite page.

It's really as simple as 1, 2, 3. Men love challenges because they love to win. (Even when we let them! And isn't that usually the way it goes?) So challenge your guy. Put up a resistance — and make sure he *comes out on top*...uh, so to speak.

One weekend afternoon start puttering around the house dressed only in a bra, panties, and one of his dress shirts. Believe me, he'll think you look *grrreat!* There's such a casual sexiness about a woman in a oversized shirt that just barely covers her backside.

You want him to start chasing you, and you'll have to goad him into it. Snap a dishtowel at his butt! Or flick a spray of water in his face — whatever it takes to get his attention. Then issue your challenge: *I bet you can't catch me!* And take off, with your laughing lover in hot pursuit. Run circles around the table; run upstairs, downstairs, outside and back in. If he catches you, wrestle your way to freedom and run again. Sure it's all in fun, but your squeals, your defiance, and all that sheer physical exertion will awaken one of his most primal instincts — the thrill of the chase.

When he finally has you cornered: *I bet you can't get my clothes off!* Fall to the floor and cross your legs, yelping and squirming. If the shirt's big enough, he'll just pull it over your head, but don't make it easy. Wrap yourself up in a ball. Fight him! The harder he works to pin your arms, the more he will savor the triumph. Make him *struggle* to pry apart your knees, and the victory celebration will be...exquisitely intense. For both of you! Recall the Equation — the obstacles you're creating are a powerful aphrodisiac.

Be sure to leave him with enough strength to finally take you — on the floor, the sofa, wherever you end up. Your battle, of course, becomes sweet surrender as you submit to his "conquest." By now, who can remember which of you really started the chase?

The Erotic Equation. It's not exactly higher math. In fact, it's lower...much lower!

Ingredients

1 Great Big Man's Dress Shirt / 1 Good Fight

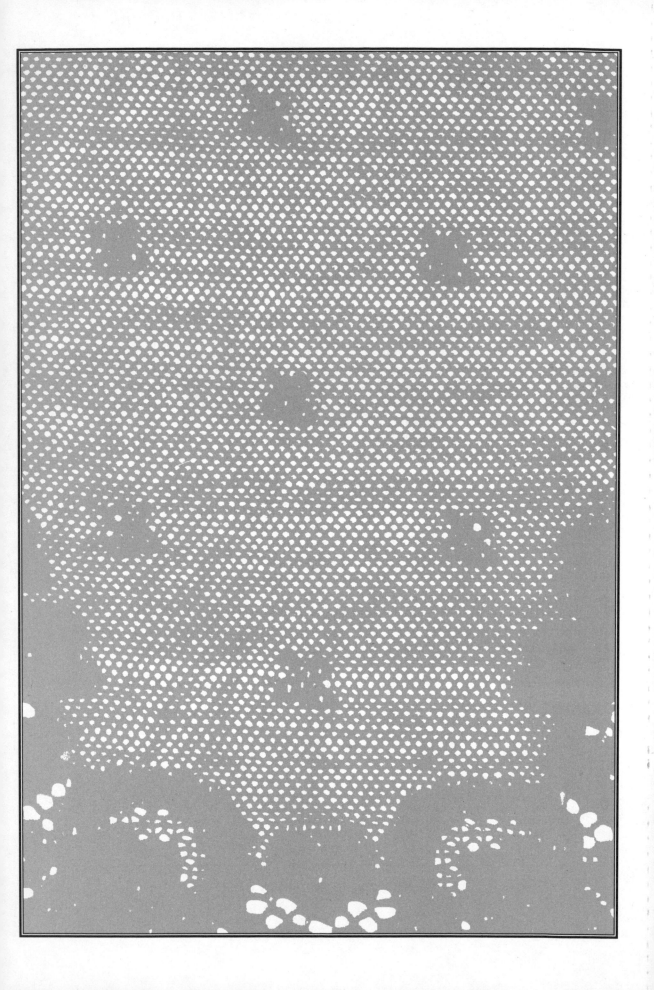

№

WHERE NOBODY KNOWS YOUR NAME

For *His* Eyes Only

LIGHT HIS FIRE
Ellen Kreidman

Most women find it extremely difficult to get fully into the role of lover in their own home. To most of us, home represents work. Even if there are no children present, it is still a workplace. There are beds to be made, marketing to be done, floors to be cleaned.

In order to feel completely relaxed, a woman needs to go to a hotel, a motel, or a resort. Trust me on this. I've talked to countless women who are surprised that they feel like completely different people whenever they get away from home for a vacation, but it's really no mystery. It's because they are separated, both physically and emotionally, from their homes and their workplace.

SECRETS OF SEDUCTION
Brenda Venus

What keeps every relationship fresh, alive, and vital is that special element of magic and mystery - we call it "romance." It's not something you can touch, smell, or see. It starts in the mind and begins to stir your emotions,. It has no rules, and yet it defines your lovemaking more than you may know. It's all about living life and loving with abandon - with a sense of adventure, fun, and play. Let your imagination run free and begin to discover the delicious magic we call romance.

Strangers in the night — exchanging glances
Wondering in the night — what were the chances
We'd be sharing love
Before the night was through?
— Francis Albert Sinatra 1966

"**Y**our name is Mrs. Jones. You're married to a man who doesn't appreciate you anymore. It's been years since he surprised you or bought you a gift or tried to satisfy you in bed. He's out of town. You're going to the bar at the Hilton tonight at six to take the edge off your sorrow. Wear a black cocktail dress and heels.

"A man named Chris will want to buy you a drink. You've never seen him before, but he'll be in a blue blazer and he looks a lot like me. Will you let him pick you up?"

That's how the script for tonight's seduction starts. Make a copy for your leading lady and put it in an envelope marked *Open At Lunchtime*. Hand it over as she heads out the door this morning.

Yes, it's exactly how it sounds — you're going to come on to your sweetheart like you did when you first met. No, I take that back; this one's *different*. The first time you laid eyes on her a voice must have warned you to *be careful. She's special. Don't blow it!*

And look how well it turned out. But this evening, you're ready to take some risks. You're looking for nothing more than a hot babe for some hot sex, and as far as you're concerned — you're out of there by morning. This means you can *come on hard*. Flirt like crazy. Tell this stranger things you'd be embarrassed to say to your lover. Use lines you know your bedmate would never fall for. She'll buy 'em. Because tonight she gets to let loose too.

No, really, you have the most beautiful eyes. You must hear that all the time from men. Well, I just can't believe your husband could ignore a gorgeous woman like you. I sure wouldn't. You poor baby; tell me about it. Can I buy you another drink?

Me? I'm on the road all the time. Man, if it weren't for my Gulfstream I'd never get back here at all. Would you like to see it? My flightbag's up in my room; why don't we go get it....

Something tells me you ARE going to get it!

Ingredients
---

1 Script / 1 Actress / 1 Quiet Bar, with Hotel Attached

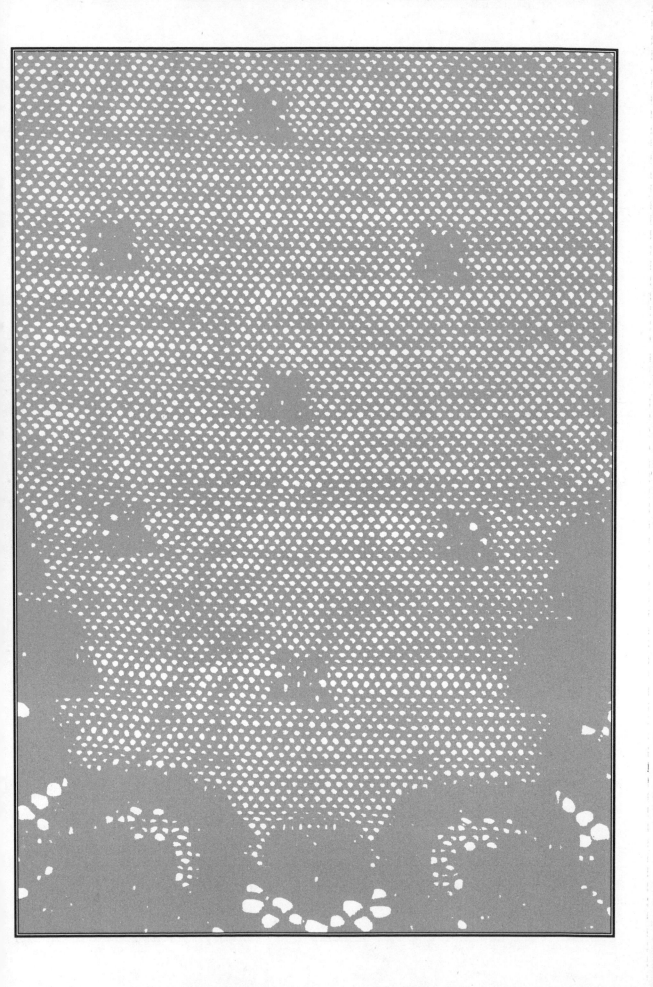

N⁰ *40*

MATING CALL

For *His* Eyes Only

MY HOT TALK
Michelle Digiacomo

When you know what REALLY turns your partner on, phone sex will seem as natural as the real thing. A wild, fun filled avenue to explore. Not only will it enhance your sex life, it will change it dramatically. When you discover the power, you'll wonder why you never did it before.

HOW TO MAKE LOVE TO THE SAME PERSON FOR THE REST OF YOUR LIVES
Dagmar O'Connor

I often encourage couples who complain of humdrum sex lives to try talking dirty with each other, either over the phone or in person. Over the phone, as we have seen, can be the best way to start because it is less threatening. One woman told me that she and her husband made frequent "quickie, obscene phone calls" to each other all day: "I get him on the phone-even if he is in the middle of a meeting-and I'll say something like 'Don't move- I just stuck my hand in your fly. Talk to you later.' We have a good laugh, but there's no denying that it's a real turn-on."

*D*o you remember the first time you ever heard a woman *talk nasty* during sex? Wow. It's electrifying, isn't it? Sad, but true — when in a relationship for awhile, most of us tend to forget the stimulating power of erotic, explicit language.

This time your assignment is to use all those unmentionable, dirty words — not to shock, but to *arouse* your bedmate. And to make it easier to free that dark, wild man inside you, you're going to do it over the telephone.

One night this week, make an excuse to go out for a while, and when she's all alone in the house, call her. You'll need a very private phone, of course. An out-of-the-way public booth might work, or one of your business phones after hours.

Hi, it's me. I miss you. You know, I was watching you all day, and I thought I should call and let you know how much I love the way you move. Uh-huh, just move around; you have this sensuous kind of walk. Well, I guess it helps that you have such terrific legs. Terrific legs and a REALLY great butt! Boy, do I love your ass.... Have I told you lately how beautiful you are? Yes, and so sexy.

What are you wearing? And under that? I'm thinking I'd like to see you UNdressed right now. I could touch you. Would you like that? Would you let me run my fingers over your nipple? But I'm not there. Umm, you'll have to do it for me. Go on, touch yourself. Does that feel good? Oh baby, I wish I could touch your tits. I'm getting a hard-on just thinking about it. I wish I could slide my hands under your panties, too. You do it...

Tell her exactly what you want. Tell her to stroke herself, to get wet, to put her fingers inside. *Does that feel good? Mmm, put the phone by your *****. I wanna hear you playing with it. Yesss...*

Go on, feed her fantasy. Get a little nasty! If you want to suck her until she comes, and make her scream with passion — tell her. *Would you like me to come home? If I come home right now, will you **** me?*

Yes, it's phone sex. Not with some underpaid actress on the other end of a 900 number, but with the woman who really turns you on. Even better, she's a woman who is *already* turned on before you walk in the door. Hey — Domino's couldn't serve you faster!

Ingredients

1 Private Phone / 1 Hot Lady

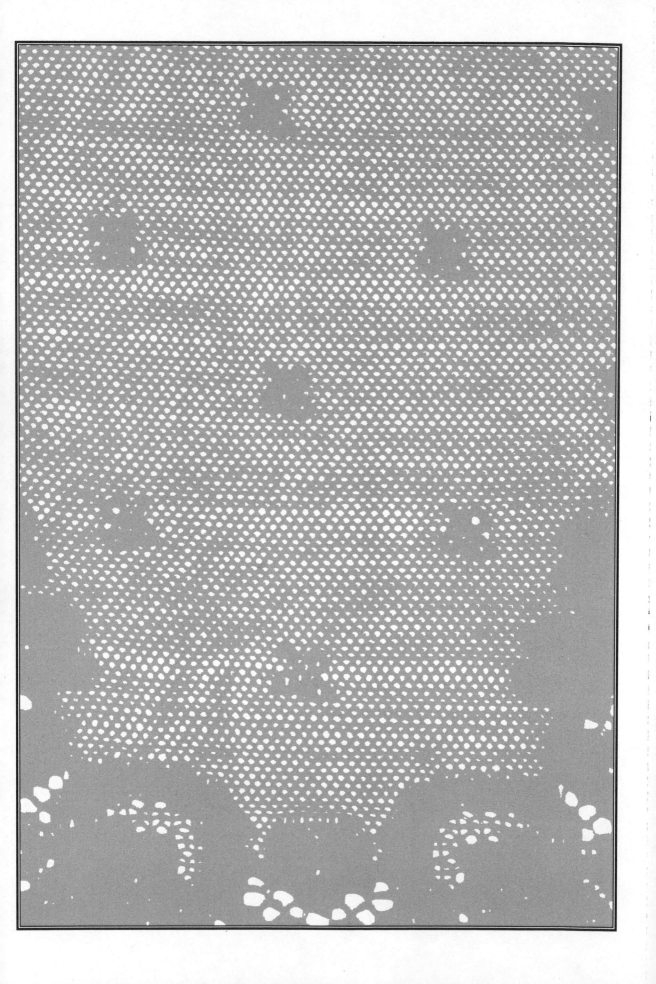

N⁰ *41*

SIXTY MINUTE MAN

For *His* Eyes Only

FOR MEN ONLY
Joseph Angelo

If your relationship isn't sexual that means trouble. Remember, sex is not about intercourse, sex is about being with the woman you love. Sex is about body closeness and physical intimacy.

When people go around thinking that sex is love, they become lunatics. If sex is love, then the longer most people are married the less they love each other. Not the case. Sex is fun and you have to practice to get good at it. Sex is more difficult than golf, tennis, or horseback riding, but most people would never think of spending four or five hours on a Saturday morning playing a round of sex with someone they love. They are too busy to practice and master sex. Nobody has the guts to admit it, and most will deny it. But then again, people used to think the world was flat.

HOT MONOGAMY
Dr. Patricia Love & Jo Robinson

Reserving a one hour block of quality time once a week for sex may increase your satisfaction with your lovemaking more than any other change you can make.

*Y*ou've seen the Kevin Costner movie *Bull Durham*, haven't you? Hmm, I'll bet you thought it was about baseball.

Nope! This movie was about seduction from beginning to end, and there wasn't a woman in the theater who didn't get absolutely *wet between her legs* when Kevin jumped Susan Sarandon while the soundtrack cranked out "Sixty Minute Man."

A couple of days before the seduction put a cake timer on the nightstand. Don't tell her what you're up to but you're going to give her one hour of divine sensual pleasure.

And it starts with a whole lotta kissin'! Set your timer for fifteen minutes and *kiss her* — short, soft kisses on her eyelids and nose; long, wet kisses on her lips and neck. Kiss her nipples, kiss her thighs, all while she's still dressed! And when fifteen minutes is up, reset the clock.

Now get your hands into the act. Massage every inch of skin as you pull her clothes away. Slip your fingertips under the elastic of her panties — remember when that was called getting to third base? *Finger her.* Spread her juices up to her clitoris; rub it all around. Women never get enough manual stimulation.

You made her wet; now lap it up. Hit the timer and start the third quarter-hour with your face between her legs. Suck all of her — her thighs, her buttocks, her lips and most especially her clit, which may be as swollen and hard as you are by now. And when that bell rings —

Slip inside. You know what to do. But, uh, pace yourself — And if your game ends up in overtime, hey, who cares?

Whew! Some workout, huh? Catch your breath as you pop the Bull Durham tape into the VCR — cued up, of course, to that famous scene. Cuddle up and have a laugh while the song goes by. You'll be her Sixty Minute Man any hour of the day!

> *There'll be fifteen minutes of kissing*
> *Then you'll holler please don't stop.*
> *Fifteen minutes of pleasin', fifteen minutes of squeezin'*
> *And fifteen minutes of blowing my top!*
> *I'm the Sixty Minute Man....*

Ingredients
---

1 Tape of Bull Durham / 1 Kitchen Timer / 1 VCR
A big bottle of Gatorade and some vitamins!

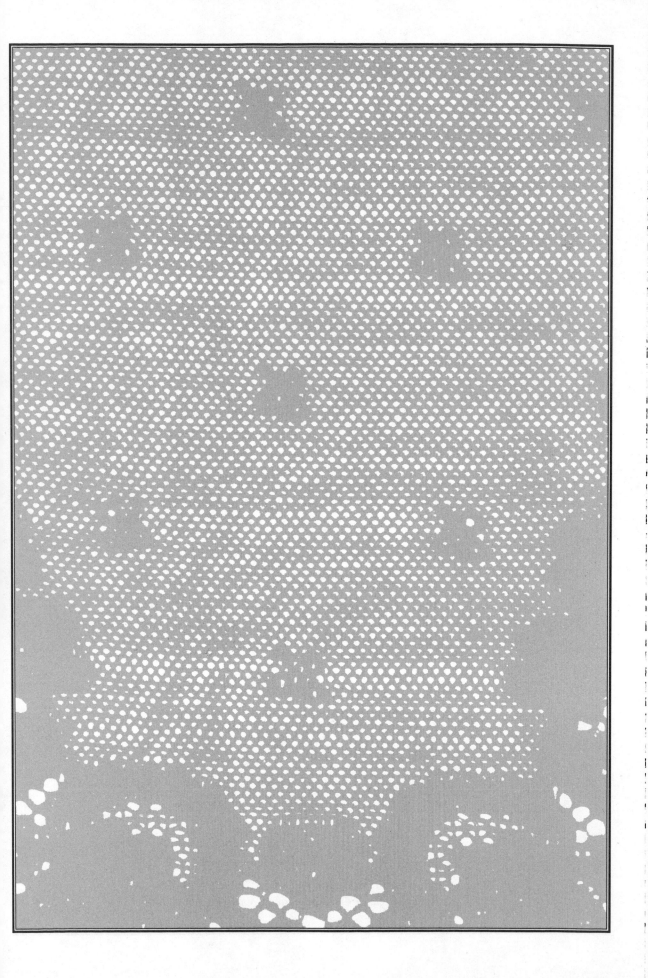

Nº **42**

TITILLATION

For *His* Eyes Only

$

WILD IN BED TOGETHER
Graham Masterton

Use your penis to massage her breasts and her nipples. Show her erect nipple will just fit into the lubricated hole in the end of your penis. Slide your penis into her underarm; press it against her cheek; wrap her hair around it. Use it. it's part of you, and it's not meant just for intercourse.

SECRETS OF SIZZLIN' SEX
Cricket Richmond & Ginny Valletti

Whether Dolly-dimensioned or luscious little love bumps, all breasts are fully loaded with sensory nerves that can be instantly activated. Size in no way symbolizes sexiness, touch sensitivity or reaction satisfaction. Although some females climax solely from breast arousal, most of us need additional nudging below the belt. Perhaps more women would take heart and hug those honey's if given some entertaining encouragement.

Rubbing nipples with Ben-Gay or similar heat-producing creams will warm more than your heart. Don't however, use analgesic products on genitals. Better yet, purchase user-friendly Hot Stuff body oils and lavish them abundantly on bosoms. Feel your temperature rising as you lift mams to your mouth and gently blow. No oil available? Simply moisten a finger with saliva or sexy secretion and apply...hummmmmmm.

Thanks for the mammaries....

*A*ren't breasts just the greatest things ever? Men can't help but look at them, and believe me, we love to show them off! Regardless of size, though, most women are a little insecure about theirs. Well, you're about to put your sweetheart's mind at ease. By the time this night is over, she'll be convinced her breasts are spectacular — magnificent! — and incredibly erotic, *and you're going to prove it to her.*

Start your seduction with a present — a beautiful, sensuous, lacy bra from Victoria's Secret. (Dig into her closet if you don't know the size.) Tell her that beautiful breasts like hers deserve the finest. You only ask that she wear it on your date this weekend.

Ooh! Lovely new lingerie, and a command performance? She'll be aroused before the evening even begins. The real fun, however, comes after your dinner or movie. You're going to focus on *stimulating her breasts,* and you've got some special tools and tricks to help you do it.

First, help her get undressed, but stop at the new bra. Tell her she looks fantastic in it — then press your face right into her décolletage. Rub the fabric across your cheek, kissing each inch of sweet flesh as it's slowly exposed. *Now get your toolbox....* First, take out a large silk scarf and drape it across her belly. Pull it taut, and draw it upwards, gently stretching her skin as you go. Tug left and then right, the buttery fabric cupping her pillows in it's satiny embrace. If her breasts are sizable, roll your scarf into a cord and wrap it completely around one. Pull it snug — even just *a little tight* — to set her nerves abuzz.

Reach for the lotion, the flavored kind that grows warm as it's applied. Take your time to rub it in, slowly zeroing in on her aureoles. They look so sexy when they perk up like that, don't they? Let's *tittilate* 'em! Take a soft string and loop it over her distended nipples. Tie it in an exquisitely small knot, and carefully, ever-so-gently *lift her breasts* by your tiny little leash. Use your imagination. A little ice...or ice cream! How about a mouthful of hot chocolate? Mmm — don't forget to share!

Now unless she is an unusually sensitive woman, you'll finally have to, uh, head south in order to finish the show. But you'll sure learn to appreciate the grrreat view from the *balcony!*

Ingredients

1 Sexy New Bra / 1 Bottle of Motion-Lotion / 1 Large Silk Scarf / 1 Soft String

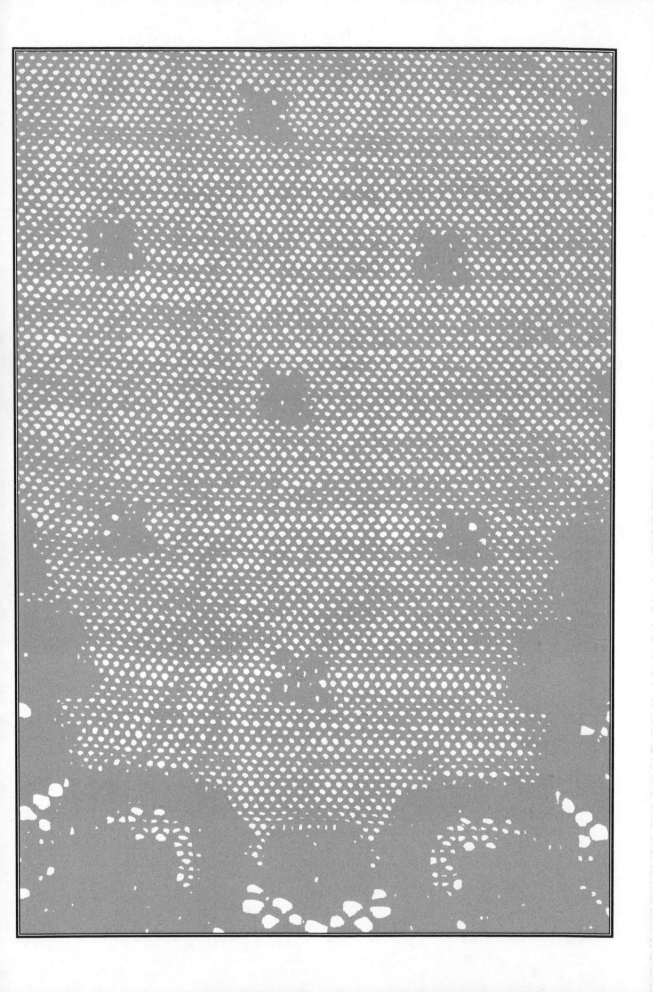

N°

LEAVE IT TO BEAVER

For *Her* Eyes Only

DRIVE HIM WILD
Graham Masterton

When I questioned men about their sexual preferences, well over 75 percent of them said that they would like the women in their lives to shave off their public hair, either occasionally "so that it grew back from time to time' or permanently.

Some women are afraid that a man who expresses an interest in shaven pubes is suppressing a secret desire for underage girls. But, largely, the opposite is true. It is the sight of a fully mature vulva, completely hairless, with nothing hidden, that most men find so arousing.

Why do men like it so much? First, because it shows them instantly that the women in their lives want to arouse them. Secondly, because it openly displays that part of the female anatomy that really excites them.

WHAT MEN REALLY WANT
Susan Crain Bakos

His is erotic variety. He wants something other than a dozen roses and a love note on the pillow.

As a columnist, I received hundreds of letters from men asking why wives or girlfriends wouldn't shave off their pubic hair; talk dirty in bed, make love in garter belt, black stockings, and high heels, or masturbate for them. The men in my survey harbored the same desires. Almost 90 percent of them rated more than one of these a turn-on and several wrote explaining why they craved stimuli women didn't.

*D*o *you know what the first dirty words ever spoken on national television were? It happened back in the fifties...when June said, "Ward — I think you were a little hard on the Beaver last night..."*

This is going to take some real daring on your part — but what a marvelous gift you're offering him! In this one moment you'll be showing your complete trust in him, your willingness to try something new. And if this doesn't get him totally, outrageously hot, then call 911 — because he's expired!

Prepare a small tray with the essential tools. Scissors, a bowl of water, shaving cream; they're all listed below. Find a time when he's not seriously occupied — looking through the paper, or channel-surfing — and slowly walk up, lay the tray in his lap, and smile.

Meet me in the bedroom in five minutes....I need your help with a little...project....(You know how men like their little projects!)

Pile up some pillows on the bed; make yourself comfortable. When he walks in, he'll find you bare below the waist, legs apart, and wearing little but your best jewelry.

Once he's picked his jaw up off the floor, have him sit between your thighs and begin. Just a short trim? Shave it into a small patch, or completely off? Whatever your preference...or his...start by having him massage a few drops of warm oil into your skin to soften it up. Mmmmm...this is getting better all the time! Crop with scissors, and move on to shaving cream and a razor.

Tell him what you've read in this book — that there's absolutely nothing like the sensation of a man's mouth against freshly shaved skin. Tell him you want him to try it, to *lick* you right now....In fact, you should show him you mean business by pushing him on his back and climbing right on top of his face, pressing your slick, pink flesh against his tongue.

For the first time, there's nothing between his mouth and the most sensitive part of you. Be prepared for heaven...because it really *is* incredibly different, incredibly arousing, incredibly sensuous. You may find yourself reaching orgasm faster than ever before...and you may find that *he* wants to do it more...and more...and more....

Ingredients

---

1 Tray / Scissors / 1 Ladies Razor / 1 Soft, Moist Towel / A Few Drops of Mineral Oil
A LOT of Trust! / 1 Bowl of Water / Shaving Cream / A Small Mirror

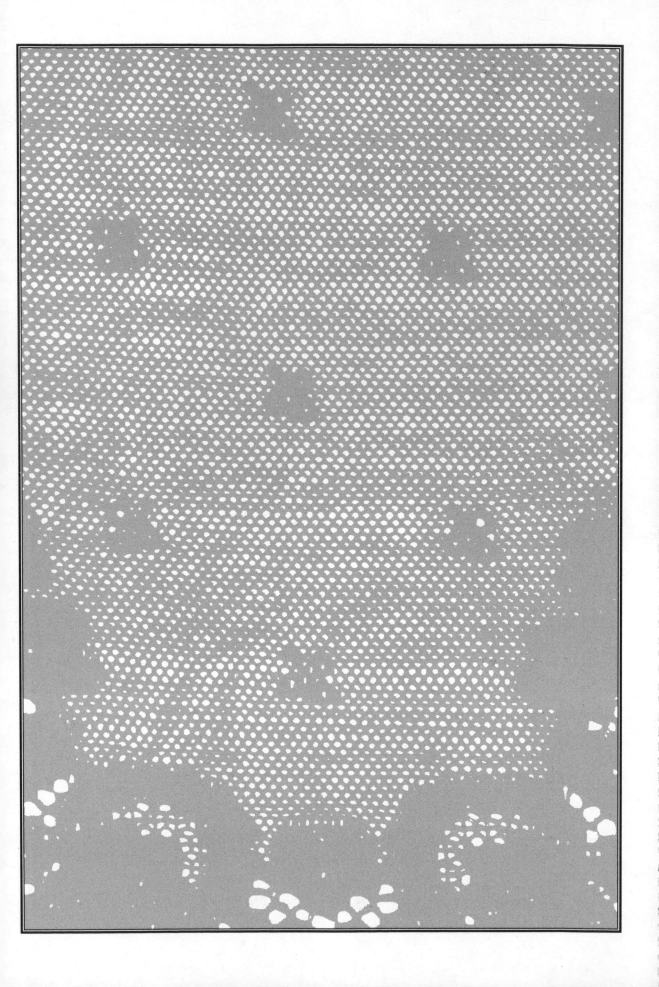

HALFTIME SHENANIGANS

For *Her* Eyes Only

LIGHT HIS FIRE
Ellen Kreidman

Most men can't resist that vulnerable little girl who resides inside all of us, but I have found that most women who were only children or the oldest in the family have a tough time being playful or using baby talk. If you heard messages such as, "Grow up and act your age," or "Stop being a baby," it may be hard for that little girl to come out. You have to experiment with what feels comfortable for you.

Practice looking adorable in front of a mirror. I know that what I've said here feels foreign to some of you, but I'm convinced that men will react favorably to you if you can make them laugh or appeal to the little boy in them. Remember, inside every man, no matter how strong, how successful, or how powerful he is, is a little boy just waiting for permission to come out and play.

IF IT FEELS GOOD
Joan Elizabeth Lloyd

Woman: Wear a tight skirt or one that's very short, hiding just enough. Wear a low-cut blouse or bra that pushes your breasts together and creates a lot of cleavage. Or wear no bra. If you never go braless because of your lack of natural uplift, do it anyway. A little sway and jiggle is very erotic. Let your erect nipples show through an open-weave sweater or a tight polo shirt. Your partner will feel that they're just waiting to be sucked.

Gimme an "F!" —
The notorious "Fish Cheer"
Country Joe and The Fish, Woodstock, 1968

*I*t's back to high school the way he *wishes* it were during this athletic, erotic seduction. Athletic for you, that is, because the time to surprise him with this "quickie" is when he's stretched out in his favorite chair, relaxed and watching sports on the tube.

You're going to be his halftime entertainment! When the players take a break and the commercials come on, pop into the room dressed in bobby socks, tennis shoes, a short pleated skirt and bulky sweater. Grab the remote and punch the "mute" button — he won't mind at all as soon as he realizes you're the cheerleader of his dreams. Shimmy and twist and jump and shout....

Take a "P," take an "E," take an "E-K" now! PEEK! Ooh, no panties!

You're my "H," you're my "U," you're my "N-K" man; you're a HUNK! Climb into his lap. A big kiss, then back to your cheer —

Here's my LEFT, here's my RIGHT, for my tits you'll FIGHT! Hey, there's no bra under that sweater! Jiggle them right in his face, and start getting physical. Let him take a run at your end zone. Oops — five yard penalty, backfield in motion....

Now, it's only minutes until the game starts again, so before they blow the whistle — blow *his* whistle! Take him in your mouth, and mutter one last cheer, this time in a sultry whisper.

Fe, Fi, Fo, Fum — I am gonna make you COME....

When it's over...when he's laying back gasping, and you're cuddling his tender little trophy...*Honey, I feel like I left something out. What's that thing those players do when they make a big score? They, uh...spike the ball?* Give him a quick squeeze — and watch how fast he calls time out!

Let him get back to his game. He'll love you all the more for understanding how much he wants to watch it. But don't be surprised if he sneaks up behind you later and suggests an Instant Replay.

Let's see that again in slow motion! Here's the pass....

Ingredients

1 Cheerleader Outfit — or something like it
1 Sporting Event / 1 Sporting Man

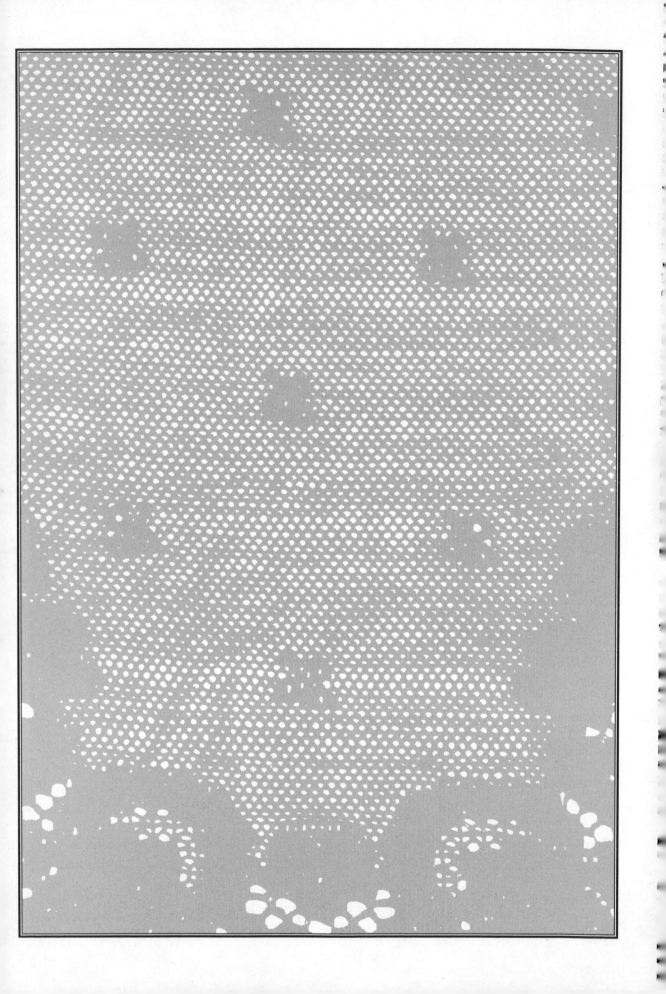

No. *45*

SLAVETIME!

For *His* Eyes Only

THE LOVING TOUCH
Dr. Andrew Stanway

Many couples add to their pleasure of sex, and to their anticipation of what is to come, by playing sex games. There are endless possibilities and it is up to each couple to write their own rules. The only limitations are a joint desire to play them and imagination.

Research has shown that there are some games that are more popular than others, although the variations are enormous and can, if required, be adapted to every couple's desires.

THE GOOD VIBRATIONS GUIDE TO SEX
Cathy Winks and Anne Semans

Half the thrill of sexually engaging with a new partner is the thrill of the unknown: the myriad possibilities of seduction, the opportunity to present whatever side of yourself you choose, the mystery of your new partner's responses. Hot sex requires an "other" to react against, and sustaining your identities as separate individuals is crucial to sustaining a sexual spark. Many long term couples know that the key to keeping their sex lives fresh is to take neither each other nor each other's availability for granted.

Wanna bet?

*T*hat's the note you'll inscribe in big bold letters on a dollar bill. Tape it to her mirror, and when she asks, explain that you want to play a game this week. Any game she likes — cards, checkers, Trivial Pursuit; it doesn't matter. But it's not until the actual night of your seduction that you name the stakes. The prize you are playing for...is *slavetime!*

Believe me, poker has never been this exciting! The real fun begins once this special game is over. Your lover — **assuming you win, of course** — now owes you *one full hour of slavetime.*

Begin by setting the mood — or better yet, command your slave to set the mood by lowering lights, arranging candles, and bringing her Master a drink. Tell her to kiss you...and then tell her that, sadly, it just wasn't good enough. She'll have to do *more* to earn her Master's pleasure. Put on some sexy music, and order her to dance while slowly removing her clothes. Ask her to model her sheerest, most sensual lingerie. Make her sit, legs apart, in the nastiest pose she can think of — and then play with her. Make her wet. Make her play with herself *while you watch.*

If you've ever dreamed of a woman drawing your testicles into her mouth while stroking you with her hand, this is your chance. If your wildest fantasy is a smorgasbord of your favorite foods licked off her naked flesh — go for it. You are in command.

There are only a few ground rules to follow, mostly designed to make sure your slave will be willing to totally trust her Master:

1. **No public embarrassment.** You can't invite the boys over to watch a strip show. (Advanced players may negotiate!)

2. **Nothing painful!** Need we say more?

3. **Nothing with any lasting consequences.** No photos, no pickups of strangers in bars, no unsafe practices.

Two final words of advice — Never forget to direct your slave to reach an orgasm of her own. Several, if possible. And always, *always* remember that you might *lose the game.* (Why, I'll bet you're even thinking about throwing it from time to time!)

Ingredients

One Deck of Cards (or any game you know and enjoy playing)
One or more private, uninterruptible hours

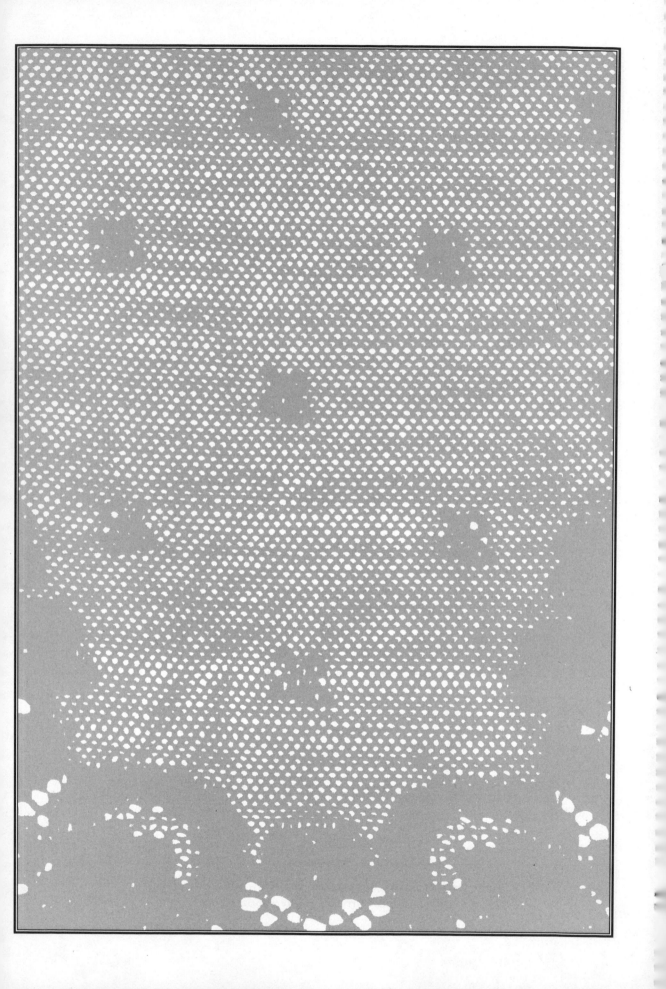

N.º 46

LE FEMME FATALE

For *Her* Eyes Only

SINGLE WILD SEXY & SAFE
Graham Masterton

Finally-let's take a look at one of the most important ways in which you can make yourself sexually irresistible to the man you love-and that's to use spontaneous compliments and displays of affection: It has often surprised me how many couples fall out of the habit of flirting with each other. Just because they've been married for a few years, each of them seems to assume that their sexual interest in the other is "understood" and doesn't need constant re-expression.

MORE WAYS TO DRIVE YOUR MAN WILD IN BED
Graham Masterton

You deserve much more than a routine sex life. You deserve excitement, arousal, and constant satisfaction. But you will never get it by feeling sorry for yourself and lying back and waiting for you husband or lover to wake up to the fact that he ought to be making love to you better. Whether the dullness of your sex life is your fault or not, you will have to make a positive effort to stir up that man in your life and do for him what another woman would do if she were out to excite him.

Don't ever leave the house without clean underwear.
You never know when you might be in an accident.
— Mom, 1968

I wonder what Mom would think of this? You're about to venture out in public with *no* underwear!

Call your sweetheart and arrange to pick him up after work. Tell him you need his help with something...or you're taking him out for drinks. Believe me, this will be worth the all the extra effort it takes to get him back to his car! When you show up, be sure to go into his office, because that's where your seduction begins. Stroll around while he gathers his stuff. Scope out a place where only he can see you, or where your back is to anyone else —

And then flash him. Yep, you're going to pull open your overcoat or raincoat to reveal...nothing! Well, almost nothing. You've got shoes, of course, and maybe a sharp hat. Stockings and a garter belt add a lot to the overall effect, but otherwise, you are standing in front of him in the altogether. Au naturel. Nude. Bare.

Wow! And wow again! A few seconds is all you need before you cover up. The damage is done; his brain is now fried. Remind him sweetly to pick his jaw up off the floor and then turn and saunter out of the building. Don't worry if he's not right behind you. It may take him a moment to remember how his feet work.

Next stop — the video store. Those high shelves should give you ample opportunity to display your wares again. Look in the comedy section for Alan Funt's *What Do You Say To A Naked Lady?* and ask him...hey, what *do* you say? (Quick peek!) Sharon Stone got a lot of attention in *Basic Instinct,* but did she do *this?* (Fast glimpse!) Oh, look dear, here's The Flash....

Don't rush home. Make him wait. Let the anticipation build as you stop by the convenience store and the mailbox. When you finally walk through your door, turn your back to him and shrug the collar back off your shoulders.

Honey, would you get my coat for me?

You'll knock his socks off! — and his shirt, and his pants, and his briefs, and his....

Ingredients

1 Long Coat / 1 Pair of Shoes / 1 Ounce of Courage

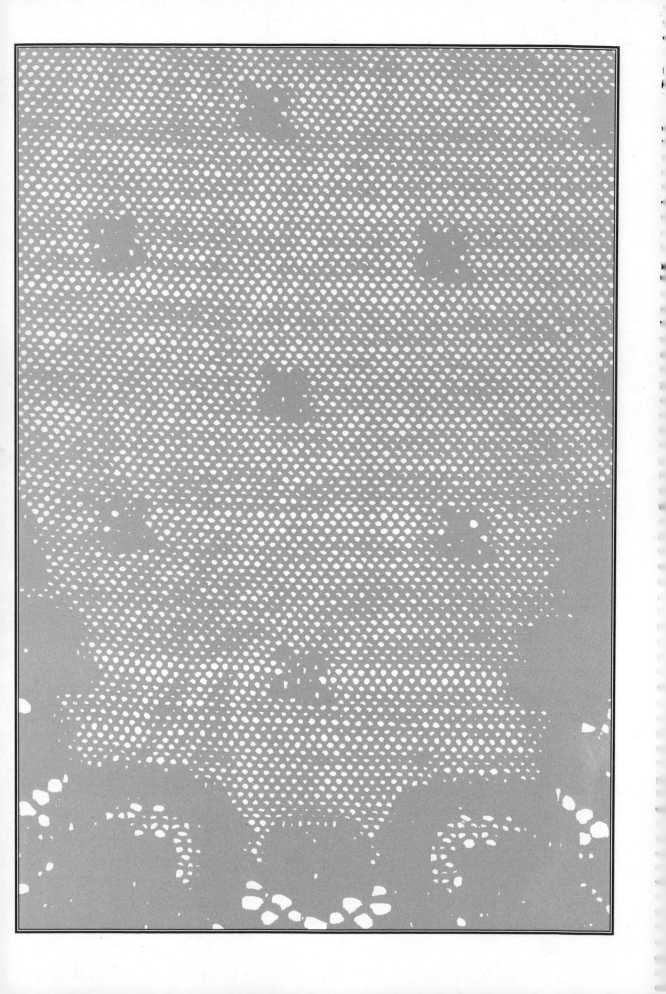

N° 47

MIRROR, MIRROR

For *Her* Eyes Only

SECRETS OF SIZZLIN' SEX
Cricket Richmond & Ginny Valletti

When viewing your nakedness in the mirror and negativity pops up...don't get hysterical! Wink, smile, seductively shrug your shoulder and affirm: "Who can resist lovable me?" Stand tall, strut, sink, pose or stretch and belt out, "Baby, you got it." Blow extra kisses to scars, wrinkles, veins or other less-than-perfect areas. Accept them as trials and recorded history of where you've been. Use the mirror to watch yourself dance or prance till it feels good and looks inviting. Giggle, laugh, sing and rejoice at being the heavenly love goddess you are. Remember, keep repeating positive affirmations until they become a part of you.

HOT AND BOTHERED
Wendy Dennis

The woman who knows her way around what one man described as "that little rim around the head of the penis where every nerve ending in your body shorts out" knows what she's doing. So does the woman who coaxes a penis to attention with soft, feathery touches and teasing licks. The woman who drags her teeth across the head of the penis does not. A great blowjob, one man observed, is like a ballet, a seamless performance involves a well-orchestrated blend of "lots of saliva-work, lots of tongue-work and lots of handwork." And, just as a woman senses a man's sincere interest in her nether regions, so does a man know when a woman's heart isn't really in the job. Since the whole point about a blowjob is having all that loving attention focused on his penis, it brightens a man's spirits enormously to meet a woman who treats it with playful adoration when it's limp, with awe and reverence when it's ready for action, and who takes a break now and then to gaze up at him with smiling eyes.

*S*ex is so wonderful when you can take the time to do it right. Slow and easy, with lots of foreplay and lots of laughs — these are the ingredients for a great evening of lovemaking.

But not today! This seduction is incredibly powerful precisely because it's so *short*. Hot, fast, and fiercely erotic, what you're about to do will simply stun your lover's senses. It's a "quickie," but the memory of it — and of you — will last him a lifetime.

Warm him up first. Flirt with him. It won't be too tough to get him thinking about sex. He is a guy, after all! But your quick kisses and subtle squeezes still won't give him a clue about the surprise you have in store.

It involves a mirror, the biggest you can find. If you don't have a full-length mirror, purchase one — they're not expensive. All you need is a few uninterrupted minutes, and I'll bet you can arrange that even if there are other people in the house — or the office, or the store, or wherever your imagination leads you. When the time is right, grab him and lead him to the mirror; kiss him hard and fumble with his belt. Tell him you've been dying to get to him all day. Then drop to your knees, free that swelling bulge and draw it into your mouth all the way, as far as you can.

He'll be shocked — literally. It's *erotic electricity,* a sensuous short-circuit between his brain and his penis. You'll enjoy feeling the changes that come over him. He'll start soft and sweet, rolling around on your tongue. In just seconds he'll grow firm, then outrageously hard. The sensation is so overwhelming he may actually tremble and grow weak at the knees.

And he can watch your performance in the mirror. He can *see* you pulling him deep into your mouth — he'll feel like the star of his own private video. Don't be too gentle! This is *fast.* Twist and turn as you devour him, press his head against the inside of your cheek. In that mirror, he should see a wildcat, a sexy vixen eager to relieve the tension between his legs. Do it. Don't slow down, and don't stop until he reaches ecstasy.

Mirror, mirror, on the wall,
Who's the hottest one of all?

It's you!

Ingredients

1 Full-Length Mirror / 1 Full-Length Man

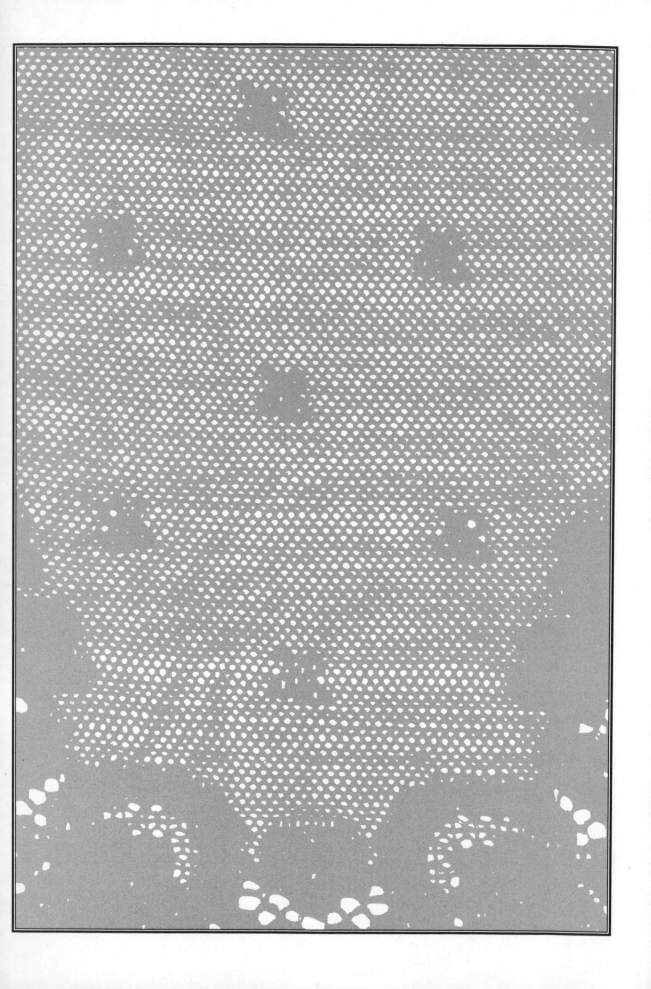

N^{o} *48*

A SUDDEN GLIMPSE OF LACE

For *Her* Eyes Only

$

DRIVE HIM WILD
Graham Masterton

First of all, remember that you're sexually attractive to the man in your life. However much you may criticize yourself (don't like your breasts, tummy's too protuberant, thighs are too heavy) the man in your life doesn't see your body in the same way. He sees the woman he's won, and he's proud of you.

It is this kind of reticence that prevents so many sexual relationships from ever really taking off. When you are involved in a sexual relationship with a man, you should give it all or nothing. If you decide to do that tonight, you'll be startled by how affectionate and attentive your partner suddenly becomes....in and out of bed.

WHAT MEN REALLY WANT
Susan Crain Bakos

The desire to touch is a human need, as much male as female. But the need to please sexually is stronger in the male. If women only realized this, we would have more sexual confidence in ourselves. We would make love with greater abandon because we would finally understand he isn't thinking about our heavy thighs when he's in bed with us.

*S*ince Eve put on the first fig leaf, men have been trying to get women back out of their clothes. Nothing arouses a man like the sight of a woman *in the process of taking her clothes off.*

This week, you're going to become an ecdysiast — a practitioner of the fine and ancient art of striptease. And to do it right, you're going to need some props. Stockings and garter are traditional; a g-string or thong-back panties, indispensable. It's worth a trip to the mall to find those sexy over-the-elbows French lace gloves and a long, long strand of pearls. High heels, a lacy push-up bra and a slinky sheer slip complete your ensemble.

The morning of your seduction, just before he leaves, he'll spy your gloves casually draped through the refrigerator handle. Hello! What's this? No time to talk, but boy, will he be thinking about it all day! When he walks in that evening, there they are — and there you are, in an attractive but otherwise ordinary dress that reveals no hint of the treasures beneath.

The gloves? Here, have something to eat. Oh, do you like them? Hmmm...how about a glass of wine? Distract him for awhile. *Would you like me to try them on? Then sit down....*

Pull on the gloves. Dim the lights. Start some very hot music. My favorite? Joe Cocker's "You Can Leave Your Hat On" — it's on the *9 1/2 Weeks* soundtrack. Off comes the dress first. Ask for his help with the buttons. Dance around him as you peel away your slip...then wrap it around his head! He'll cheer each item you toss his way. What do you think he'll appreciate more? The stunning look? Or the effort you put into it? And you did it all for him....

Now go, sister, go! Shake those things he's staring at — press your breasts right into his face. Turn and bend over as you pull the pearls between your thighs. Plant your bottom right in his lap and *squirm!* And don't forget the classic Gypsy Rose Lee hook, the move that put the tease in striptease. Grab something — a hat, a pan, a big book — and cover yourself while you pull off your lingerie. Oh, he'll get to see it, but only a glimpse at a time. He'll get to have it, too, but not until the show is over.

And guess what — he's going to *finally* start noticing your outfits. (But I'll bet he's thinking more about what's under them!)

Ingredients

Your Sexiest Lingerie / 1 Pair of Opera-Length Gloves
Your Hottest Music / 1 String of Pearls

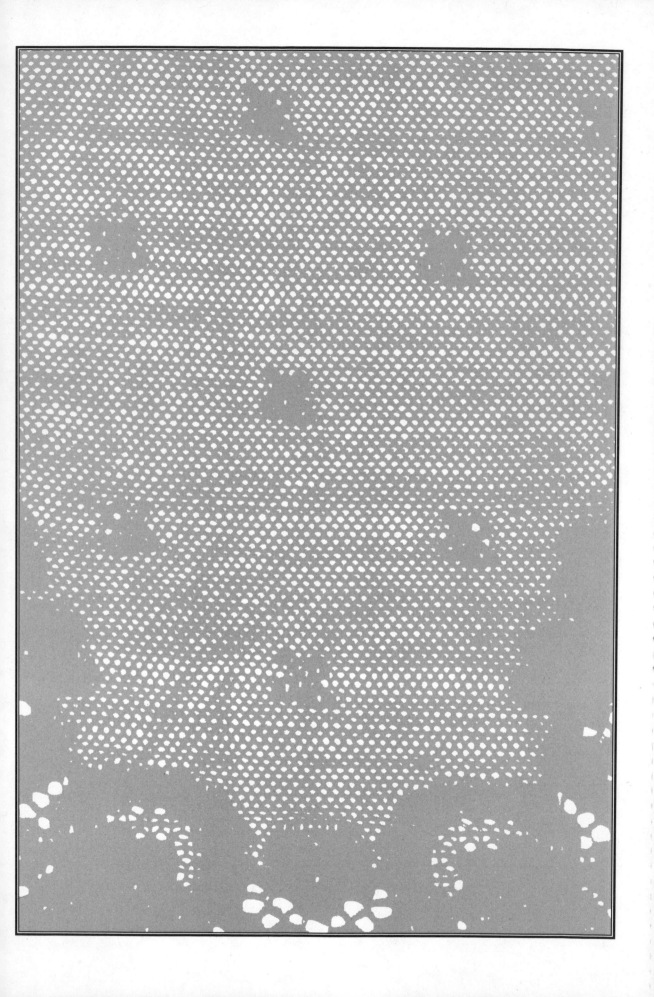

N.º 49

NIGHT MOVES

For *Her* Eyes Only

$$

LOVE POTIONS
Cynthia Mervis Watson, M.D. with Angela Hynes

Setting the stage for sex is a little like planning a party, producing a play, or preparing a celebratory feast; getting ready is half the fun. The more you enjoy putting it all together, the more fun you will have when the guest of honor arrives.

IT WAS BETTER IN THE BACK SEAT
Sherry Lehman, M.A.

A couple's imagination is what is needed to keep the marriage crackling. Imagination costs nothing. Everyone has one. It is an unlimited commodity. The more an imagination is exercised, the greater the personal reward. It can be the most challenging adventure of a couple's life to keep each other sexually aroused and erotically involved. Planning to infuse a marriage with sizzle and keep it romantic can be a wonderful pastime for any couple. Don't forget how enjoyable it was to play dress up as children. Choosing different clothing was helpful in being able to play "let's pretend." Just because a person grows older does not mean the same games cannot be enjoyed.

*S*timulating conversation, extraordinary food, moving music — these can all enhance an erotic encounter, and I always encourage their use. Of the seductions in this book, however, this is the only one that uses a technique that can actually *alter your state of mind*...producing not just Grrreat Sex but, as you'll see, some remarkable side effects as well!

You'll need a *strobe light* — one of those bright, rapidly flashing lamps used in dance clubs. Small, inexpensive units are available at Radio Shack, and you can probably rent one from a photography store. Set it up at home in a room that can be made completely dark, and then get ready for your private little party. You'll want to wear something you can tear apart — with buttons up the front. Party food? You bet, and don't forget the music.

Your evening starts normally enough — talking, eating, a little kissing and a lot of laughing. But then it takes an *unusual* turn. Put on some music that makes you want to dance; turn it up loud. Flip off the main lights, and activate your strobe. Immediately the room takes on a whole new cast. It seems somehow...wilder, more mysterious. Every twist of your body, every toss of your hair is frozen in time. The lightening-quick strobe creates more dark than light, so he simply *can't see* your hands as they fly over his body, unbuttoning his shirt, unzipping his trousers. The flickering blast is disorienting. It's suddenly harder for him to think, and harder to resist his more, uh, basic instincts. Now push him back on the couch, and — rip your blouse open.

Oh, the effect is quite startling. He's entered an unreal world of erotic *snapshots*. One sexually charged image flashes by after another — it's a wet dream come alive. Leave your tattered shirt in place as you pounce on him like a lioness. *Force* him to kiss you; squeeze your lace-covered breasts into his face. His own animal nature is in command now, and he'll follow your lead by tearing at your clothing. Don't kiss when you can bite; don't lick when you can suck, and *suck hard.* Your aggressive sensuality will be amplified by his, and after all this foreplay, intercourse could be brief, but it will be extremely intense.

Pulsing lights, pounding music, a powerful climax — by now he may have entered a different state of consciousness; he might actually be *hypnotized.* It couldn't hurt to find out. Draw close to his ear and whisper your commands...*I want a new caaarrrr...I want to go to Hawaaaaaiiiiii...I want you again rrriiiight nnooowww!!!...*

Ingredients
---

1 Strobe Light / 1 Dark Room / 1 Disposable Blouse / 1 Loud Stereo

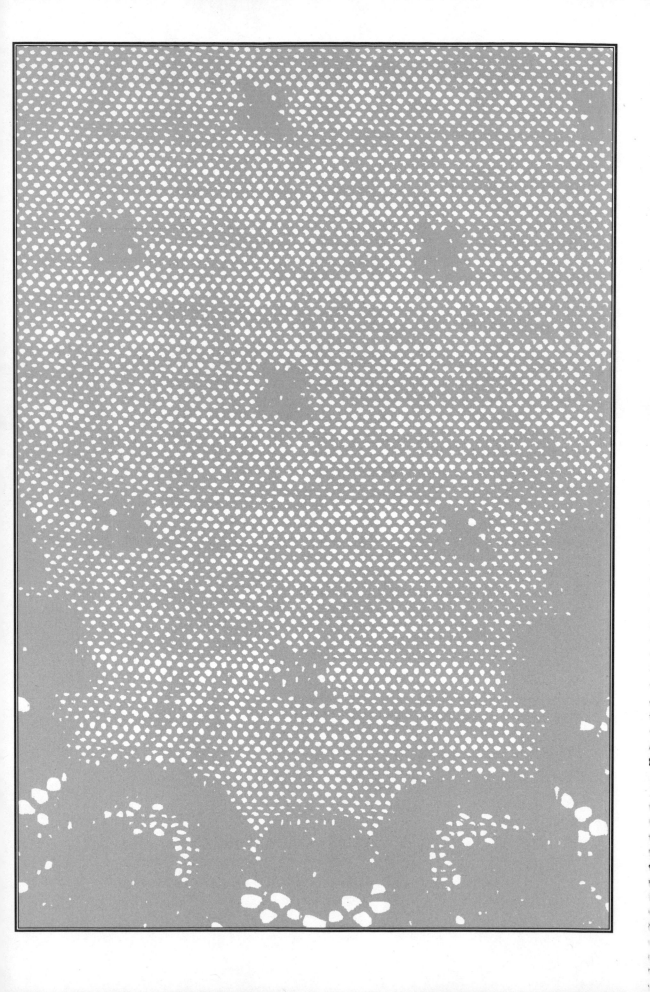

№ 50
—————
SUBLIMINAL SEDUCER

For *His* Eyes Only

$$$

DRIVE YOUR WOMAN WILD IN BED
Staci Keith

With women, it's a little different. They want you to want them more than you've wanted anyone in the history of the world. Again, that maddening fairy-tale princess mentality creeps in! Because every woman is a goddess inside. No matter if she is four hundred fifty pounds, bald, and wears a pith helmet, every woman wants that goddess paid tribute. That's why women melt over those traditional emblems of worship - roses, poetry, gifts: they're an offering on the shrine of their womanhood.

FOR MEN ONLY
Joseph Angelo

If you learn anything from this book, learn that women are different from men. Stop treating women as if they were men with tits and vaginas. They aren't. They are different creatures.

Loving women is difficult because they are so different from men. Women speak an entirely different language. They feel differently; they do things differently. But most of all, women perceive events differently from men. The simplest way to understand this is to think about sex. Men have an exterior probing, prodding, and pushy unit that gets very excited quickly and then fades. Women have a soft, warm, interior membrane that gets excited very slowly and stays that way for a long time. When you think about it, only love could allow these two units to connect.

*H*ere's a seduction that's one long tease, from morning to night, and it begins, appropriately, with a little sunrise flirtation.

As soon as you awaken, snuggle up behind your bedmate in the classic spoon position. Nip her shoulders lightly with your teeth. Tickle the base of her neck with warm, fleeting kisses while pressing your body into hers. Let her feel your arousal against her thighs. About the time she starts to purr and snuggle back —

Get out of bed, take your shower, and get dressed for work! You've accomplished your goal. You've planted the thought of sex squarely in her mind. Before you leave, scatter a dozen or more Post-Its™ around the house — you know, those semi-sticky little yellow notes. Your messages are short and to the point.

I love you. I miss you. I want you. You're gorgeous!

No kids around? You can be a little more explicit — *Sex. Sex. Wanna ****? Sex. Orgasm. SEX!* Each one will bring a smile to her lips as she stumbles across it.

Send her a bouquet of roses surrounding one lone *anthurium.* Your florist will grin when you order this special flower! The blossom is in the shape of a red heart, and jutting out from the center is a gold pistil that looks like nothing more than tiny, fully-erect penis. Your card reads: *Study this carefully. Anything come to mind?*

Build her sense of anticipation by taking her out for dinner. Occasionally, when you think no one else is looking, reach into your pocket and whip out a prepared flashcard. Just a little three-by-five card with more of your naughty words — *Do me. Eat this. Sucksucksuck. Sex!!!* She'll have to struggle to stifle her laughter as you whip each one past her eyes.

"You know, honey, I get the feeling you've got something on your mind tonight...."

Indeed you do! And if she hasn't grasped your subtle hints by now, you'll be happy to make it *quite* clear as soon as you get home!

Ingredients

6 Red Roses / 1 Hawaiian Anthurium / 1 Special Dinner
1 Set of Erotic Flashcards / 1 Pack of Post-Its™ / 1 Special Card

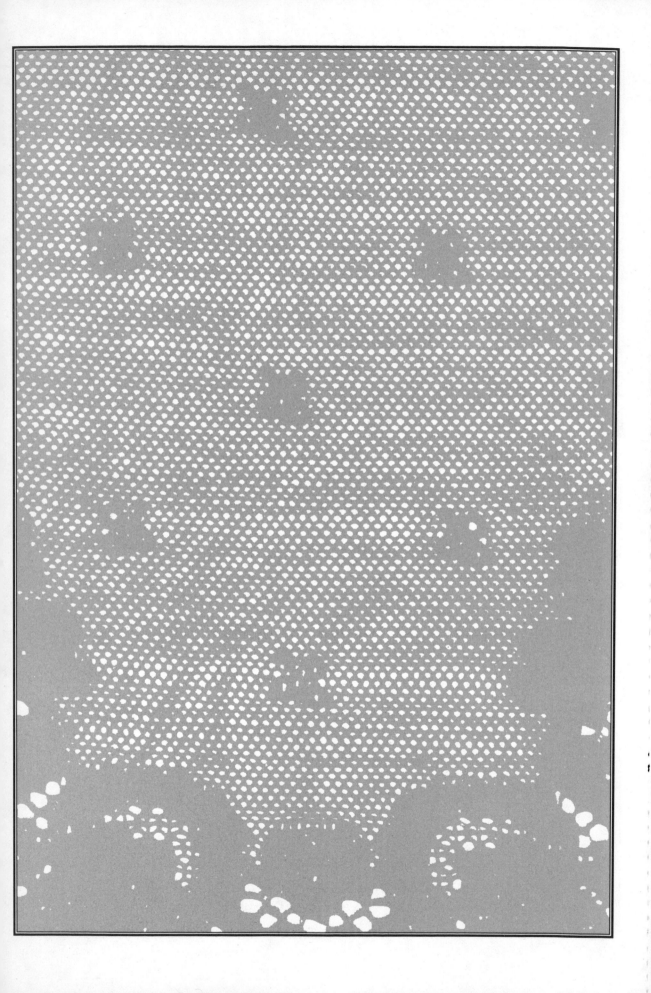

N°

51

RADIO PURR-DUCER

For *His* Eyes Only

DRIVE YOUR WOMAN WILD IN BED
Staci Keith

There's nothing like doing something sappy and adolescent to win her heart, so why not call a radio station and have them dedicate a song to your sweetheart? Every couple seems to have "their song" - one that, to them, perfectly epitomizes their feelings for each other. If you don't have one yet, pick one. And watch her heart strings quiver!

THE LOVING TOUCH
Dr. Andrew Stanway

Almost all couples play some sort of love games, if only from time to time. These can be as different as simply having a private language so that they can communicate sexy things in public, to organized, formal sex games that involve dressing up or acting out various roles.

Many couples play sex games simply for the fun of them. It is a form of recreation - like playing tennis - and for the creative couple sex games add to the fun in their lives just as other hobbies and pastimes do.

Sex games can also be used as 'presents' to one another when they feel particularly loving, sad, depressed or just grateful. Playing a game that you know your lover will enjoy can be a wonderful way of saying 'I love you'.

RED HOT MONOGAMY
Patrick T. Hunt M.D.

Noted meteorologist, Dr. E. Lorenz, found that minute changes have profound effects on complex systems like weather. He described this as the Butterfly Effect because, as he put it, a butterfly flapping its wings in Brazil might create a tornado in Texas. What this means to you is that a small effort can cause a big change in your relationship. By investing as little as a minute, you can markedly change things for the better. And your sex life will be fantastic.

*O*ver the years I've been a guest on lots of radio programs, and I can tell you that the men and women who run those morning shows are some of the brightest, funniest, hardest-working people in America.

But just think - they have to get up at 3:00 or 3:30 each morning. Can you imagine how that might put a crimp in your sex life?

Well, now you're going to have a little erotic fun, make a wish come true, and maybe put a little zing into the lives of these poor souls whose days start when most of us are in dreamland. Do your job right, and you'll end up with some free concert tickets!

You're going to be a *Radio Purr-ducer*, and here's how it works. First, before going to bed, get some paper and write down a wish; something you want her to do for you...make a favorite meal, wash your car, perhaps a special sexual treat. Let your lover in on the rules, but keep your wish a secret.

Then, when the alarm goes off the next morning, hit the snooze button — and get busy. In the few minutes before the radio comes back on, you're going to try to make your bedmate *purr*...or moan, or laugh, or make some sound of pleasure. If she does...you win! She has to fulfill your secret wish.

Now since this seduction indirectly involves your favorite morning radio team, let them in on it too. Call up and explain the game. (Don't be surprised if they already know about this book!)

Trust me, the morning crew will be interested. They spend most of their time getting people *out* of bed — what a rare treat to help someone stay there, especially when *they* get to be part of the foreplay! So ask them to help sweeten the pot. In return for a follow-up report, complete with a testimonial from your purring arousee, might they be willing to part with some tickets for the next big show in town? A word of warning: Once they figure out what time your radio pops back *on* in the morning — you may be startled to hear the team, and the town, cheering you on!

Remember to put this page back in the book. Even if you can't get through to your favorite station (and isn't their phone line *always* busy?!) you *can* enjoy your partner's attempt to beat you next time at the Radio Purr-ducer game. Those deejays will tell you that the battle for higher ratings was never this much fun!

— *Ingredients* —

1 Radio with Snooze Button / 1 Purring Bedmate / 1 Telephone
1 Wild but *Very* Lonely (or Very Horny!) Morning Radio Team

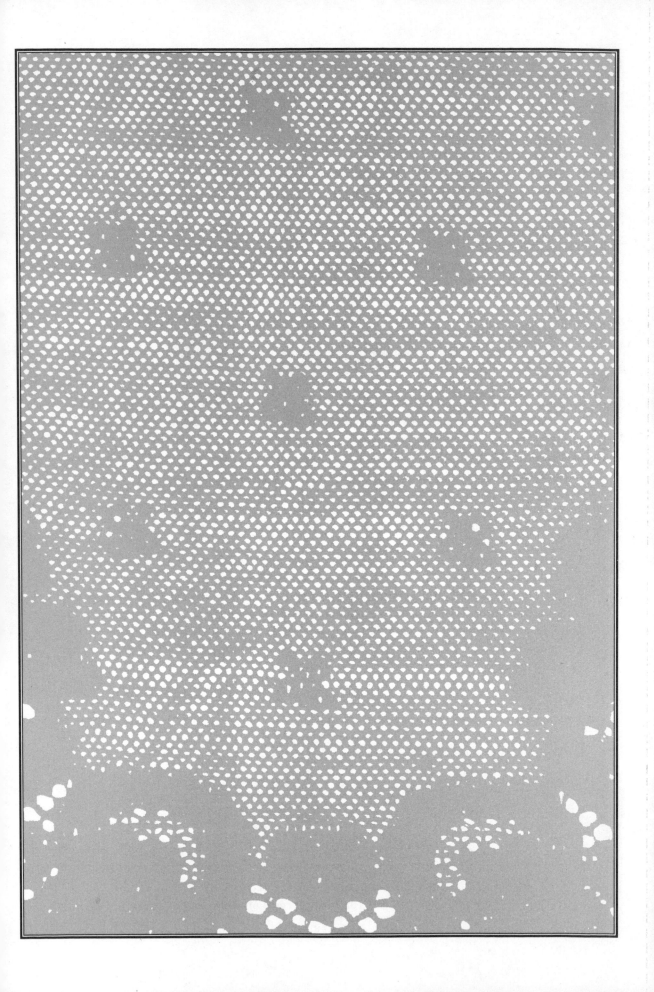

No.

MORNING GLORY

For *His* Eyes Only

DRIVE YOUR WOMAN WILD IN BED
Staci Keith

Few things feel more exquisitely erotic than having a man perform oral sex on you after having drunk a very hot beverage. Or a very cold one. Perhaps you can vary the temperature, thereby discovering which one she likes best. You will need to keep the drink handy so you can maintain the extreme hotness or coldness but for heaven's sake, don't use ice cubes directly on her vagina! Most women, in fact, prefer the hot beverage to the cold; the chill tends to numb their full range of sensation.

SECRETS OF SEDUCTION
Brenda Venus

Cunnilingus is much, much more dependent on your technique and expertise than intercourse. During Cunnilingus, a woman's body sensations are quite different than the ones she experiences with your penis inside her vagina - even though they're both nirvana. It's not possible to excel in this art without knowing our lady's intimate anatomy; ergo, the lesson preceding.

Your mouth is a highly mobile organ set in a highly mobile head and therefore provides great sensitivity by the touch of the tongue. It is also vastly superior to your penis. Why? Because if she finds it difficult to orgasm with "Mr. Happy" or if "Mr. Happy" is tired, you will still be a success! A woman can enjoy a series of orgasms of varying intensities before she's completely content.

*W*hat's the taste of passion?

On radio and in interviews, I've talked to a lot of men over the years. They can all name favorite aromas that put them in the mood for love — flowers, a special perfume, even a certain favorite meal on the stove can trigger hot memories. All men seem to love the smell of a woman's freshly washed hair.

But when it comes to taste, there's just one that's always guaranteed to, um, raise the flag, if you know what I mean. It's the glorious, fragrant, slightly sweet and always highly evocative flavor of *pussy*. This week, believe it or not, you're going to sneak a bite when your love isn't looking!

Pick a day when you both can sleep in a while without interruption. First thing in the morning, encourage her to stay in the sack. Cuddle up close to her; she'll love being held as she drifts in and out of that drowsy half-awake state. When she slips back into dreamland, crawl out of bed and head for the kitchen, where you'll make some coffee or tea or some other hot drink. Bring her a cup, but before you present it to her, take a big sip —

And climb under the covers. Way under. Try very hard not to wake her before you run your tongue right across her belly and down to her sweet sex.

Wow! What a way to come awake. The drink has heated your mouth and moistened your lips. Your tongue is creating steam everywhere it touches.

She might still be dreaming...sweet dreams, no doubt! But soon she'll come to realize the magic you're making is no fantasy. Don't expect conversation from your little sleepyhead this morning — but a deep sigh and a few moans will let you know you're on the right track. As for you...*enjoy*.

Mmmm — Breakfast of Champions!

Ingredients
---

1 Sleepyhead / A Little Sleepy Head!

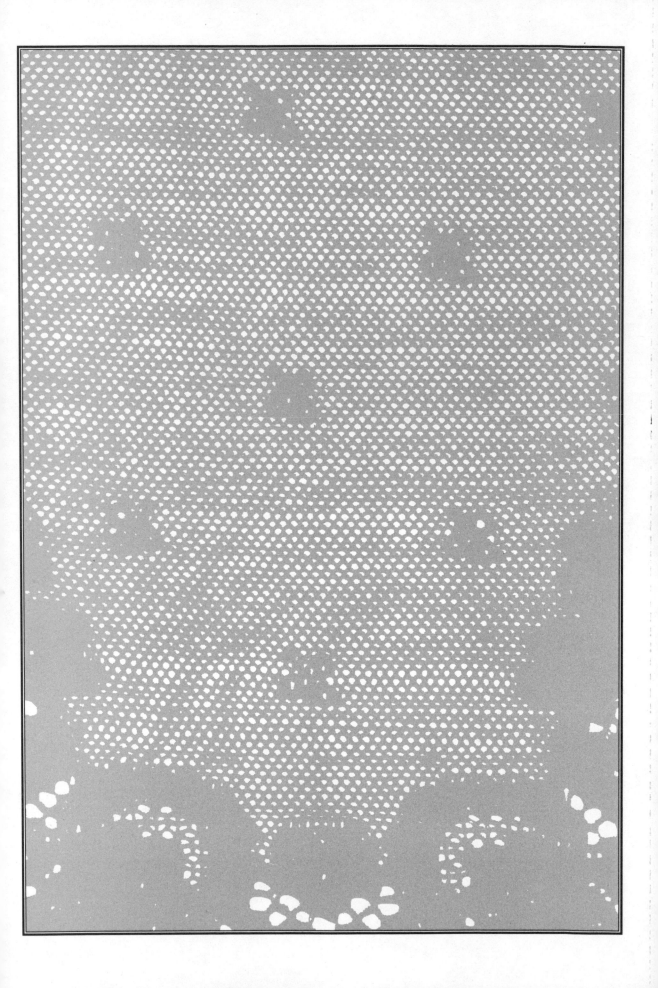

№

ON TOP OF SUGAR MOUNTAIN

For *Her* Eyes Only

WOMEN ON TOP
Nancy Friday

Ah, the joy of seduction! To take a man, lay him down and you on top, orchestrate his sounds of slow surrender with the shifting of your weight, the forbidden dirty words whispered in your female/mother voice, watch his gradual loss of control- no, control his loss of control- until ultimately, with the pressure and release of delicate vaginal muscles on his swollen penis, he comes. What power to give another human being an orgasm. No, let me change the verb because it is important, what this chapter is about: What power to make someone come. "I'm the dominant one doing all the work and he's the receptive one," Sue describes her seduction. "My pleasure is in knowing what abandonment he has felt...seeing him change from cool sophisticated male to a man in the throes of sexual release."

203 WAYS TO DRIVE A MAN WILD IN BED
Olivia St. Claire

The foot fetish - During intercourse, whenever you're in a position to reach his feet easily, you might consider this little trick. Just as he's about to have his orgasm, grasp his toes and pull gently. It seems that a man's toe bone is connected to his genital bone, and this extra stimulation increases the intensity of his ejaculation.

Leave a note taped to the door he walks through after work.

Class starts at eight. There will be a test afterward.

*Y*ou won't be dressed like any teacher he ever had...outside of his adolescent fantasies, that is! A sheer robe over a skimpy teddy, high heels — men just *love* barely-dressed women in heels — and an enticing fragrance should put him in the mood for this kind of homework. Today he'll be studying the *female superiority complex.* You're going to practice five different positions, all on top, and he has to decide which one's best. Life should only be filled with such tough choices, eh?

First Get him thoroughly aroused and then straddle his thighs, facing him. Slide his penis the length of your lips, spreading your wetness just across the head. Dip it in half an inch...then pull it out again. Rub your clitoris all over the swollen end, then slide it in a little deeper. Repeat.

Second Drop all the way down, engulfing his erection in your tight, wet warmth, and lean forward. Stretch out on top of him, your legs over his, your face cradled against his neck. Rock your hips. Push down until you feel your clit pressing directly against the base of his shaft.

Third Sit up and squat over him, feet just outside his thighs, hands against his chest for balance. In this position you can really fly, riding up to the tingling tip, then pounding back down. Every smack of your bottom against his hips will drive him one step closer to ecstasy.

Fourth Turn around. This time, lean *back* after guiding him inside. Lay against his chest; let him reach around and caress your breasts. Pull your legs together on top of his and *squeeze....* The powerful muscles of your thighs and buttocks are a velvet vise tugging at his manhood. *Hold on! There's just one more....*

Fifth Still facing his feet, kneel over his hips and lean forward. For him, this is an incredibly erotic position. He has a spectacular view of your beautiful bouncing bottom; he can actually watch himself slip in and out. You've made him wait long enough. Tell him to *come right now....*

Good boy. Next time he'll be ready to move to the, uh, *head* of the class!

Ingredients

One Hand Written Note / A Lot of Energy!

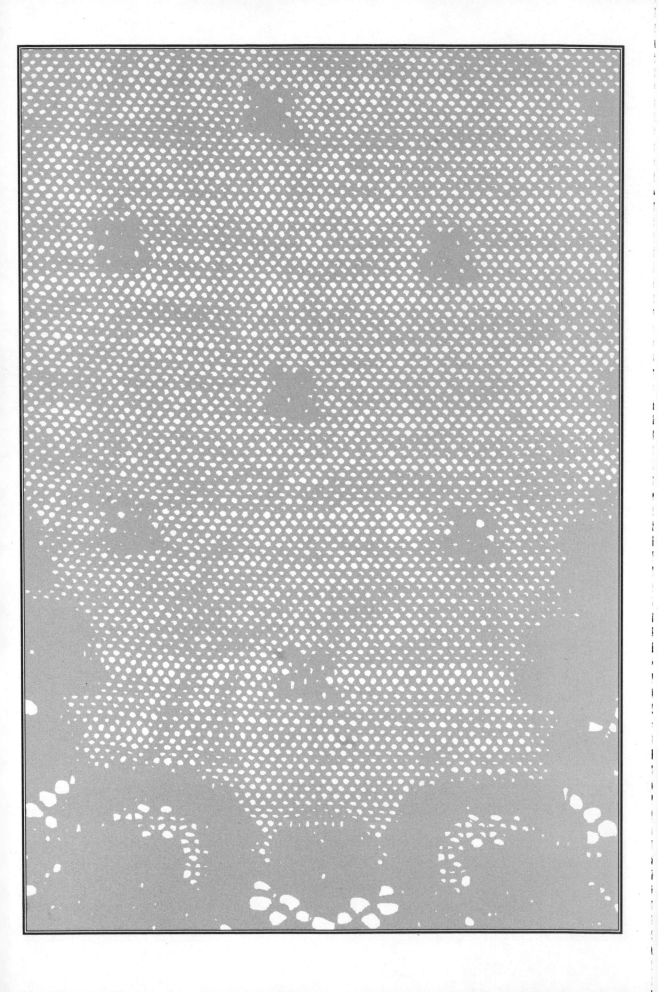

N° 54

SLIP AND SLIDE

For *His* Eyes Only

$

THE NEW MALE SEXUALITY
Bernie Zilbergeld, Ph.D.

Couples who have good sex over time are adventurous in a childlike way. They play at exploring their own and each other's sensitivities, and they are willing to try out new things, although I hasten to add that this does not mean they try out every new fad that comes along. It's not so much how many different activities and positions they try, but their attitude as they do whatever they do. Many new things don't work - it isn't really that easy, after all, to have intercourse in the bathroom of a 747 or even to get two people into that tiny a space - but they have fun finding this out. They have a healthy sense of humor about the whole business.

People who have good sex over the years seem not to take sex all that seriously, or maybe I should say somberly. They play at it rather than work at it. They have fun.

Playing at sex also means not having rigid rules about it, being tolerant for what it is and what it can give. These couples really do take sex any way they can get it rather than having to have it a certain way.

*C*owabunga! We're heading to the beach!

Actually, we're bringing the beach into your bedroom, for a seduction that starts with a big laugh...and ends with a *big* bang....

Head to the toy store for an inflateable children's pool. (If your kids already have one — *don't use it.* You'll never be able to look at it the same way again!) Set it on top of the bed, and build your beach around it. A heat lamp, some Beach Boys on the stereo, a couple of exotic drinks with fruit and tiny paper umbrellas — let your imagination go wild. When you call her into the room, you'll be lounging in swimsuit and your wildest party shirt, Ray-Bans on your nose and a smile on your face.

Crazy? Sure! And she'll probably still be chuckling as you both get undressed and climb into the pool with nothing but a bottle of tanning lotion. The first time you get oiled up and try to embrace, you'll be laughing hysterically! Be prepared to slip and slide all over the plastic pool — and over each other.

But soon your bodies will take over. The sensation of hot, slippery naked skin is a bit overwhelming, and you'll find yourselves laughing less — and moaning more. Keep exploring, and keep the lotion flowing until you're both covered head to toe. There's something indescribably erotic about the touch of her slick cheeks as she slides into your lap, don't you think?

All this lubrication means lots of *locomotion* — moves that might otherwise simply chafe become intensely sensual. *Squeeze* her breasts; *pinch* her nipples. Climb on her back and slip your erection between her legs. Have her press the head of your penis directly against her clitoris while you glide your hips over her bare butt. Her fingers, her flesh, your oil-drenched joystick all grinding together will have you both on the edge of orgasm, and lends a whole new meaning to the phrase "riding the wave...."

Phenomenal sex, no crowds, and no sand in your shorts — I'll bet that Frankie and Annette never had *this* much fun at the beach.

Of course, they never had to explain what a kiddie pool was doing in their bedroom, either! Hang ten, Mahalo!

Ingredients

1 Plastic Pool / 2 Pairs of Sunglasses / 2 Exotic Drinks / 1 Bottle of Suntan Lotion
(actually, pure mineral oil is much less likely to cause rashes in, uh, *sensitive* places)

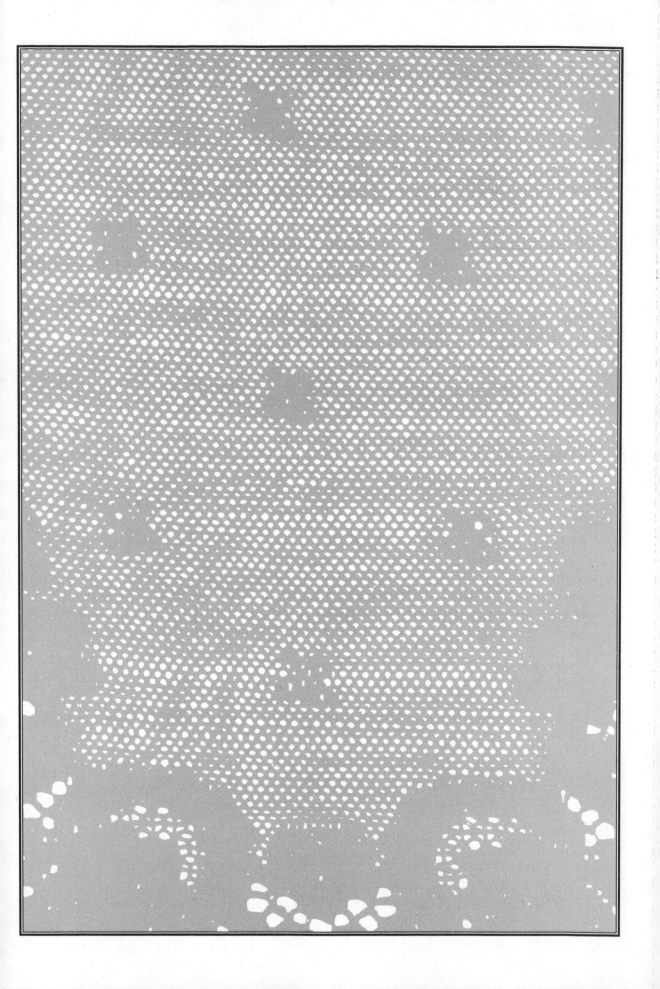

Nº
55

SWEET SURRENDER

For *Her* Eyes Only

$

HOW TO PUT THE LOVE BACK INTO MAKING LOVE
Dagmar O'Conner

"What I really want you to do is to bring sensuality into all of your life. Sensuality has a wonderful way of trickling from one part of your life to another. I have always maintained that if you learned how to eat sensually - to chew languorously, to run your tongue around the inside of your mouth, to smack your lips, to savor the texture of each morsel and the subtleties of each spice - you would automatically begin to make love more sensuously. And vice versa."

THE LOVING TOUCH
Dr. Andrew Stanway

Some men like the contrast between hot and cold that can be given by being sucked by a woman with ice cubes in her mouth. Others find ice cubes too hard and prefer the woman's mouth filled with cold yogurt or some other creamy substance. For the woman putting soft fruit or wine into her mouth before she fellates her man can be a memorable experience as well.

"You're going to need two showers today."

*T*hat's the cryptic message your lover will find on a folded card tucked in his mailbox, or placed at his breakfast table. Well! You've aroused his curiosity with those seven words, but he won't have a clue about your real plans. Tonight, *he* is going to be the feast!

Spend some time at the grocery store picking out the ripest, lushest fruit you can find. Apples and strawberries; cherries, grapes and bananas — anything that looks delicious and has a lot of juice will do. Just before your seduction begins, slice the larger pieces into bite-size morsels and arrange them around a platter; pile all the smaller berries in the center. Clear your nightstand to make a place of honor for your sumptuous treat, and invite your paramour into the bedroom.

Your usual fun and games will bring you to your birthday suits, and then — let the banquet begin. Grab a handful of fruit and decorate his body. Place big, sopping wet pineapple chunks on his nipples. Pop a cherry into his bellybutton! Slurp them up as noisily as you can, and then go back for more. Dot his thighs with banana slices and then smear them into his skin with every messy bite.

His turn! Squish the nectar from an apricot over one nipple — then lean over him and let it drip into his mouth. Bite an apple, and pass it to him in a sweet, luscious kiss. Mmm... here's a dish he's sure to love — rub a plump sliver of ripened peach between your thighs, thoroughly soaking your ridges and folds, and then straddle his face. Ooh, you'd think he'd been starving, the way he's lapping it up!

Hey, you need your vitamin C, too. Squeeze an orange over his own little bowl of fruit, and then suck it all away. Let him taste the syrup on your lips. It's a good thing he's eating such healthy stuff. He'll need the energy if he's going to satisfy his sweet tooth tonight!

An apple a day keeps the doctor away.!

Ingredients

1 Big Plate / 1 BIG Pile of Fruit / 1 Hot Shower / Hungry Lovers

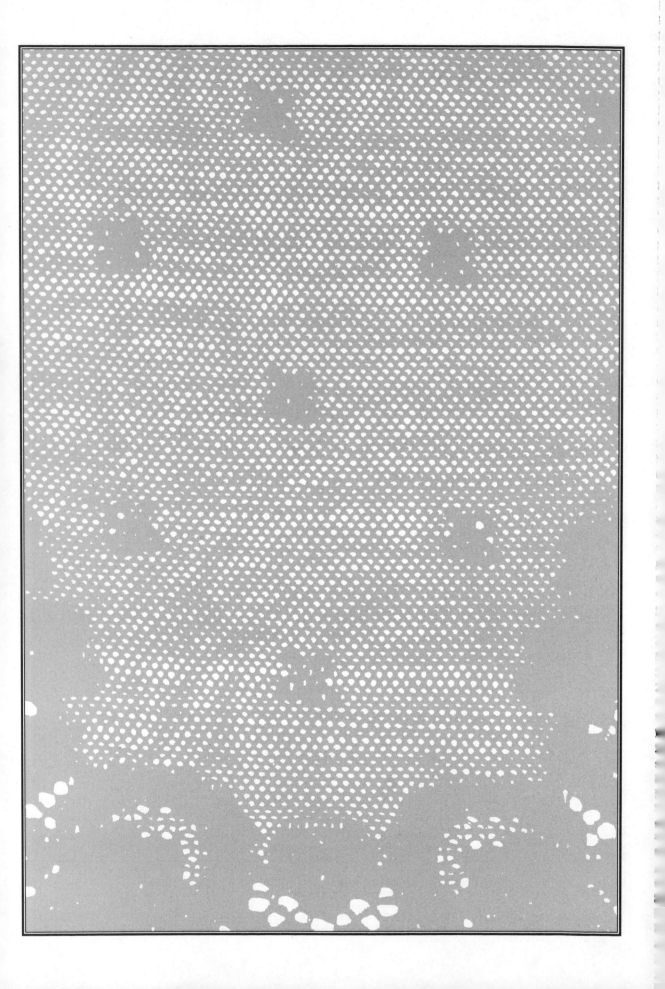

Nº 56

THE PERFECT TOUCH

For *Her* Eyes Only

THE PERFECT TOUCH

15 BODY PARTS	10 ACTIONS
1. Any place above the waist	1. Four long ice cream licks
2. Penis/Vagina	2. Fifteen little nibbles
3. Right nipple	3. Five deep noisy sucks
4. Navel	4. Ten various kisses
5. Left buttock	5. Three circles with tongue
6. Tiny toe on right foot	6. Eight gentle bites
7. Middle finger	7. Long massage with mouth
8. Inside of elbows	8. Massage with fingertips
9. Back of knees	9. Seven flicks with tongue
10. Bottom lip	10. Wet with tongue and blow
11. Back of neck	
12. Inside of left thigh	
13. Left ear	
14. Palm of right hand	
15. Any place below the waist	

THE WONDERFUL LITTLE SEX BOOK
William Ashoka Ross

Sex is not a serious subject. Important yes, serious no. A person who has a healthy interest in sex is not a serious person. A person like that may be lighthearted, loving, caring, tender, dedicated, good natured, and playful, but not serious. Seriousness and good sex don't mix.

Four long ice cream licks/inside of left thigh.
Fifteen little nibbles/back of neck.

*T*here can't be any losers in a game that has instructions like these! And besides the, uh, obvious rewards, you'll have a lot of laughs as you take each other on a Pleasure Trip.

Let your bedmate see you making up the game cards a few days before your seduction. You can tell him they contain special instructions that he has to follow exactly. You can tell him he'll like it — Oh, he'll like it, all right! — but he *can't look at the cards* until his special night arrives.

When it does, make sure you've got some uninterrupted time. Turn off the TV; unplug the phone. A bottle of wine and some nice music should complete your scene. When the two of you are good and relaxed, pull out your cards. *Remember these, honey?*

You've got twenty-five index cards, written in two different colors and placed in two different piles. Fifteen of them name parts of the body. Ten of them name sensuous actions that can be performed on those parts. The object of the game is to pick one card from each pile, put them together, and...

Well, I'll bet you've figured this one out already! So do it, and put your heart into it. If he's ticklish, eight gentle bites on his right nipple may make him laugh till he cries. Some of the other suggestions are more silly than sensuous. Have fun with them; it's a game, after all. And when you turn up the really *interesting* combinations — the kissing, the sucking, the flicking, the massaging, on highly sensitive areas — take your time. There's no clock running on this game.

Take turns. Shuffle the decks. And feel free to make up your own rules — Do your clothes come off before you follow the card's instructions, or after? Are ice cubes in your mouth forbidden...or required? Do you dare slip a wild card into the deck?

Remember, everybody wins, because the end doesn't come — until you do!

Ingredients

25 Blank Index Cards / 1 Bottle of Wine / 2 Felt Tip Pens (different colors)

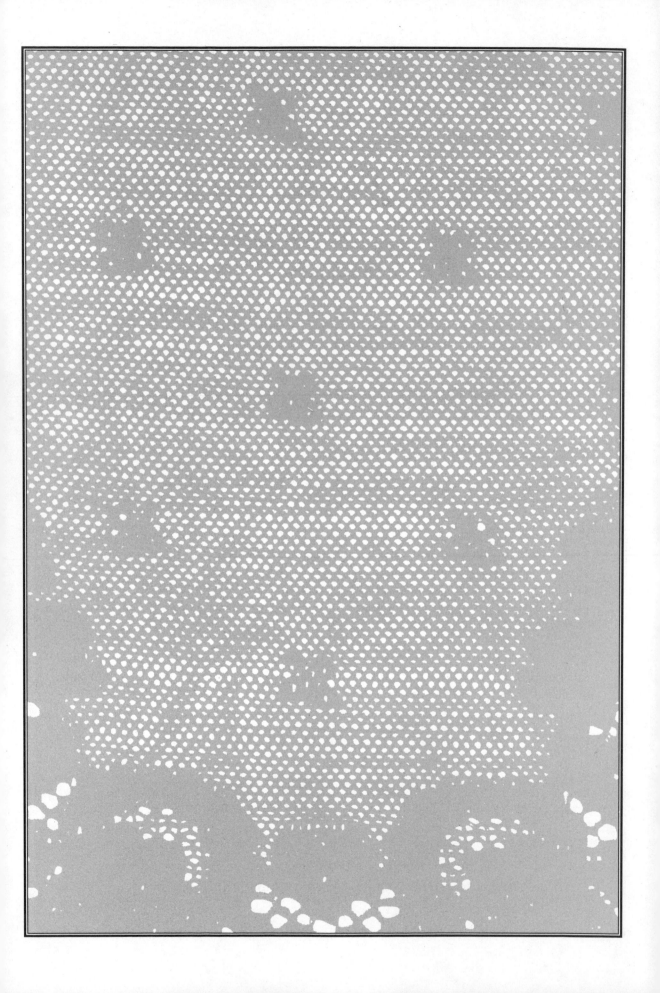

N.o 57

TICKLED PINK

For *His* Eyes Only

$$

THE LOVING TOUCH
Dr. Andrew Stanway

A common complaint women have of men is that they are boring in bed. This can be a cruel irony because often the very same man has a rich fantasy life and would be willing to be much more adventurous if his woman made her needs known. Unfortunately, the woman who complains may be too shy to tell her man what she would most like.

HOT MONOGAMY
Dr. Patricia Love and Jo Robinson

For some couples, this category might include gymnastic positions, sex games, sex toys, erotica, shared fantasies, or the use of various props, such as food, seductive clothing, feathers, or ice. Adventuresome sex can be hilarious as well as erotic. It can bond you together like no other activity.

ESO
Alan P. Brauer, M.D. and Dona J. Brauer

Most people make love on a bed. You may want to provide a special sheet for ESO to protect your sleeping sheets from the lubricants you will use. You don't have to change the sheets. Just put the special sheet on top. There's nothing wrong with making love on the floor, on pillows. Create a nest, a comfortable place. Be deliberate about it.

We didn't get much sleep.
but we had a lotta fun —
On Grandma's featherbed!
— John Denver

*W*hen two people are absorbed in the throes of passion, it doesn't seem to matter where they make love. In life, as in the dictionary *comfort* is always second to *climax*.

Not this week, though! You're job is to create a perfectly comfortable, cushy, even luxurious lovenest for your bedmate. It'll require a little shopping, of course. Genuine down-filled pillows are easy to find. Most lingerie specialty stores carry feather boas. And if they don't also have those enormous about two feet long- beautiful, hand-dyed ostrich feathers, you can order one from a catalog listed in the back of this book. The morning of your seduction, leave this magnificent plume on her dresser as a hint of the fun to come.

Blindfold your love before you lead her into the room, and help her undress. Is she ticklish? *Good!* She'll have a fit of giggles when you drape the boa around her. Pull it past her breasts and between her thighs; wrap it around her shoulders and pull her close for a kiss.

When you get to the bed, your tickles develop a slightly more erotic edge. Moisten her nipple with your tongue...and then draw the big ostrich feather across it. Brush her nose with your gossamer quill, then run it down over her lips, her chin, her belly, her thighs. Part her legs and stroke her *most* ticklish part, alternating between tongue and feather. Which makes her wiggle more?

The blindfold can come off as your fluffy foreplay heats up. She'll love rolling around on your new cozy new pillows. One of them, though, has been sabotaged. What's this? A slit in the pillow? And all those downy little feathers are puffing out?

Sounds like an excellent excuse to start a pillow fight! Soon your bed will be a cloud of feathers, caressing your bodies as the battle turns into sweet, soft surrender. Remember what they say —

Birds of a feather f*** together. Or something like that.

Ingredients

Feather Boa / 1 Ostrich Plume / 1 Down Pillow
1 up woman (Cleanup's a snap! Just gather your sheet up into a bundle) HOT

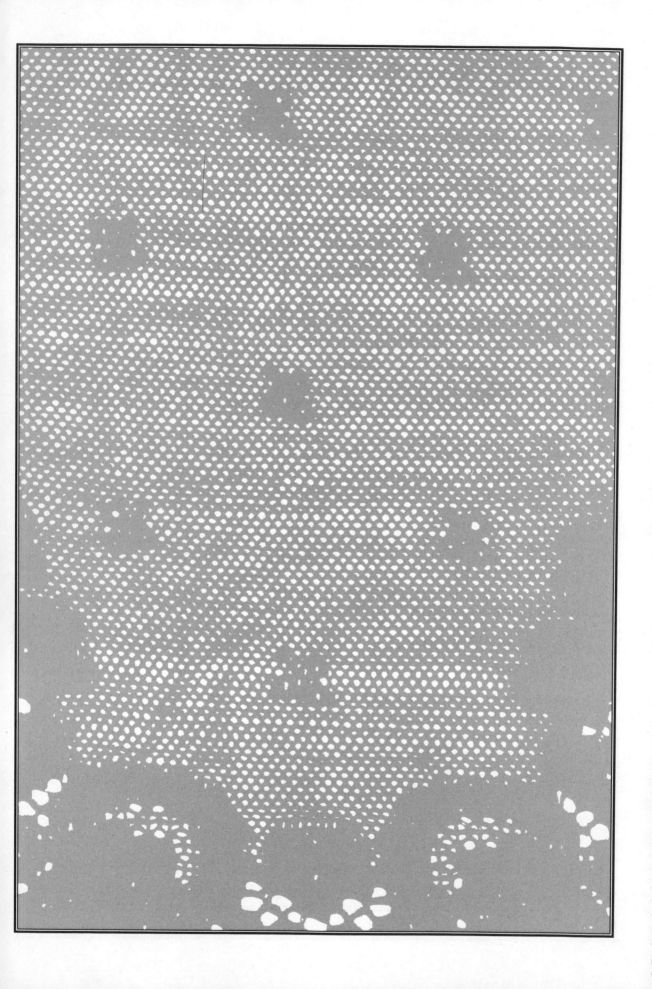

№ *58*

THE SENSUOUS SQUEEZE

For *Her* Eyes Only

$

THE LOVE MUSCLE
Bryce Britton

Most women are totally unaware of the crucial role their love muscle plays in their orgasm. Most of us now are familiar with the idea of fitness, if not actively involved in it. So the idea of exercising a specific muscle is no longer strange. At this point, I can sum up all the scientific research for you - if you don't use it, you lose it. As far as I'm concerned the evidence is conclusive: "An orgasm a day keeps the doctor away." A strong muscle, whether you wish to orgasm or just keep sexually fit, is your best insurance for your future happiness and good health.

203 WAYS TO DRIVE A MAN WILD IN BED
Olivia St. Claire

Here's another great vaginal exercise. Place a dildo, vibrator, candle, cucumber, or the like inside your vagina. Sitting straight up and using only your developing sex muscle, try to keep it there. Don't let it slip out. See if you can walk around while still holding the object in place. Now lie down and try to push it out. Practice until you can squirt it out forcefully. First you keep it locked inside, then you send it flying. Just think what you'll be able to do to him!

You can give him an almost unbearably delicious thrill by learning to flex your sex muscle. By that I mean your pubococcygeus, or PC muscle. This is the muscle that allows you to stop the flow of your urine; the same one that contracts when you have an orgasm. The twitching of the PC muscle against your man's penis is a wonderfully erotic and highly stimulating sensation for both of you. Try inserting three fingers into your vagina and flexing that muscle. See what I mean? As with any other muscle, the PC muscle gets stronger with use. To develop a superbly sexy vagina, practice contracting your PC muscle at least twenty-five times every day. Soon you'll have an exquisitely toned man pleaser.

*L*et's face it — exercise is just no fun.

Oh, the consequences are great. When you're in good shape, you can walk farther, ride faster, play longer, and of course you look better. But exercise itself? It's a lot of sweat and sore muscles.

Except for this one. What you're strengthening this week is your love muscle, and not only are you going to enjoy the workout, you're going to love showing off the results! In addition to the suggestions on the opposite page, you're going to need to buy a Kegelcisor. This feminine fitness device is a sort of dildo that functions as a miniature vaginal barbell. Practice with it! If you're going to master this remarkable new skill, you'd better start right now. And when you're not using it, leave it out for him to discover. A tool he's never seen? You bet he'll be curious!

When playtime finally rolls around, lean back into your pillows and tell your bedmate you need his advice. Take his hand and put it right on your vulva. *Notice anything different, honey? No? Well here, rub it this way. Go ahead, put your finger inside.*

Now squeeze. Contract that muscle. *I've been working out. Can you tell? Think that'll feel good when your **** is inside me?* Believe me, he'll be amazed. But not half as impressed as when he sees your new trick. *I've been working on this all week for you. Watch this....*

Pop it in. Show him your new exercise program. When was the last time you saw him totally dumbfounded?

*Again? Okay, one more time. But then come here and **** me.*

When the opening act is over and the main feature's under way, continue your sensuous squeeze. *You feel so big! (squeeze) Omigosh, you're so hard (squeeze) I love it, I can't get enough (squeeze) I don't think you've ever felt so good (squeeze!) you're ooh, ooh, you're filling me up....(squeeeeeeeze!!!)*

He'll believe you. He *wants* to believe that he is making you hotter than ever before. But in fact it's your erotic language and new, powerful grip that will be launching him into ecstasy.

Tomorrow morning, slip a little souvenir into his pants as he's heading out the door. *Is that a barbell in your pocket, or are you just glad to see me?*

Ingredients

1 Kegelcisor — See Specialty Page / 1 Love Muscle

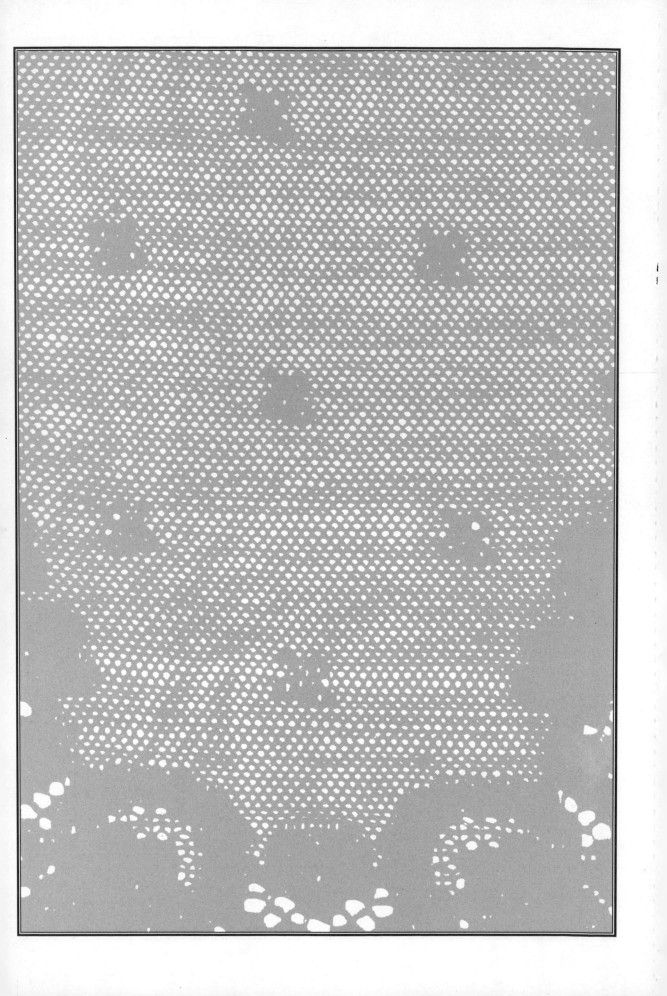

N.º **59**

DELICIOUS DETOUR

For *Her* Eyes Only

TALK DIRTY TO ME
Sallie Tisdale

"My mouth on her body, my tongue savoring her crevices was like plunging my face into a bowl of ripe summer fruits and inhaling their mingled fragrances - peaches, apples, pears," wrote Richard Rhodes. "All of her was fresh. All of her was beautiful."

Mysterious and compelling, this urge to bury our faces in each other, to retreat from isolation and distance into the most humble smells and tastes, the quivering of muscle and the crawling of skin, rough hair and wetness. To submit to another's belly, or another's mouth. Oral sex may be the most potent of sexual acts, completely divorced from biology, never mentioned in the presence of children, the most secret and secreted of acts. It is an act of power derived from the most vulnerable kind of intimacy.

RED HOT MONOGAMY
Patrick T. Hunt M.D.

What Really Turns A Man On:

1. A woman taking the initiative

2. Perfume

3. Lacy lingerie

4. A women using sexually explicit
language while making love

Ladies, taking the initiative with men can also pertain to situations outside the bedroom. Unexpectedly unzipping his pants and giving him oral sex in the car on the way home will always put a smile on your lover's face.

*S*ure, cars are useful things. But here's the real reason we love our cars so much — we get to fool around in them! Necking, making out, mashing; the words may change, but the act remains the same. Most of us had our first intimate experience inside an automobile...and that's where you're going to have your next one.

Get his motor running early in the week by taping a local road map to the refrigerator door. You'll need to do some homework. Think of some scenic spots — lover's lanes, if you will — and every day or two circle one on the map with a big bold heart and mark the route to it. *Whatcha doin', honey?*...Oh, just mapping out a little trip...a trip to paradise!

Finally, when you've got some free time together, hand him the map and tell him you need some fresh air. Think he'll get the hint? He will in the car when you cuddle close, nibbling his neck and brushing your wet tongue against his ear. Remind him to keep his eyes on the road! No small task, since you're practicing the sweetest kind of torture on him.

Reminisce about the earliest days of your relationship, filled with long, passionate kisses as you said goodbye. Tell him you miss the time when most of a date could be spent talking and touching in his car. And when you find your private parking place, don't waste any time. You're starry-eyed high school sweethearts desperate to make the most of your few minutes before curfew. And the most powerful influences in the male universe — automobiles and erections — are about to come together.

Squeeze his stiffening sex through his pants. He may actually gasp with relief when you pop it free from its suddenly-too-small home. He will certainly grow flush with anticipation when you whisper in his ear...*I'm going to wrap my lips around you now ...umm, you taste good.*

What a scene! It's a fantasy he's had since he first sat behind a wheel. He is literally *in the driver's seat.* He sees your hair, slowly bobbing up and down. He senses the wet heat of your mouth, and the velvet touch of your tongue. He is feeling sixteen again. Which does have its advantages. At sixteen, after all, he'd be ready to go again in only a few minutes....

Just long enough to get home! Sure hope Dad's not waiting up!

Ingredients
---

1 Map / Felt-Tip Markers / 1 Car
(and try to avoid bucket seats with high center consoles. Ouch!)

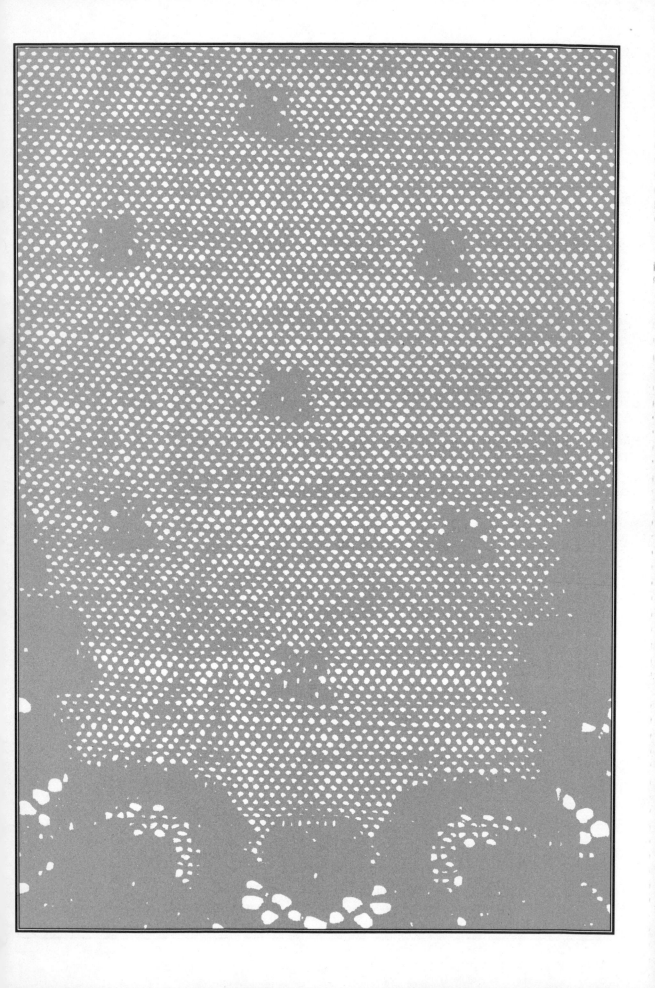

N° 60

TRICKS OF THE TONGUE

For *His* Eyes Only

DRIVE YOUR WOMAN WILD IN BED
Staci Keith

A lot of men ask, "How long should I do it?" and I answer, "How long can you last?" This is where stamina becomes important.

THE FOLLOWING METHOD IS THE BEST, EASIEST, AND MOST EFFECTIVE WAY TO BRING YOUR PARTNER TO ORGASM. Even women who report having orgasms without this particular method say the orgasm is far more intense and quicker to achieve this way.

1. Lie directly between her legs.

2. Spread her vaginal lips far apart.

3. Locate her clitoris.

4. With just your tongue, slightly pointed (keeping your lips away from her vagina), flick lightly across her clitoris. Side to side.

5. (Optional) Insert a finger into the vagina itself, twisting it in and out.

HOW TO HAVE MULTIPLE ORGASMS
Janalee Beck

There's a connection between how someone kisses and how he'll perform intercourse or cunnilingus. Don't you agree? There are exceptions to every rule, but on the whole, a good kisser makes a wonderful lover. Describe a good kisser. We all probably have personal quirks, but why did so many women love Kevin Costner's line in Bull Durham about long, soft, deep, slow kisses? It's universal.

*T*he Latin term is *cunnilingus*, but fortunately, great oral sex is much easier to learn than Latin. In fact, it's as easy as ABC!

Like any good student, you must first get comfortable in your classroom. So kiss her belly; rub her soft, bushy little thatch of hair against your cheek. Drink in that heavenly aroma as you part her thighs. And then...start with one simple lick...like an ice cream cone! Slip your tongue between her lips and run it slowly to the top of her folded flesh.

Unwrap her with your tongue. The ridges and folds of delicate pink tissue will start to swell as you part them with your lips and tongue, mixing your saliva with her own sweet juices.

Now your class begins. If you've been caressing her softly — press harder with your tongue. If you've been flicking rapidly across her clitoris — slow down into long, deep strokes. From minute to minute, you should *change your style*...and along the way you will quickly discover what kind of approach she really wants. Feel the way her body responds to each change; listen for her sighs as you zero in on the moves that make her tremble.

Try nibbling — ever so softly — on her inner lips, the *labia minora.* Draw her clitoris into your mouth by gently sucking on it...in and out; tugging, then releasing. As it swells, it may pop out from under the hood of flesh that protects it — be careful! That dear little exposed nubbin is extremely tender. Start by circling your tongue around it, or gliding lightly across the base before attempting to touch the tender tip.

Make her shiver! Pick up a straw and blow a steady stream of chilling air against her; follow up with your hot, warm breath from closer in. Back to the straw — direct your frosty jet in a slow loop around her most sensitive flesh.

Ready to earn your Ph.D in oral sex? Use your tongue to trace the letters P, H and D across her clit! And since you're becoming a man of letters, try the ABCs, or start spelling out her name. Find the one letter that makes her knees go weak. Don't stop to dot your "I," and don't slow down. Focus on O, as in Omigodimcomingdontstopdontstop....

And finally, remember the advice of the wise old man when the lost little boy stopped him on a New York street. "How do you get to Carnegie Hall?" he mused...."*Practice, practice, practice!*

Ingredients

---

1 Loose Tongue / 1 Short Straw
A Working Knowledge of the Alphabet (and for extra credit — learn it in Greek or Cyrillic!)

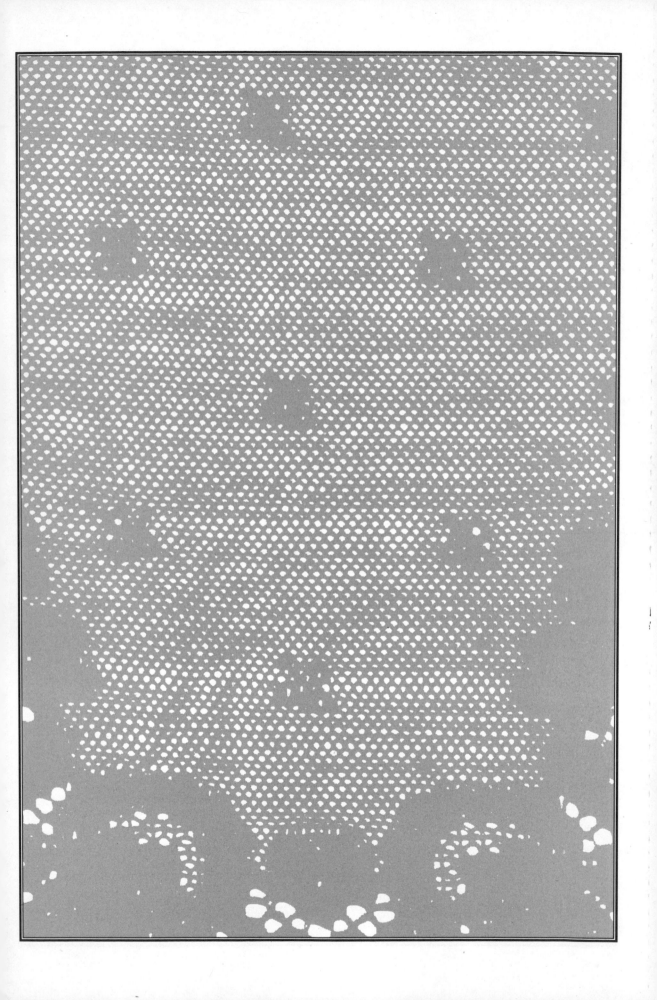

N^o **61**

SEVEN SINFUL FLAVORS

For *Her* Eyes Only

$

CHOCOLATE SEX
A. Richard Barber, Nancy R.M. Whitin & Anthony Loew

The smell of chocolate. Its velvet brown color. Its taste.

Long after the last morsel of chocolate is consumed, the memories remain...are they lustful sighs, or heart-pounding flashbacks?

Scientist have found that substances in chocolate combine with the body's natural chemical makeup to raise one's blood pressure, heart rate and glucose levels, resulting in a sensation that can be likened to only one other feeling: orgasm. ©

IF IT FEELS GOOD
Joan Elizabeth Lloyd

A few comments about orgasm. We have been conditioned to believe that orgasm is the outcome to strive for during sex. We've been taught that foreplay is a way to get us sufficiently excited for penetration. This is ridiculous. Most of the fun can be had during the minutes or hours it takes to get to the moment the penis enters the vagina, not only during the few seconds of actual intercourse. Everything you do from the time you first get together can be part of sexual pleasure. Looking, smelling, tasting, and feeling are not means; they are ends in themselves. Savor your enjoyment.

Sugar and spice and everything nice...
That's what little girls are made of.

*N*o wonder men have a sweet tooth!

This week, visit a gourmet candy shop and pick out seven cream-filled chocolates...but don't eat them! *Giftwrap them,* and present them to your lover with a promise of the most delicious seduction he's ever had.

Stand before him in a sensuous, silky robe, and pull your sash away. Your robe falls open, but he'll catch only a glimpse of flesh before you tie the sash over his eyes.

His task is to guess the flavor at the center of each luscious chocolate. Each time he's right, you'll remove a piece of his clothing. And even when he's wrong, he wins...because each sample has been artfully applied to the most interesting parts of your body!

ORAL ORANGE — Smear over your lips and the tip of your tongue. Give him fleeting little kisses around his mouth, and slide your tongue from one corner of his lips to the other. When he guesses the flavor, remove one of his shoes.

COQUETTISH COCONUT — Apply on both sides of your neck, (like perfume) and kiss his eyelids as he sucks the flavor off. When he guesses, remove his other shoe.

STIMULATING STRAWBERRY — Rub on your earlobe and brush it against his lips so he can nip at it lightly. When he guesses, remove one of his socks.

PENETRATING PEACH — Dip your finger into the creamy flavor and trace the outline of his lips. Part them with your fingertip and wiggle it around his tongue. When he guesses, remove the other sock.

RAVISHING RASPBERRY — Put the cream on the nipple of one of your breasts, touch it to his cheek and slide it down to his lips. When he guesses, remove his shirt.

VIRGIN VANILLA — Cover your other nipple entirely, and feed it to his eager mouth. When he guesses, remove his pants.

CREAMY CHERRY — Saving the best for last pour the sweet cream over your labia and let him lap it up! He'll probably stop guessing, and you won't care! BON APPETITE!

--- *Ingredients* ---

7 Creamed Filled Chocolates / 1 Silky Robe with Sash

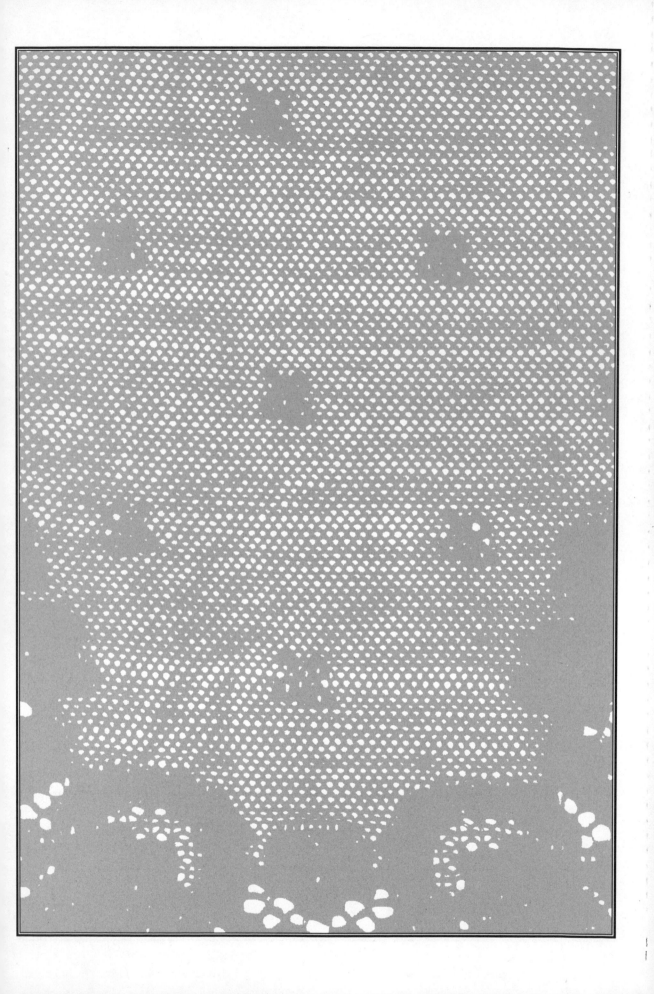

THE SPECIALITY OF THE HOUSE

For *Her* Eyes Only

RED HOT MONOGAMY
Patrick T. Hunt M.D.

Sometime right in the middle of sex, stop and start giving your lover oral sex. Ladies, this coitus interruptus followed by knobus slobus will have your man melting.

THE LOVING TOUCH
Dr. Andrew Stanway

Sharing the pleasures of oral sex is one of the most intimate ways of making love. For a man fellatio is particularly exciting because it is so different from 'conventional' intercourse. The lips, lined as they are with tissues similar to the vagina itself, feel like a new vagina. It also shows a high degree of intimacy and it gives the man a chance to feel worshipped and play a passive role, which he may welcome from time to time. It is also an extremely effective way of restarting a man for a second round of lovemaking.

COSMOPOLITAN THE NICE GIRL'S GUIDE TO SENSATIONAL SEX
Nancy Kalish

The combination of concentrated stimulation, a bird's-eye view (not possible in most intercourse positions), and the complete lack of pressure to perform gives fellatio an irresistible erotic kick for almost every man alive. So if your man hasn't asked you to "go down on him," it's probably not because it doesn't have immense appeal to him, but because he's afraid it will have absolutely none for you.

In addition, being adept at the oral arts comes in handy for those times you feel like having sex, but not intercourse, such as when you're menstruating, want to have more control over your orgasm (you can masturbate while performing fellation - either with or without his knowledge), or if you simply forgot (oops!) that darned diaphragm or your other birth control.

*T*onight you're taking him on the road to *Grrreat Sex* — Highway 101! You'll be, uh, getting off at Teaserville....

Do you have some kind of countdown clock? A kitchen timer is ideal. Put it right in the middle of the bed, where your love can't miss it when he gets home from work. (After all, that's where he throws his dirty clothes, isn't it? *Men!!!...*)

Tonight's seduction starts normally enough...lots of flirting, lots of kissing. Leave the timer where it is when you push him down on the bed! If it gets in the way as you roll around on your comforter, *good* — it'll only make him more curious about the mystery behind your special evening.

When your clothes are gone...well, mostly gone...sit up and smile. Hand him a vitamin pill and a glass of water. *Go on, sweetie; you'll need it.* Now grab the timer, crank it to fifteen minutes, and set it aside. Let him lie back as you start to practice your best penilingus. Yum! Don't you just love that first rush of excitement as he starts to swell in your mouth? Brush that little devil against your cheeks; swirl your tongue around the rim. Get him completely steamed up, and then — stop.

Is that a look of panic in his eye? It won't be there for long, because now you're going to climb on top of him and slip his penis between your *other* lips. Go slow! Drop your hips inch by lascivious inch onto his. Pick up the tempo; let him feel the slap of your seat. But watch his face for *that look...*

Because you're going to stop again. Give him a moment to cool off — and then gobble him up. Nibble and bite and suck, but before he blows his top, *stop* — and switch again! It's the most exquisite torture. Each time, you're breaking his concentration just enough to slow him down, and each time you're revving him right back up again. Mouth to vagina and back again; keep it up until the bell rings. And this time, give it all you've got....*Let me have it, baby, I want you to come, I want you to come right now....*

Did I say road-trip? Running a marathon is more like it! He'll need no more than, oh, a week or two to recover....

--- *Ingredients* ---

1 Cake Timer / 1 Class in CPR!

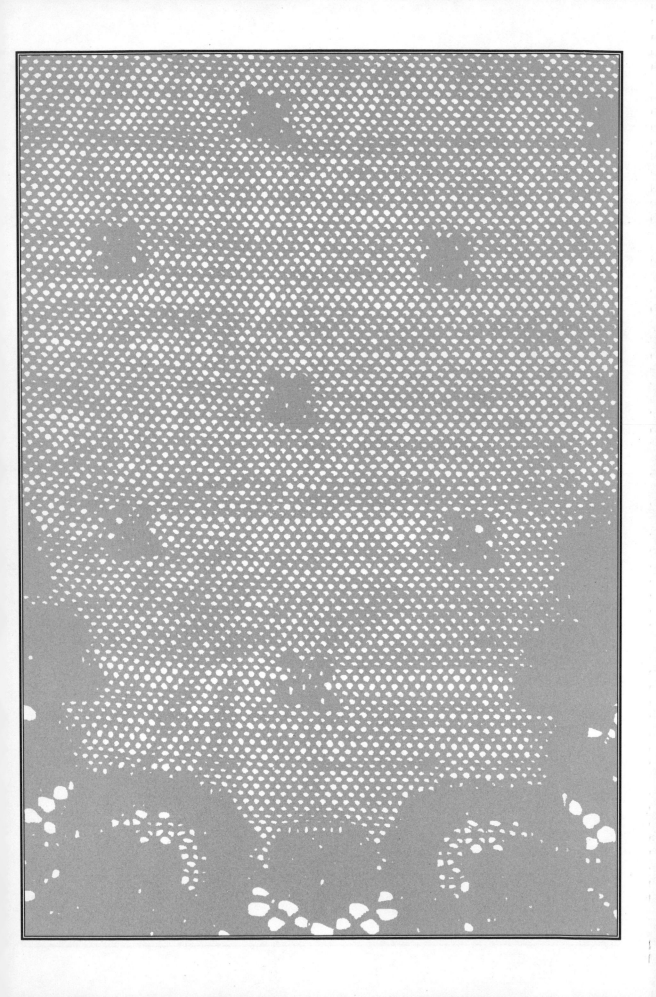

N°

THE PIZZA MAN ALWAYS RINGS TWICE

For *His* Eyes Only

$

WILD IN BED TOGETHER
Graham Masterton

So many people regard sex as a repetitive unchanging act. You feel thirsty this evening, you have a cold beer. You feel thirsty next Thursday evening, you have a cold beer. You feel thirsty on Sunday evening, you have a cold beer. But sex is not a simple thirst or a simple appetite. It's intellectual as well as instinctive, it's emotional as well as physical, and you need to nurture and develop and change your lovemaking as time goes by - otherwise it will become boring,, and routine. In other words, you will have allowed it to become no more meaningful to your life than just another cold beer.

RED HOT MONOGAMY
Patrick T. Hunt, M.D.

Ladies should always come first - Men, I'm sure you are all aware of the fact that women take longer to reach orgasm.

Try to let your partner have an orgasm before you even get close, using whatever method you like, vibrator, manual, or lingual. (For those of you into extremes, I would suggest maybe belt sanders or tire jacks.)

The average time for a woman to reach orgasm is eleven minutes. By contrast, our furry friends aren't as lucky. Our close relative, the poor baboon, takes a mere eight seconds and 15 thrusts to complete intercourse. Lions average four seconds - I think that's about where I was in high school.

Men, after your lover thinks she's satisfied, whisper that you can't hold out any longer, it's coming. However, men, I want you to fib a little. Tell her this when you're, say, only eighty percent of the way there. Moan and groan like it's happening.

The excitement of your expected orgasm often will push your lover to a new level of ecstasy.

*H*oo boy! Great pizza *and* great sex — life just doesn't get any better than this....Tell your sweetheart not to worry about dinner tonight. You've got it taken care of — you'll be getting a special *Love Pizza* delivered to the house. She'll be curious, but don't tell her any more; make the rest of your preparations in secret.

Go down to your favorite pizza delivery place and talk to the manager. Can they make a heart-shaped pizza? That would be great, but if not, don't worry. The essence of your Love Pizza is the card that comes with it. Pay for it in advance, and offer him a few dollars more to make sure your sealed envelope gets firmly taped to the box your pizza will be delivered in.

When evening rolls around, call in your special order... and start the seduction. Kiss her, grab her, rush her to the bedroom. This is no time to take it easy! That pizza's due to arrive in thirty minutes — *or less!* — and you're running against the clock.

She may be startled, but she'll certainly be delighted by your sexual hunger. Be aggressive; concentrate on *her* pleasure. The spell will no doubt be broken by the doorbell, but if takes her a moment to come to her senses, you can tell her to take her time... *the Pizza Man always rings twice.* It's policy!

She will, however, have to get the door. You, um, can't quite fit into your jeans at this point. What she'll find is a large envelope on the pizza box inscribed READ ME FIRST. Inside is your card:

The pizza's paid for. So — did you come yet? Mmm, pepperoni and p**sy! My favorite combination! Now get rid of the delivery kid and come back to bed. P.S. — ***BRING THE PIZZA!***

She'll be laughing out loud as she sends the pizza guy away...and as she realizes why you hurried her to bed so fast. This is the kind of race *nobody* loses! She'll be really touched, too, that you went to all that trouble for her — even if the pizza came first.

When she walks back into the bedroom with a pizza and a big silly grin, ask her — can she guess what you have in mind for *dessert?*

Ingredients
---

1 Understanding Pizza Store / 1 Telephone / 1 Special Card / 1 Special Woman

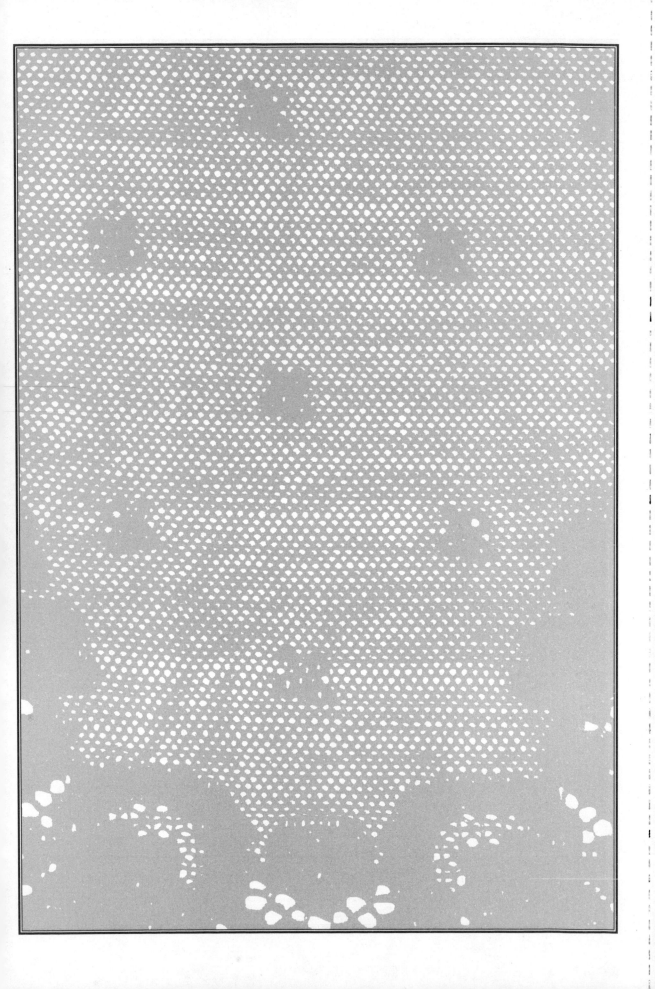

N° **64**

CHEMISTRY CLASS

For *His* Eyes Only

MAKING LOVE A MAN'S GUIDE
Whit Barry

When you and your partner were first getting to know each other's bodies, you went to great lengths to find out what she liked. Did she go crazy when you put your tongue in her navel? Did she like you to pay a lot of attention to her toes? Was oral sex a requirement for orgasm?

Having by now presumably found out what turns her on, you may see no need to do any more research. This is a mistake. You have changed. She has changed. You are both more relaxed with each other now; you know your own bodies better. You know what you like now and what you don't.

COSMOPOLITAN
THE NICE GIRL'S GUIDE TO SENSATIONAL SEX
Nancy Kalish

A recent survey by Philip and Lorna Sarrel, two Yale University sex therapists, concluded that "the ability to share thoughts and feelings about sex with your partner is the single factor most highly correlated with a good sexual relationship." In fact, this study has only proved the theory that every therapist on the planet has been pushing for years: that open communication is the key to stellar sex - and a rock-solid relationship.

Luckily, your man is on your side. Like Joe most men are extremely eager to please when it comes to sex. He may never learn how to load the dishwasher correctly no matter how much you nag, but gently hint that using a bit more suction on your nipples will send you into spasms of lust, and his mouth will be on your breasts before you can finish your sentence.

*P*ay attention, young man. Class is about to begin. Your assignment is to study the female form, and its reaction to certain sensual stimuli. Your subject also happens to be your teacher, and if there's anything all those years of school should have taught you— it's that it *always pays to kiss up to the teacher!* So start your week by leaving one bright red shiny apple on her nightstand. Under it place a sealed envelope marked as follows:

Professor — please hold this until after class. Do not open.

The evening of your seduction, run a bath for her. Invite her to soak for as long as she wants. When she's dry and totally relaxed, take her face between your hands, look into her eyes, and tell her you want to learn some things tonight. For instance —

Do you like to be kissed like this? Brush your lips past hers. *Or do you prefer this?* Firm, full-on-the-lips, and just slightly moist. Don't let her get away by saying she likes both! Tonight, she is your instructor, and you await her guidance at every turn.

Do you like it when I nibble your ears like this...or when I use my tongue like this? Down here on your neck, what's better for you — little licks, or...mmm big bites?

You already know where all her buttons are...but in this seduction, she finally gets to tell you exactly how she likes them pushed! Very important — don't just ask if she likes a move you make. Of course she'll say she does. Instead, give her a choice each time between two different styles. One's good, but the other might be *ohmigodyesyesyes* much better. Memorize it!

Your nipples...gosh I LOVE your nipples...do you prefer light kisses, or when I suck them hard? Harder? Or softer? Down here, should I put my finger inside you when I lick, or not? One finger, or two? Keep them still, or move them like this? When you come, should I stop — or speed up?

Once she's taught you how to give her the very best orgasm in the world — ask her to hand you your envelope. In it is your diploma. Simple or fancy; all it needs is your name and the phrase "Ph.D in Se.X." *Whaddaya think? Do I get to keep it?*

If you've been a very good boy, you do. And if you've been a bad boy, well — I guess you'll just have to stay after class for extra lessons! Hmm. Which do *you* prefer?

Ingredients

1 Teacher / 1 Apple / 1 Hand Made Diploma

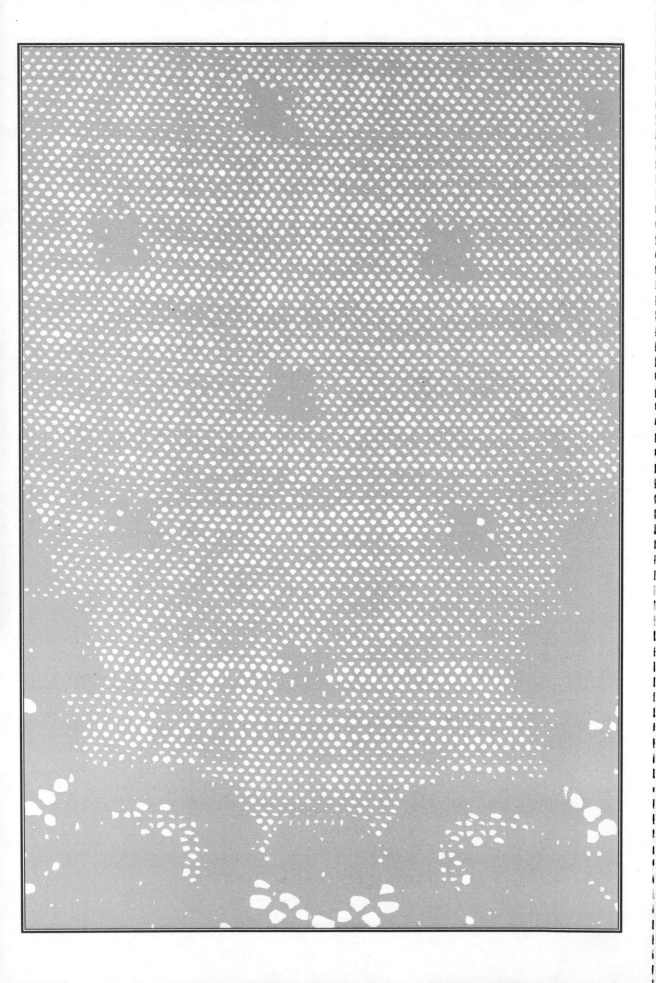

N.o **65**

WINNING HAND

For *His* Eyes Only

ORDINARY WOMEN EXTRAORDINARY SEX
Dr. Sandra Scantling and Sue Browder

We tend to think that what we experience in life depends on the sights, sounds, tastes, textures, and smells that are "out there." But increasingly, we are beginning to understand that what you perceive "out there" depends on what you're inwardly ready to perceive. The high absorbing supersexual women we met are somehow more ready to see, smell, or feel the beauty in a rose or to appreciate a sunset. They have a special mind-set that allows them to appreciate the world around and inside them, and to enjoy sex in brand-new ways.

HOT MONOGAMY
Dr. Patricia Love and Jo Robinson

Hovering, which involves the lightest of touch, is done by holding your hands just about the surface of your mate's skin, brushing the fine hair. Many people find this a tantalizing experience. It can send chills up your spine and make you squirm with sensation. For the toucher, it is a rare opportunity to focus completely on your mate. It can be a very sensual and loving experience.

*T*here are different techniques in massaging and touching a body to relieve tension, or to relax the muscles. Here is a different approach which has a titillating effect with a slight tickling sensation. It's almost not touching at all, which results in the ultimate tease!

Gratifying her sense of touch in this way requires you to bring out the gentle side of yourself. A man's tendency is to rub too harshly, so he can feel the flesh of his woman under his hands. However, this is for *her pleasure alone.* You are going to use a method that will intensify her anticipation for you, as her lover!

Have her lay naked on the bed but cover her with a sheet to keep her warm and comfortable. Fold the sheet down as your hands go over her body. The sensation she will feel occurs by the static electricity of her fine body hair coming in contact with your hand. You will be doing a hovering movement over her body, which will cause her to have electrifying sensations!

Using your fingertips, and barely touching her, let them brush over her face, follow the outline of her forehead, the crevices of her eyes, the line of her nose, the outside of her ears, and down her neck. Glide your hands in a very *slow motion* over her skin. The effect is greater when you can flatten out your hand and use the hovering method from her neck to her feet. Do this type of massage for at least 10 minutes, rotating her from front to back. Don't worry, you won't relax her into sleep, but you *will stimulate* and *excite* her sense of touch.

Now, you will search out the erogenous areas of her skin by going back and giving a fingertip massage to the same areas of her face. Continue down, and let your hands sculpture each soft curve of her body. When you get to her vulva, use the palm of your hand to massage the entire outside, then the heel of your hand to press in the center, and finally your fingers to stroke from the top of the clitoris down to the entrance. Repeat these steps with your hand, (palm, heel, fingers) until your hand is shiny with her wetness!

She will be in a very erotic mood for a sexual encounter when your are through!

Chances are, when you touch her between her legs, she'll have been wet for some time without either of you realizing it!

Ingredients

1 Naked Woman / 1 Cover Sheet
1 Man with Sensitive Hands / 1,000 Hoose Bumps

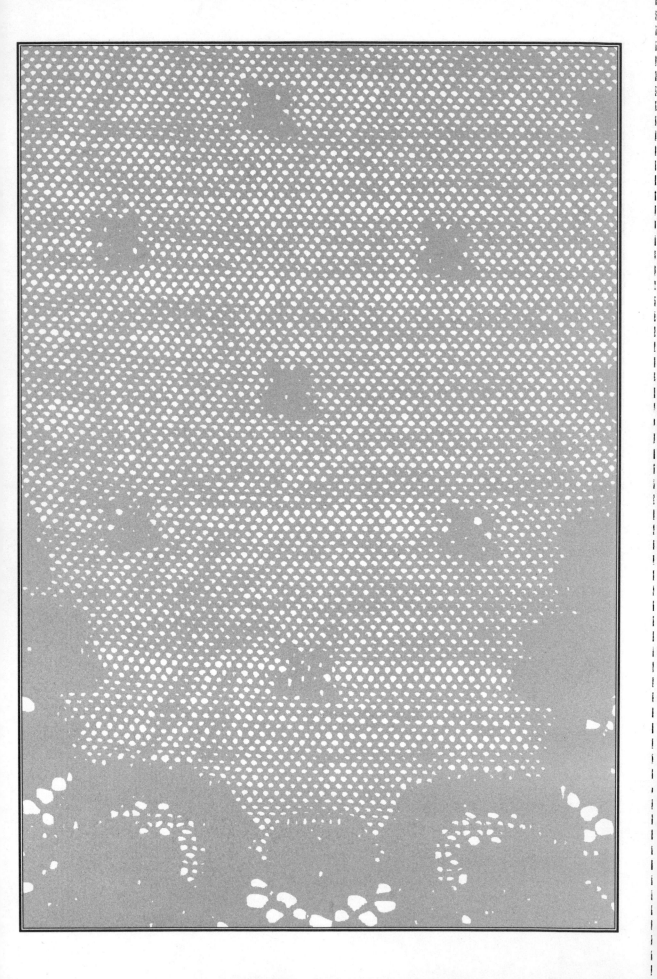

N.º **66**

THE FRENCH CONNECTION

For *His* Eyes Only

THE MAN'S GOURMET SEX BOOK
Peggy & Evan Burke

Your kisses can be the most important part of sexual foreplay, and these kisses are not doing all they are capable of doing if they are confined to her lips and face. Body kissing can arouse her as no other thing can do, so tonight, as the folks who publish the yellow pages of the telephone directory might say, let your kisses do the walking.

HOW TO HAVE MULTIPLE ORGASMS
Janalee Beck

Kissing is a unique, special mode of communication. A definite turn-on. If a man hasn't kissed you on the neck, shoulders, forehead, breasts, butt, toes, armpit, back, earlobe, or behind the knees—you haven't really been kissed adequately. (Minimally, he should choose seven out of ten places) And let's not forget to return the favor!

THE LITTLE BLACK BOOK OF ANSWERS
Laura Corn

I asked 2,000 women:
What spot on your body is seldom used as a erogenous zone
—but is actually very sensitive to a kiss?

The top three answers in order are:

1. The intersection of cheeks and thighs.

2. The back of her knees.

3. Just under her arms and down her ribs.

*D*id you ever play "Connect-the-Dots" as a kid — creating a picture by drawing lines from one dot to the next? This is the grown-up version of the game...and the picture you're going to create is definitely X-rated!

Start by covering your lover's eyes with a blindfold. Already you'll have aroused her curiosity, and by blocking off one of her senses, you're heightening the rest. Undress her; lead her to the bed and have her lay face down across it.

Mmm....She looks good enough to eat, right? And so you shall —

Break out a bottle of chocolate syrup and slowly squeeze out little drops on the back of her calf, behind her knee, the top of her thigh. Squish a big one onto her cheeks — draw a little star on either side of her buttocks! Continue dripping chocolate up her back to her shoulder, out to her wrist, and then back down the other side. Her backside may be the most sensitive part of her, and it's finally getting the attention it craves.

And now the real fun begins. Re-trace your path with your tongue, lapping up all that rich, gooey goodness one single droplet at a time. Change your technique with each dot. Lick one like an ice cream cone that's melting too fast. Long, wet strokes will have *her* melting in short order! For the next one — lap it up, hard and fast, flicking your tongue across her flushed skin.

Remember hickeys? I'll bet it's been a long time since someone gave her one. Do it! Then blow a cool stream of air at the same spot to chill things down.

Take your time connecting the dots. The longer, the better...and the wetter she will be for the grand finale, when you pull her up to her hands and knees at the edge of the bed. Kneel on the floor behind her and pour a little more syrup on her cheeks, and over her lips. Feel it mix with her own sweet juices as you lap it up.

Stand up. Slide inside. Forget about the chocolate; it's time to go for a ride. Be sure to take the long way home.

And if you're in a nice restaurant one day and find yourself growing inexplicably *erect* when the waitress rolls the dessert cart around, well....Don't say I didn't warn you!

Ingredients

1 Blindfold / 1 Bottle of Chocolate Syrup
The Phone Number for a Local Chapter of Chocoholics Anonymous

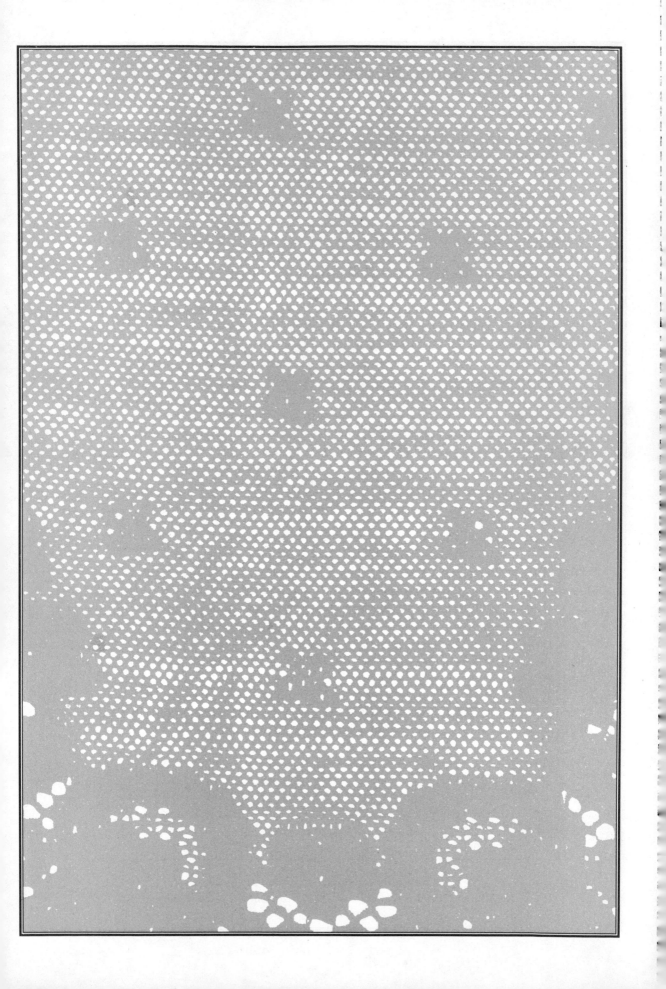

_No._ 67

TENDER OUTLAW

For _His_ Eyes Only

$

BEING A WOMAN
Dr. Toni Grant

This is it: the ultimate female fantasy of being "taken," transported, ravished, "swept away," carried over the threshold of love in the arms of a valiant hero. It is a theme of countless books and movies, perhaps the most popular of which is that spectacular scene in Gone With The Wind where Rhett carries Scarlett up the stairs. The sight of the gargantuan brute King Kong scooping up delicate little Fay Wray in his huge hairy paw is another great cinematic vision of ravishment.

Surrender. The very word conjures of visions of defeat, of shame, of submission. Yet in love, as opposed to war, surrender is sweet, for it enables the woman to fulfill her deepest feminine potentialities, both sexually and emotionally.

THE LOVING TOUCH
Dr. Andrew Stanway

Many women experience great pleasure from being dominated during intercourse. Such women enjoy sex particularly if the man is in control and makes everything happen. The missionary position is ideal for this. The man, being on top, controls the thrusting and can pin the woman down to the bed and take her roughly and at his pace.

Being 'taken' like this can be highly exciting to some women. For the woman who is at all guilty about her sexual needs and appetites this position leaves her free of guilt, because she can think of herself as being overpowered by a much stronger man.

*R*omance novels are consistently among the top-selling paperbacks in the country. Women love these stories! And why not? Most of them play up to a woman's fantasy of being seduced by a *bad boy* — Tough on the outside, but tender and loving on the inside, he lives by his own rules.

This week you're going to step right out of the pages of one of those novels. Make up a wanted poster with your picture on it. The caption reads:

BEWARE OF THE TENDER OUTLAW
WANTED FOR NUMEROUS ROBBERIES
HE STEALS HEARTS AND TAKES ADVANTAGE
(Expected to hit town on Saturday!)

Roll up the poster and leave it for her one morning. By the time Saturday rolls around, you've outfitted yourself with a toy gun and holster, and the black mask of an outlaw. Sneak up behind her, wrap your hand over her mouth, and tell her she's now the prisoner of the Tender Outlaw. She won't be hurt — if she stays quiet and does exactly as she's told.

Mmm, she's a mighty pretty filly...and you think you just might need to steal a kiss from her. Pull her to the sofa or take her on the floor; *ravish her* — and don't be surprised when this sweet little frontier girl turns out to have some outlaw blood of her own! I'll bet you won't mind at all if she tries to take your, um, family jewels out of the ol' vault. Now remember, you're a bad guy, not a rude guy — you can't leave without tasting the specialty of the house. Tug her panties off. Tell her she better spread 'em wide if she knows what's good for her...and then give her what's good for her! When it's over and you're both flushed and slightly breathless, get up and pick her panties off the floor.

*Ma'am, I think these'll be going with me now....*Put them in your pocket, blow her a kiss, and quietly leave the room. When you come back, your disguise is gone. But that night, when she finds your mask under her pillow, she'll remember every detail of her mysterious stranger, and smile.

And if you find the mask under *your* pillow, well...I guess it's time for The Return Of The Tender Outlaw! Yeeee Haa! Who says crime doesn't pay?

--- *Ingredients* ---

1 Black Mask / 1 Toy Gun, with Holster
1 Wanted Poster (Make one from a photo and construction paper)

N.º

68

PUSS 'N BOOTS

For *Her* Eyes Only

$$

DRIVE HIM WILD
Graham Masterton

You may be interested to know that a high proportion of men have erotic fantasies not about rape or pillage or having their wicked way with vainly protesting women. Quite the opposite. They daydream of being tied up and whipped and humiliated by a cruel and unforgiving dominatrix. Monique von Cleef, one of the most successful prostitutes I ever knew, told me that the men who came most regularly to her house in the Hague for masochistic sexual services were captains of industry, police chiefs, and politicians.

The fantasy of being sexually helpless is a very potent stimulus for all of us — both men and women. It is recreational as well as highly erotic.

"...Anyway, we played out this slave fantasy one morning and to my total surprise it was very, very erotic. I think that I got into it even more than he did. I wore a soft green suede jacket and black suede thigh-boots and nothing else at all. God knows what any of my friends would have thought if they had looked through the window and seen me. He was completely naked except for a black studded strap which I buckled between his legs and around his testicles. We laughed a little at first; nervousness, I guess. But then we really got into the spirit of it. I made him get down on his hands and knees and wash the kitchen floor. Then I made him clean the bathrooms and clean the windows and polish all the furniture. Most of the time he had a huge erection, and even when he wasn't fully hard his penis was quite swollen... it obviously turned him on, and it turned me on, too. I kept coming up to him and flicking him with a thin leather strap, just enough to give him a red mark on his bare bottom. When he was finished I walked around and inspected everything while he had to kneel on the floor. I strapped his thighs for leaving polish-marks on the table. Then I bent over a chair and said, 'As a punishment you have to fuck me.' By that time, both of us were pretty well worked up, and we fucked like tigers. I can remember screaming. I'd never been so excited in my life."

*T*his is the big one — every man's secret sexual wish, so dark he may not have ever shared it with you. But you found this book! And now you're going to take him on the ride of his life.

The key to this seduction is your outfit. A mask and boots will not only set the tone for the evening, it will help you get into character for your role as tease and tormentor.

The night before, leave your mask dangling from his rear-view mirror. He may find himself a bit...*distracted* at work all day! When he brings it home, have a good laugh. Flirt and touch and talk like always, but the moment you put on the mask, your whole demeanor must change. You are *investing the mask with power,* and he needs to learn to take it seriously. Tell him to take his shirt off. Don't ask. Tell him to lay on the floor at the foot of the bed. Climb on him, kiss him; tell him how good he feels under you. In fact, you think you just might need to keep him there.

Roll over onto his arm, the one nearest the bed. Pin it while you spring your trap. You've already secretly tied one end of a soft cord to the bedpost or mattress frame. Now quickly knot the other around his wrist. *Oooh, now that I've got you — what am I going to do with you?*

Here's what. Start by sliding your hand inside his trousers and giving him a quick squeeze. Smile, and say you'll be right back. Go put on your costume. Sensuous lingerie, boots...after you don each item, stroll back in and taunt him some more. On one visit, press your leather-clad toe against his pride-and-joy. Ask if he's been a *good boy*. On the next, free his penis from it's zippered prison, but don't touch! Kneel over his face; command him to lick. Grab his hair and pull him against you...mmm! When you've had your fill, lay down nearby. Run your fingernails under his balls and just tease him. Brush your lips against his head. Circle it with your tongue. He wants desperately to push into your warm, wet mouth but it's *so hard to reach*. When you finally take your prisoner don't let him enter all at once. Make him beg for relief. Make him wait. His climax, when it comes, will be quite shattering.

Wow. Finally, a seduction that isn't just about sex. Or power, for that matter. It's also a *Grrreat* excuse to buy a new pair of boots!

Ingredients

Boots — the higher the better / 1 Mask, any kind
1 Soft Cord, like the sash from a bathrobe

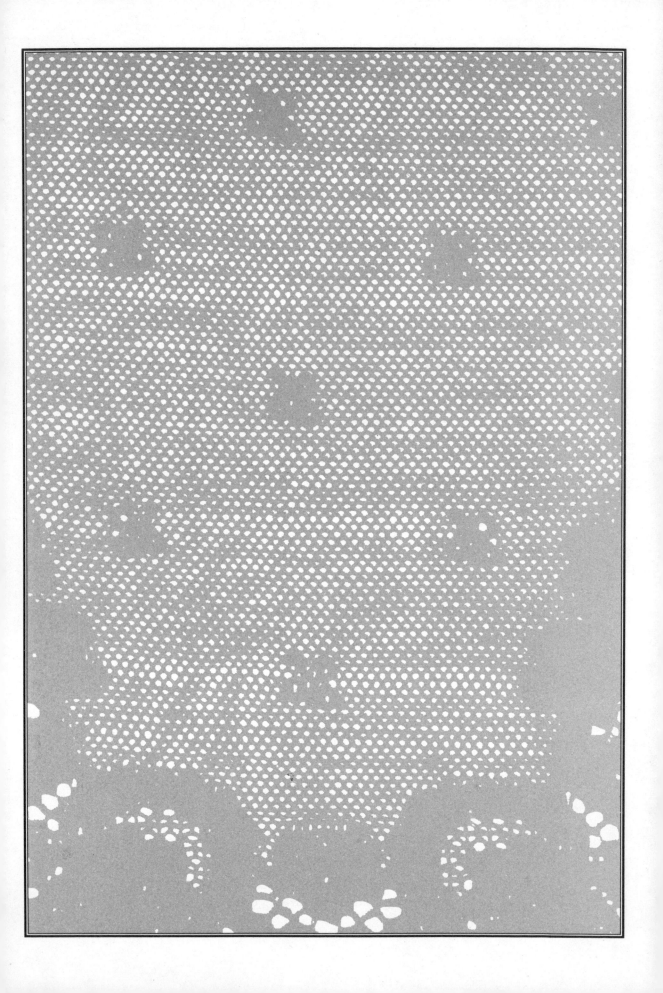

N^o **69**

THE CAT TECHNIQUE

For *His* Eyes Only

THE PERFECT FIT
Edward Eichel and Philip Nobile

Partners make a small but significant adjustment to get into position for the CAT technique. The man slides forward higher up on the woman. He assumes the "riding high" posture with his pelvis over-riding hers. The base of his penis is brought into direct contact with her clitoris. Taking the weight off his elbows, he lowers his chest, resting his torso on the woman. His head and shoulders veer over her left or right side to a position that is comfortable for both partners. The weight of the man's body gravitates forward over the woman; he should not allow his body to slide backward, causing his pelvis to slip back down under hers. The woman wraps her legs around the man's thighs with her ankles resting on his calves. Her knees should not be raised because that immobilizes her pelvis.

A rhythm of movement is established in the CAT technique that is interdependent and unique. The motion of one partner corresponds to the motion of the other. The patter of movement is basically identical for the man and the woman. The upward and downward strokes of movement should travel a distance of about two inches. Movement should not be too hard or too fast. The partners maintain full bodily contact.

Meeee-oowww!

*G*iven a choice, I think every cat in the world would do nothing but spend the day eating, sleeping, and, uh, *making more cats,* if you know what I mean. And if they could only master the CAT Technique — they might be willing to give up food and rest!

Get your love's attention early in the week by presenting her with a cat of her own. Leave a small figurine or a cute stuffed toy on her dresser, but please — none of those Garfields that stick to car windows! If your budget permits, make a tiny little kitty collar out of a breathtaking new gold bracelet or watch. *What's the matter, honey? Cat got your tongue?*

When it's time for your seduction, give her all your attention. Sneak up behind her and nuzzle her neck — ooh, standing in back puts you in such a nice position for *touching.* Glide your hands over her breasts and her belly; unbutton her blouse and slip your fingers just past the edge of her bra. Take your time unveiling her flesh. Reach *under* her clothing while you stroke and scratch and massage her sweetest spots.

Lay back on the bed or sofa and pull her on top of you, her back still nestled against your chest. Slip your hand between her thighs and whisper in her ear....*Spread your legs for me. Uh-huh, just like that; I wanna feel you. Oh, yeah, that's so nice....You are soooo beautiful God you feel good....*

As the temperature rises, and your clothes come off, grin and tell her about the CAT. No, it's not how felines do it, but it should have you both howling like cats in heat! Pin her to the bed with her knees against her chest, ankles over your shoulders. *Come inside.* Oh my — is there any better feeling in the world than that first sensation of steaming wet heat engulfing your erection?

Now shift forward while she wraps her legs around your calves. Ride higher than usual, so high that the base of your penis rubs directly against her clitoris. You're not thrusting in and out, but rather moving your pelvic bone in slow circles against hers, with nothing but her extremely aroused clitoris between you. The stimulation is intense, the position easy to maintain. The climax...is simply explosive. *Wow!*

CAT, meet pussy. Pussy — CAT. You're going to be gooood friends!

------------------ *Ingredients* ------------------

1 Toy Kitty / 1 Horny Tomcat / 1 Sex Kitten

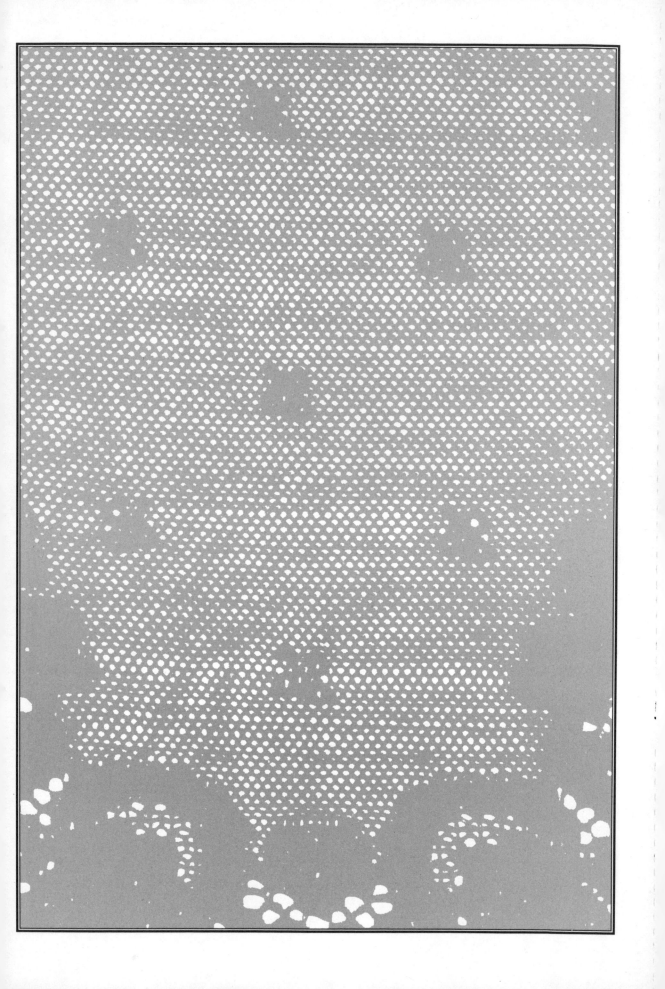

N.º 70

WET AND WILD

For *His* Eyes Only

$

IF IT FEELS GOOD
Joan Elizabeth Lloyd

The smell of a woman's hair and skin is as individual as her walk, the shape of her face, or her voice. You can make use of that fact. An erotic experience can be sparked by completely changing your scent - not just your perfume but your shampoo, your face lotion, and your soap. Change your scent and you can change a lot about your attitude.

MAKING LOVE: A MAN'S GUIDE
Whit Barry

Caressing each other under water adds a dimension of sensuality not possible on dry land. Skin feels smoother and is more responsive to the touch. The water buoys up your body to some extent; the weightlessness you feel can transport you and your partner into a world where abandoning your inhibitions and literally "going with the flow" becomes almost automatic.

"Being in a hot tub with my lover is like being in a warm, protected cocoon." Angela said. "I can't always tell where the water stops and our bodies begin. When I close my eyes, everything disappears but the physical sensations. It really is the ultimate."

Of course, not everyone has access to the ultimate. Most people do have tubs or showers, however, and these too can become bowers of sensual delights. In a tub or shower, you can use scented soaps to lather each other up and get slippery-sexy.

*U*nless you once stumbled into one by accident, I'll bet you've never been to a shower. Women throw them for other women, and mostly they just hand out gifts and talk. That's sort of the idea with this seduction. There's a shower, and gifts, and oooh, are you gonna give her something to talk about!

Send her a shower invitation — there's a whole section of them in any card shop. Fill it out with the date, time and location. You're the host, and naturally, she's the guest of honor. She'll get a little thrill when it shows up in her mailbox...and a bigger charge when she realizes it's you, up to your amorous tricks again!

Set the scene for your private shower. She'll love the attention to detail. Candles casting a soft glow about the bath, fluffy towels folded neatly on the rack, terrific music on the stereo — she may be speechless, and that's fine. You're not there to chat. Right now you're there to *kiss* while you help her peel her clothing away. Drop your robe, and lead her to the shower.

The surprise isn't over yet. You've got two presents, neatly gift-wrapped, and yes, she's supposed to open them right there under the steaming spray. One's a bar of French-milled soap, and the other is shampoo, the exotic strawberry-scented kind you can only get in specialty stores. And now the real fun begins.

Pour some shampoo in your hand and tenderly wash her hair. You wouldn't believe how many women get turned on by this one simple act. Take your time with it. Once the rushing cascade rinses her hair clean, take the soap and lather her up. Pay special attention to her bottom....Work your hand back and forth, slipping in and out between her cheeks, gliding your soapy fingers from swollen clitoris to velvety anus and back again. Hmm, it seems you've got something else to slip between her thighs. The sound of skin slapping against wet skin is just so...sexy! And speaking of sexy — that's a lot of freshly washed woman there in front of you. If it turns out your shower is big enough for foreplay, and no more, well, there are all those towels conveniently draped across the bed. What a coincidence.

"You scrub my back, and I'll scrub yours." It's not just a good plan for living — it's one of the foundations for Grrreat Sex!

Ingredients
---

1 Bar French-Milled Scented Soap / Shampoo / Lots and lots of towels
1 Shower Built for Two / 1 Bottle Strawberry / 1 Printed Invitation / Presents, Gift Wrapped

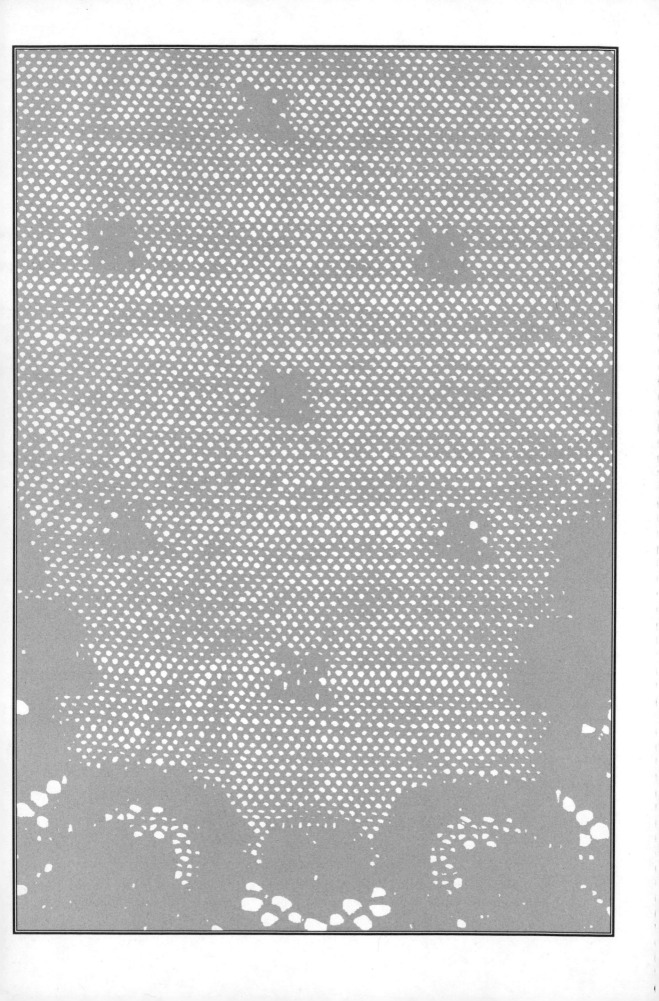

N° **71**

RED LIGHT DISTRICT

For *Her* Eyes Only

$$

THE WONDERFUL LITTLE SEX BOOK
William Ashoka Ross

It's worth your while, if you want great sex, to create a bedroom that's ideally conducive to intimacy, but it should be clean and uncluttered, have pleasing colors, and not be merely utilitarian; it should inspire a sense of beauty. The bed you use for sex ought to have a special, exotic, other-worldly feeling, almost evocative of an altar. There should be an air of reverence. Some people enjoy making love under a canopy, and you may want to construct one. Soft lighting is immensely helpful, and so is quietly pulsating music. When the whole room feels like a retreat from the hustle and bustle of everyday life, won't you relish the thought of spending time there with your beloved?

IF IT FEELS GOOD
Joan Elizabeth Lloyd

Each of the five senses has a part to play in imaginative lovemaking. Any creative lover can use these senses to enhance the sensuality of the moment.

*R*ed is the color of passion. Red sparks the senses and stirs up the appetite. Red is the color of smoldering embers, which you're going to fan into flames of passion when you invite your man into your boudoir, decorated for the evening in...*red*.

Send him an invitation — on crimson note paper, of course — to meet you in your bed promptly at nine. A single red bulb in your bedside lamp casts a deep, ruddy glow about the room. Arouse his sense of smell with a few drops of scented oil on the warm light. Try rose oil, said to be a sexual stimulant for women, and cardamom, the legendary Fire of Venus and an aphrodisiac for the opposite sex.

When he arrives, he'll find you dressed, naturally, in red. Scarlet stockings, lingerie, lipstick...and you *do* have red high heels, don't you? Oh, every woman should. And of course you're stretched out on bedsheets the color of a rich, dark claret.

There may be no song in the world that generates more steam than Ravel's Bolero....That sultry, driving beat will weave it's hypnotic spell as you pour two glasses of a full-bodied burgundy and propose a toast — to *red hot sex!*

Interrupt your sensuous playtime long enough to pluck a ripe strawberry from the bowl on your nightstand. Put the small end to your lips and kiss it. Let him stare as you slowly work it into your mouth, nibbling and sucking it like a — well, you know! Roll a maraschino cherry around your lips; let him taste the sweet juice. Ask him if he'd like one of his own, and when he says yes...draw back your *other* lips and pop it in!

Come and get it!

When you're ready to return the favor, dribble some of the cherry juice over his own hanging fruit, and slurp it up. Think of it as the Red Light Special for the evening, with a hidden surprise waiting for you inside.

But be careful if you get in the car with him tomorrow. He may be a menace in traffic. After all, he just spent a whole night learning that red means *go*...go go GO!

Ingredients

The Essentials - Red Light Bulb / Red Wine / Strawberries and Cherries / *Bolero* by Ravel
The Luxuries - Red Sheets and Pillowcases / Red Jewelry / Rose & Cardamom / Red Lingerie

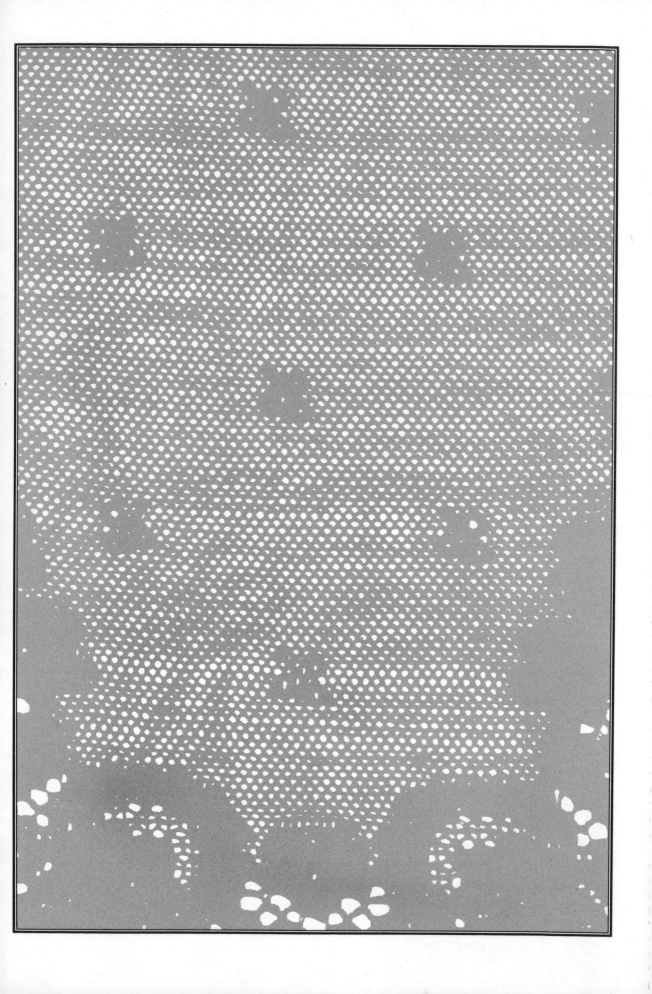

N.° **72**

CYBORGASM

For *Her* Eyes Only

$

ORDINARY WOMEN EXTRAORDINARY SEX
Dr. Sandra Scantling and Sue Browder

As children, many of us were told that daydreaming is an impractical, "lazy" waste of time. Yet the vivid fantasy lives these women learned to develop as children seem to have benefited them later as adults and helped them become more immersed during lovemaking. In a study done by Wendy E. Stock and James H. Geer at the State University of New York at Stony Brook, most of the women who listened to a ten minute erotic tape became sexually excited. But women who reported that they fantasized while masturbating became measurably more excited than those who seldom fantasized. The original research that inspired this book (Scantling, 1990) also found that women who enjoy sexual fantasy- and fantasize frequently- report more intense sexual arousal and sexual enjoyment during both masturbation and sex with a partner.

THE SEXUALLY SATISFIED WOMAN
Dr. Ronnie Edell

The Joys of Fantasy-sharing. You may have "done it" while swinging from a crystal chandelier or on the back of a camel trudging across the Mojave Desert. But I am not exaggerating when I tell you that fantasy-sharing is the most intense sexual experience you will ever have the opportunity to enjoy.

The important thing is that you use your sexual fantasies as aural aphrodisiacs, crank up the levels of pleasure in your lovemaking.

*T*his is a scorcher.

I mean it's *really* hot. The power of this seduction comes from a startling and intensely erotic invention, so new you may never have heard of it.

It's the closest thing yet to *virtual reality sex.* It's a recording of people making love, in digitally enhanced state-of-the-art stereo, and it's an incredible turn-on. This compelling audiocassette is called *Cyborgasm.*

To gain the full sensual effect, you'll also need two sets of headphones, and a headphone jack splitter — these are just a few dollars at Radio Shack, and allow you both to hear the tape at the same time. Put them in a pretty package along with the tape and present it to your lover, but make him wait to the weekend to open it! Only when you're both completely relaxed, alone, and in robes will he be ready for the Cyborgasmic Experience.

The day of your seduction, tie a blindfold over his eyes. Play his favorite music through the headphones. His world is now centered on your hands as you massage his feet, his calves, his thighs. He'll smile in anticipation of the treats to come...but he can't possibly predict the sensual power of the Cyborgasm tape.

Pop it in. And brace yourself! You're suddenly surrounded by people making fiercely passionate love in full 3-D stereo sound, and it's so real it's as if they were right there. He *feels* like they are, because suddenly a warm, wet mouth is engulfing his penis. It's you, of course, following along with the action on the tape, and finding your own temperature rising with his. Cover your hands with Astroglide or some other body oil and fondle him all the way through cut fourteen. You can squeeze hard and stroke fast — the lubricant protects his skin, and supercharges his senses. When cut fifteen comes on, climb right on top of him. The most awesome, incredibly concentrated stimulation of his life will bring him to climax in minutes.

But here's the real magic of Cyborgasm. It's so new, so amazingly arousing, that he'll be ready to try again in seconds. I hope you have fresh Energizers in the tape player — like that famous bunny, he'll want to keep going, and going, and going....

Ingredients
---

1 Tape or CD Player / 2 Headphones, 1 Splitter / 1 Blindfold / Astroglide or similar sexual lubricant
1 Cyborgasm tape or CD available at record stores or see specility shop page

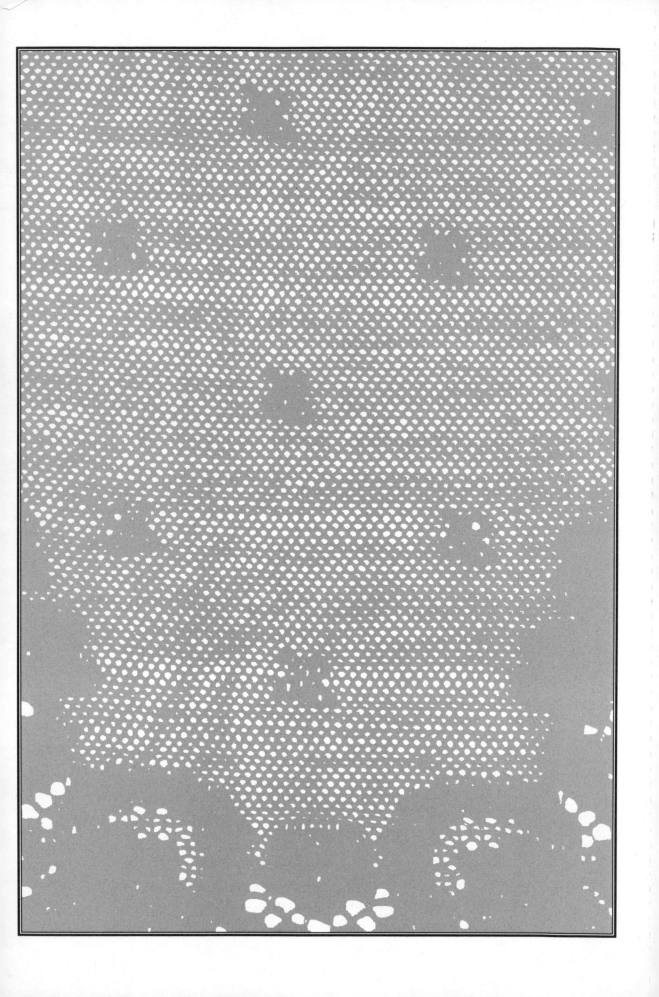

N.º **73**

DOUBLE THE PLEASURE

For *Her* Eyes Only

WHAT MEN REALLY WANT
Susan Crain Bakos

Men treat the X-rated video as a sex aide. Men feel the films are best enjoyed with a female partner. Like her, a man would be bored after the first fifteen minutes, too, if he did nothing but watch. This is participatory erotica.

Whether pornography encourages people to experiment or sparks their passion or merely feeds their fantasies, it has become increasingly a sexual tool for couples. Much has been made in recent years of the growing violent content of some forms of pornography. The less discussed new trend is couples-oriented videos featuring romantic storylines, softer photography, and romantic music. Many are produced and directed by women, most notably former porn star Candida Royalle, owner of Femme Productions. If you have been refusing your man's suggestion of bedroom erotica, rent one of Royalle's films. You might change your mind about porn.

THE NEW JOY OF SEX
Alex Comfort, M.D. D.S.C.

Pornography - Name given to any sexual literature somebody is trying to suppress. Most normal people enjoy looking at sex books and reading sex fantasies, which is why abnormal people have to spend so much time and money suppressing them.

*D*id you know that thirty percent of the customers renting x-rated videos are women? Well, it's about time! More and more women are finally exploring their own sensuality and developing their own sexual confidence. It's exhilarating — and empowering. Let yourself be a part of that thirty percent and make your sex life, as well as your partner's, more exciting!

There's no secret here — Men are very visual creatures. They get turned on by what their eyes see. Take advantage of this gift from Mother Nature. Share this fantasy with him and *you'll* be the one to reap the erotic benefits — guaranteed!

Before you begin, you'll have to go to a video store and rent a few x-rated tapes. Watch them ahead of time and pick out the one you're most comfortable with. I'm always amazed by how much I learn this way. (The top selling/renting videos are: Insatiable, The Masseuse & The Best From Europe...I love them all!) If you're sure no one else will be visiting your home, you can leave it out in a conspicuous place; when he asks, tell him you rented a special video you'd like to watch with him later. Pick a time to meet in the bedroom...and tell him he better not be late, or you're starting without him!

While he gets over the shock, get your room ready. Pull the shades, dim the lights, make a couple of drinks...and pop the tape into the VCR. Snuggle up to him and watch at least half of the movie together before attempting any sexy moves, even if he tries — and he will! Whisper to him that your favorite scene is coming up. Oh, go ahead and touch yourself; tell him how wet you're getting! But play hard-to-get. The tape may tantalize, but it's nothing compared to the tease laying next to him.

When your special scene comes on — so will you. Whatever the actress is doing on screen, you'll be copying in bed. When she starts to play with her partner's erection, you'll match her stroke for stroke. When she takes his penis into her mouth — so will you. You will quite literally *double his pleasure* as he watches two women performing identical acts. It's more than any man can control...and he won't control it for long.

You've heard computer wizards talk about virtual reality? Well, think of this as *virtual sexuality* — the cutting edge of home entertainment! This exotic twist on voyeurism really stimulates the sexual appetite, so don't plan anything else for the evening except staying right where you are...having grrreat sex!

Ingredients

---

1 Television and VCR / 1 Sexy Copycat / 2 Adult Videos

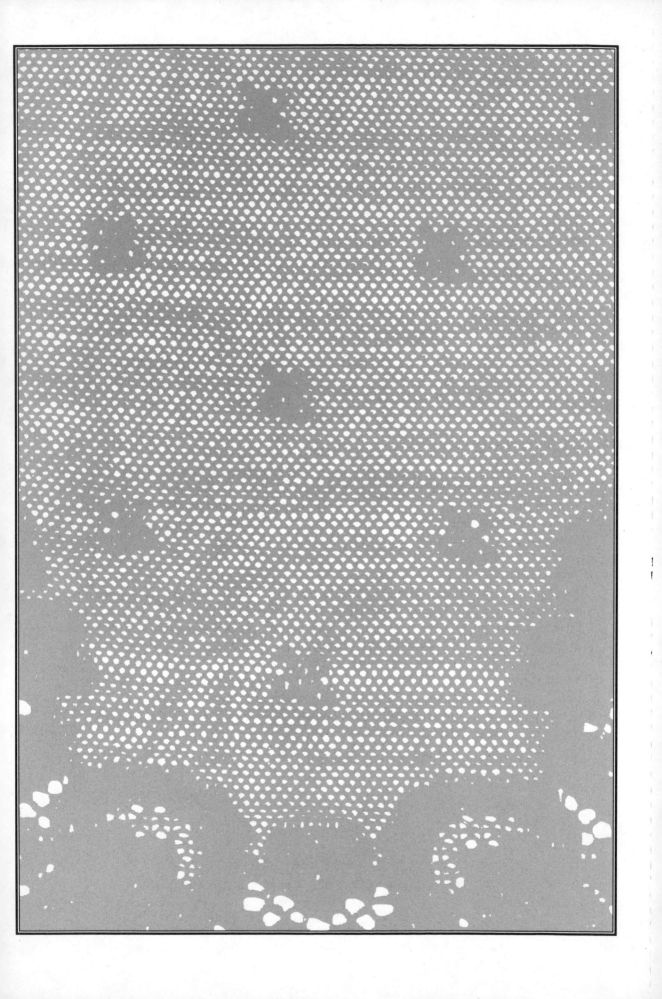

N° 74

BODY TEASE

For *Her* Eyes Only

SECRETS OF SIZZLIN' SEX
Cricket Richmond and Ginny Valletti

Lotions and oils have been part of sensuous rituals since ancient times. Slick chicks knew then what you're about to learn: Lubricants applied to your own or a fellow passenger's skin help us discover where our bodies are most receptive to touch. Smoothing on key components keeps motors purring and adds fuel to middle-of-the road masturbation.

You're at the wheel when it comes to pumping up sexual satisfaction. Skin slicks are another vehicle that can spark up a deflated routine. One thing's for sure - lubes are the ticket for a smoother ride. Buff over your chassis, his rear bumper, instrument panel, or ...ah um, spare tire. You'll speedily discover "auth-erotic" doesn't mean loving your car.

SECRETS OF SEDUCTION
Brenda Venus

I call "foreplay" anything before the act of intercourse that gets you excited. Massage is a great prelude to lovemaking. It breaks the touching barrier, and relaxes the whole body and mind. In a matter of a few minutes you can soothe, energize, or arouse. You're the musician, so learn to play muscles, nerves, skin, and all other erotic connections. It always works!

There's nothing quite so sensuous as a good back rub. Mmm, it melts your troubles and frees your mind. A lot of couples will tell you that their friendship took an amorous turn when one started working the kinks out of the other's neck!

This week you'll be giving your playmate an *ultra-massage*. Prepare him for the experience by putting a large folded blanket on the floor of the living room or bedroom. Leave it for a day or two. The morning of your seduction, unfold it. If it hasn't caught his attention yet, it certainly will when he comes home and finds it surrounded by candles and towels.

Let him think about it through dinner. Move to the blanket for wine and dessert. Then ask him to undress for his massage while you carry in a large tray with your essentials. On it are two bottles, one sitting in a bowl of ice. Steam rises from a wet and very hot towel, which you gently drape across his shoulders. Straddle him and pull the warm cloth down his back, letting the moist heat soak into his skin and relax his muscles.

Pull the lotion bottle from the ice and, without saying a word, squirt it down his spine and rub it in. *Gasp!* Make him shiver! Grab an ice cube and trail it down the cleft of his buttocks — ooh!

Let's heat him up again. The other bottle contains warm, unscented almond oil. Apply it to his neck and work down, finally smearing the warm cream over his bottom. Lean forward and add your own body heat to the mixture. Grab his arms and pull yourself forward, gliding slowly over the slippery film of oil. He'll love the weight of your breasts, the soft feel of your downy *mons* as you slide across his back.

Time to turn him over. More hot lotion is in order, but no need to repeat the entire process. His skin is already singing! Ask him to hold an ice cube between his teeth — lean over him and brush your breast against it. Let him feel your nipple rise and come alive against his lips. You've no doubt noticed something else rising as well. Friction is your friend as you squeeze him against your bosom or clamp him tightly between your well-lubricated thighs. The oil may be warm, but his explosion will be hot as he releases his passion all over your flushed skin.

Ooh, what a mess. But that's okay. Cleaning up is half the fun!

Ingredients
---

1 Blanket / 1 Steamed Towel / Several Candles
1 Bottle of Warm Oil / One Bottle of Cold Lotion / More Towels

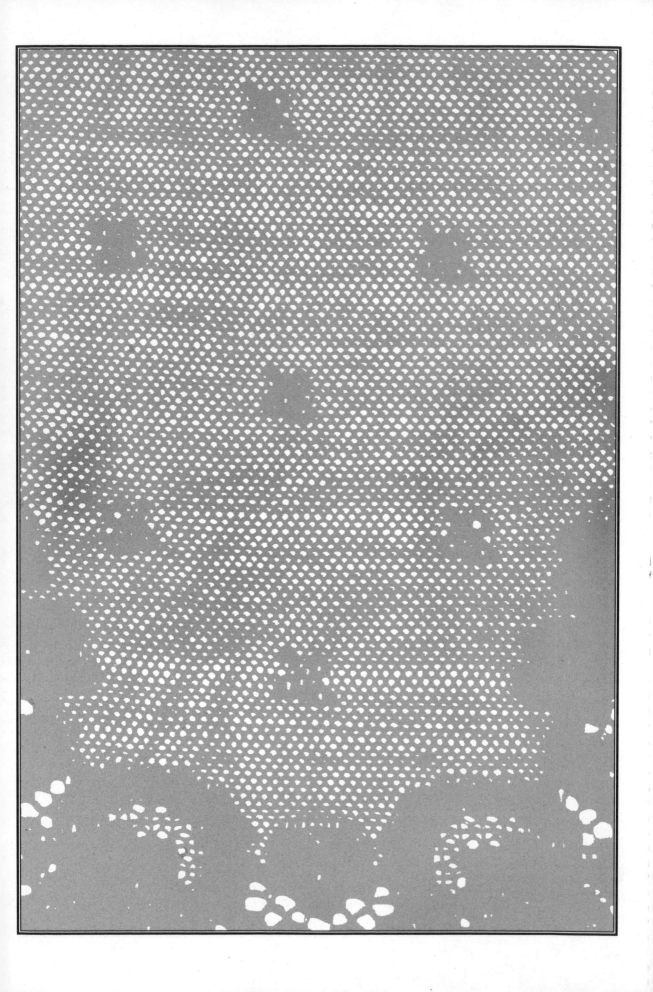

_N^o_ **75**

THE KISS OF LEATHER

For _His_ Eyes Only

$

THE NEW JOY OF SEX
Alex Comfort, M.D. D.Sc..

Leather:
Probably the most popular superskin turn-on: black hide also looks aggressive or scary and, being skin, all leather fixes natural sex odors.

WOMEN WHO LOVE SEX
Gina Ogden, Ph. D.

The consensus is that there are many things in heaven and earth that are more sensational in bed than even the most versatile penis. A penis may be able to throb, plunge, pulsate, saw, hammer, grind, ejaculate, sometimes even caress, but it cannot lick, suck, nibble, spank, give a full-body massage, flick like feathers, or vibrate for an hour. And there are many places on the body from which sexual satisfaction can be triggered.

SECRETS OF SIZZLIN' SEX
Cricket Richmond & Ginny Valletti

I especially enjoy massaging my breasts while wearing latex gloves. The material imparts a silky feel that's indescribable. Imagining it's my lover's hand caressing me, optimizes the pleasure. For variety, don gloves made of lace, fur or leather.

*W*hat is it about leather that makes it so fascinating? A woman looks totally hot in a leather miniskirt. A man in black leather strikes us as powerful, even foreboding. Our fantasies are often not of exposed skin, but of a *second* skin of soft, supple leather.

Find a good-sized leather swatch — free leather sample's from a custom tannery or furniture store is ideal. Drape it over a lampshade in the bedroom. Give her the day to think about it, while the leather charges the air with its earthy bouquet.

When evening rolls around and your flirting turns to touching, make a dramatic move. Yank off your leather belt, grab it by the ends, and rope her in. Pull her hard against you for a kiss. Slip the strap down her back, stopping every few inches to cinch it in, especially when you've got it tight against her butt. Now help her get undressed, and if there's any kind of leather jacket in the house, ask her to put it on, skin to skin.

Wear gloves so that your every touch is a kiss of leather. Use your swatch like a silk scarf, dragging it across each inch of her flesh, one side slightly course, the other butter-smooth. Draw it snug against her face for the overwhelmingly sensual aroma. Bite her nipples *through* the tender hide.

As she stretches out on the bed, straddle her back facing her deliciously bare bottom. Massage her thighs and calves. Part her cheeks with your leather-clad hands; trail your fingers between her legs. Is she wet? Is she soaking the tanned skin? Now ask her to turn over; spread her legs wide. Take the very end of your belt and *dip it inside her.* Get it soaked with her nectar. Place the tip squarely over her clitoris and, with only a light squeeze, gently slide it off. The slick friction, the pressure, the exquisite *pop* as her clit comes free from it's leather restraint will have it singing. Do it again. And again, faster and firmer. Each soft snap of leather on flesh pushes her closer to the edge. Alternate with light strokes from your fingers. Make it quicker, and wetter, and when she explodes, press all your toys against her steaming lips. Let her drench them with her honey.

Now what are you going to do with a belt that carries the very faint aroma of *sex?* Well, if she pulls it out of the closet for you one evening — it's a sure bet she doesn't want you to get dressed for dinner!

Ingredients

1 Pair of LeatherGloves / 1 Belt — one you *don't* need for work!
1 Swatch of Finished Leather or Suede (As an alternative, pick up a chamois at the auto parts store)

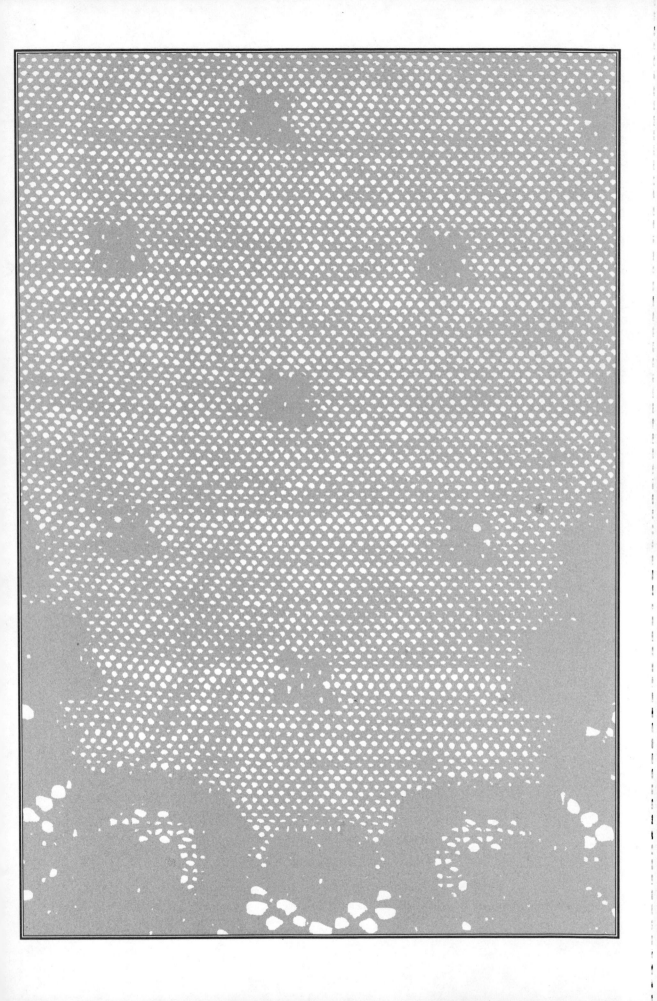

N⁰ **76**

EPICUREAN DELIGHT

For *His* Eyes Only

TOTAL LOVING
"J"

It's such a lovely way to spend an evening— or afternoon— or morning— or anytime! Isn't it a shame that when so many couples plan their day they consider lovemaking their least important activity? It may be heresy, but if I had to choose between a sensuous interlude of sex and getting the grocery shopping done or attending that obligatory PTA meeting, I'd take the sensuous interlude every time. And so would most of the happy Lifetime Lovers.

In a good love relationship, sex has top priority. It isn't endlessly shuffled aside to "Wait until it's more convenient."

Perhaps the strongest sexual don't of all is:
DON'T LET YOUR SEX LIFE FALL INTO THE HO HUM RUT.

LOVE POTIONS
Cynthia Mervis Watson, M.D. with Angela Hynes

The most basic sensations— hunger, fright, rage, joy, love, hate, sexual arousal— are moderated by the limbic brain, where impulses speed through first the internal pathways, then along routes to other forebrain regions and the cerebellum. Whereas the sensations of sight, sound, and touch must cross many synapses to reach the limbic core of the brain, the sense of smell is the most direct link to the limbic center. Because of this close connection between the nose and the limbic system, people may unknowingly make a decision to either embrace or retreat from an experience based on olfactory information.

Truly *grrreat* sex is, well —

Messy.

*I*f it's done right, that is! And that's never more true than in this seduction, in which you get your hands on some, uh, hot buttered buns. *Literally!*

Yes, you're actually going into the kitchen to play pastry chef this week. And if your culinary skills are lacking, don't panic; it doesn't matter if you can really cook. What's important is the atmosphere — and the aroma! — you create.

One morning when your sweetheart can sleep in, get up early and head for the kitchen. Whether you simply warm up some cinnamon buns or make an honest effort at baking from scratch, the scent of sweet dough and sugary frosting will soon fill the whole house. Mmm — I'll bet she wakes up with a smile!

She'll be grinning by the time she wanders into the kitchen and sees you puttering about. But, oh boy, what a wreck! It seems you managed to get flour *everywhere* — on your face, in your hair, and all over the counter. Walk up to her and kiss her...and smear a streak of flour on her cheek!

Hey, you look cute that way! You need another one over here....

Now spread a matching stripe on her other cheek. She'll giggle — and wiggle, as she tries to get away, but not before you manage to plant a white handprint right on her bottom. Feed her samples of your work, and be as sloppy as you can about it. If she takes the bait and flicks a little flour back at you, it's *war* — a romantic battle that'll leave you both covered in white. The real heat is no longer in the oven. It's building between you two as you wrestle in your indoor snowstorm. Pull your mate to the kitchen table and let your fun play turn to foreplay.

Does this all sound familiar? You've just played Jack Nicholson to her Jessica Lange in your own version of *The Postman Always Rings Twice*. Might be fun to rent the video later, to see how you compared. Be sure not to confuse it with *The Witches Of Eastwick*, though — that's the one in which Jack plays a horny old Devil.

Hmm. Come to think of it — you might be perfect for that role, too!

Ingredients

1 Cookbook (or some packaged cinnamon rolls) / 1 lb. Flour
1 Kitchen / 1 Sturdy Table

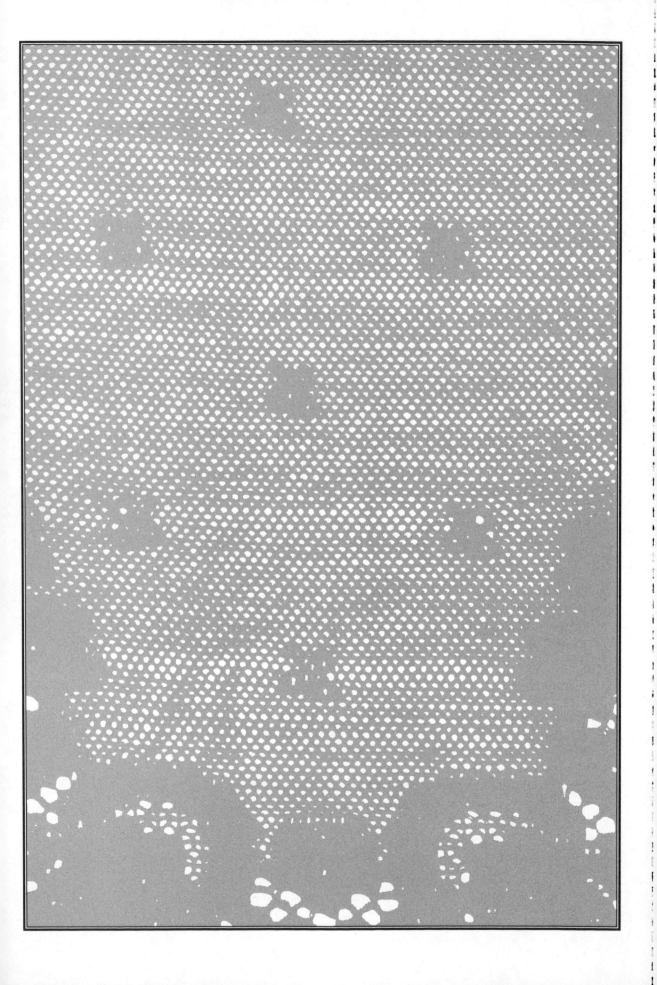

N<u>o</u> 77

WILD CARD

For *His* Eyes Only

$

LOVE POTIONS
Cynthia Mervis Watson, M.D.

Even today, mating rituals usually require that couples exchange food, either as gifts of candy or wine or as meals taken together. Dining out is the most popular form of dating, and everyone knows that cooking a meal for a prospective lover is full of implication. A well-known restaurateur who has spent a lifetime observing mating rituals told me that in the early stage of courtship, couples eat out; but once they start making love, they will more often eat at home.

Given that the act of eating together can be deliciously sensual and intimate, almost any meal could be said to be an aphrodisiac. Slowly sucking a strand of linguini into your mouth as a lover watches, sharing a forkful of cheesecake, or licking barbecue sauce from a lover's fingers can turn those foods into aphrodisiacs, although none of them would appear on any expert's list of love foods.

*H*ave you ever watched a really sexy part in a movie that made you wish you could have the same experience? This week you get to play opposite Kim Basinger as you recreate that memorable refrigerator scene in "9 1/2 Weeks...."

You'll have to do some planning ahead of time. Run to the grocery store and stock up on foods that carry a special sexual charge — cold lobster, to be sucked out of its shell...chilled wine, to be dribbled into your mouths...a ripe juicy peach to be shared for dessert...a bowl of Cool Whip, perfect for dipping fingers and decorating bodies!

She'll be thrilled when you volunteer to take care of dinner Friday night. And she'll be completely puzzled when you tell her the dress code — pajama's only! When it's time for your seduction, shoo her to the bedroom while you prepare your feast. When she comes back to the kitchen, you've got a sheet across the floor and nothing but the glow from the open refrigerator lighting the room.

Sit down and dive in to your erotic picnic dinner. Take turns reaching inside and grabbing anything you can with your fingers. Whatever you choose, you must feed it to her whether it's food or something to drink.

Don't try to be neat. Just grab your specialties, plus fruit, yogurt, whatever you can find. Pop morsels of food into each other's mouth. Stick fingers in jars and have the other suck it off. Let her pour the wine...right into your mouth! I'll bet you can get *really* creative with chocolate pudding. Let it all dribble down your chins and drop on your robes — it's all part of the fun!

The messier it gets, the more your passion will be aroused. Kiss often, tasting the different foods you are feeding each other.

Now — can you think of some way to burn all those extra calories off? Sounds like time for some sexual aerobics!

Ingredients
---

1 Opened Refrigerator / 1 Sheet / 1 Kitchen Chair / 20 Happy Fingers

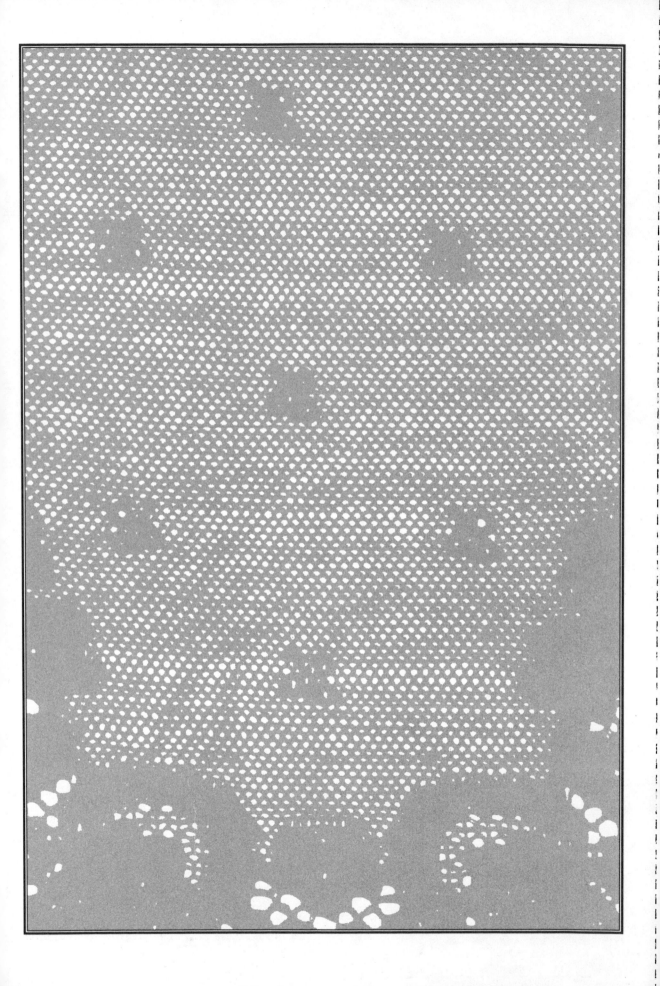

Nº 78

MUSTANG SALLY

For *Her* Eyes Only

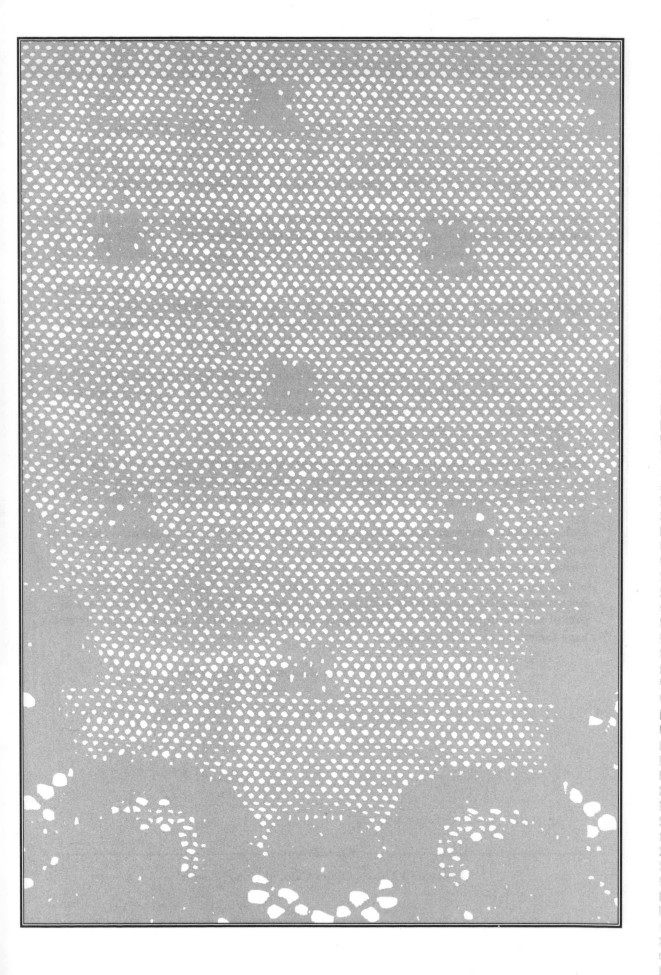

N⁰ 79

MERCY!

For *His* Eyes Only

THE NEW MALE SEXUALITY
Bernie Zilbergeld, Ph. D.

Express yourself sexually. Although men are supposed to be the big talkers when it comes to sex, many women say their partners rarely say or express much of anything. A great many women say that after years of being with the same men, they have no idea of what they like most in sex or if they even enjoy it. As surprising as it may sound, hundreds of women have told me that their men are so inexpressive in sex that the only way they know he's had an orgasm is when he stops moving.

Many women interpret this lack of a differentiated response to mean that the man is withholding information or that he isn't interested enough to give a relevant answer. So pay attention and express your desires and pleasure. If you like what she's doing to you right now or what she did to you yesterday, tell her. Use words, sounds, and movement to convey your enjoyment.

TALK DIRTY TO ME
Sallie Tisdale

I find myself thinking: Every orgasm is different. Then I must instantly amend myself, because every sexual event is different. Every point of arousal, every plateau, every intersection of desire with the desired is unique.

The move toward orgasm is a move toward preoccupation with one's genitals. Whatever the stimulus, sooner or later the conscious self gets shoved down into the crotch, nose to nose with desire.

THE LITTLE BLACK BOOK OF ANSWERS
Laura Corn

I asked 2,000 women:
If a man wanted to intensify your orgasm,
what words should he whisper in your ear right before?

The top three answers, in order:

1. Your the sexist woman alive!
2. I love You.
3. He shouldn't talk with his mouth full!

It's so nice to have a man around the house!

You take care of us, you make us feel beautiful, and you're *so good at fixing little things!* Well, most of you, anyway. Of course, you also work too many hours, you drop your socks on the floor, you never do your share of the housework....

None of that matters; we love you anyway. But do you know the one thing that really, seriously bugs us? The thing you all do that just drives us nuts?!!

You don't talk to us. You don't tell us what's on your mind, or what you want, or how you feel about us. And when it comes to sex, well...!

You're going to surprise your true love. You're going to startle her, and thrill her. You're going to *seduce her with your words all week long,* and in the process discover an entirely new path to arousal. Start with flirty words, the language of romance. Ring her up at work — *Hi! No, no special reason. Just missed you, I guess. I was sitting here thinking about you, and I thought I'd call to say I love you....*

Sounds so simple, doesn't it? But you just knocked her socks off.

When you see her later, your tone is more sensual. *Hey, you look terrific today! Come here, give me a hug. And you smell great — is that new? Ooh, I like! Mmm, I think I need a kiss.*

And when you get to the bedroom, you can get downright uncivilized. *You know what I'm thinking? I'm thinking I want you to come. Yes, in my mouth, I want to taste your sweet juices.If I suck right...here...think you could come? Ohh...you smell so good. I've been dreaming about this all day long....*

It takes more than words to communicate in the bedroom. You might be having a jolly old time, but if you're quiet and still, she feels like a failure. So let her know how much you like what she's doing! Moan, sigh, move, gasp, grab her and whisper *yes Yes YES OII GOD YES!* That's a powerful reward for all her effort —

And a powerful incentive for her to do the same thing again!

Ingredients
---

1 Voice, and a willingness to use it
1 Penis, and a willingness to let it be used!

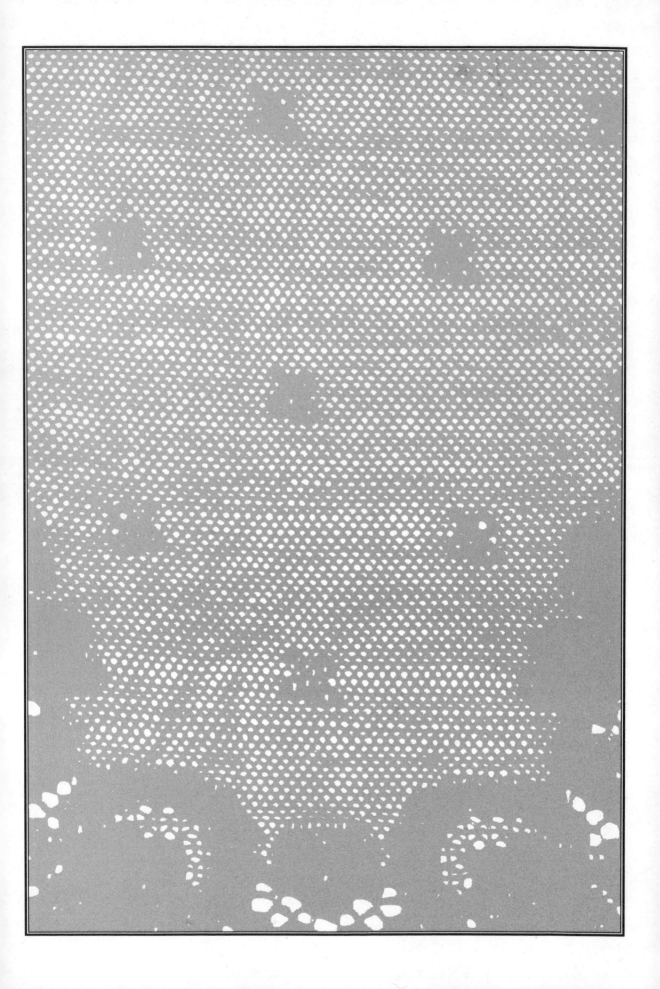

Nº 80

SEX IN A SHOE BOX

For *His* Eyes Only

THE LOVING TOUCH
Dr. Andrew Stanway

Sex is usually concerned with warm things, but the thrilling cold of ice has a special place in foreplay, for it can have a stimulating shock effect.

Be careful not to use ice directly from a deep freeze. Supercooled ice sticks to any moist surface and can burn like a red-hot iron.

But normal ice, which is on the point of melting, leaves deliciously cool damp trails across the skin. Test the ice on your tongue before you begin.

Ice will certainly stimulate the nipples - a single touch will have them erect in seconds - and many find the touch of a cold cube on the genitals a turn-on too. For some women, having a cube of ice put into their vagina first, before having regular intercourse, can be a real turn-on for them.

THE SEXUALLY SATISFIED WOMAN
Dr. Ronnie Edell

New techniques: for example, using food during lovemaking. You might get creative with your vegetables or bring a little ranch-style dip to the bedroom to add tang to the evening.

*T*his week's seduction is a game — a guessing game, like Twenty Questions, except there's an orgasm at the end. *Wheee!*

To start, you need a box, at least the size of a shoe box. This is all your love gets to see, so go ahead and dress it up with a bow or giftwrap — and then leave it out for her to find!

There's nothing in it now, of course; your special ingredients are all hidden elsewhere. But sometime this weekend, after you've kissed and cuddled and gotten close, ask if she's a bit curious about your mystery box. She is? *Oh, too bad...no peeking.* She can guess what you have in there, but —

She can't use her hands. She has to wear a blindfold. And the only time she can feel each item is when you apply it to her skin!

Tie a silk scarf over her eyes and go fill your box. From the refrigerator, pick out a carrot, a cucumber, and a small squash, all thoroughly scrubbed. From the freezer, grab some ice and put it in a glass of water. From the pantry, fetch a squeeze bottle of Magic Shell — that's a chocolate syrup that becomes solid when poured over ice cream. Microwave the syrup and half the vegetables until they're warm...*not hot...* to the touch.

Now go play. Use your tongue to make sure she's quite wet, and apply the warm carrot. Rub the rough length of it slowly past her clitoris. Follow with quick, tiny little tugs, on one side of her clit then the other, back and forth. Can she tell what it is?

She'll have no trouble guessing the ice cube when you slide it across her nipple! Follow it with the warm syrup, and then more ice, until the syrup hardens into chocolate candy. Mmm...don't forget to share! When the cube is small and melting fast, glide it over her mons and between her labia. Quickly pop it into her vagina — not too far! — and just as quickly suck it back out.

Go through your collection, alternating between warm and cold. The two extremes add up to *hot!* Keep it up until she identifies each item — or runs out of orgasms. And when you're done, why, you've got all the fixings for a delicious salad.

A kind of a *box lunch,* you might say. Mm-mm-good!

———————— *Ingredients* ————————

1 Shoe Box / 1 Blindfold / Magic Shell Chocolate Syrup
Assorted Veggies and any other edibles you like / Ice

ESO
Alan P. Brauer, M.D. and Dona J. Brauer

Only by your teaching, verbal and nonverbal, can your partner learn to stimulate you effectively. You are the only final authority on your own sexual response. People often believe that they should know instinctively how to satisfy their partners. But every human being's response to sexual stimulation is different. So no one, man or woman, can know your response in advance. They have to be taught.

That teaching requires trust. If, when you say "That feels uncomfortable. Try a lighter touch," your partner gets mad and says "Oh, the hell with you. If I'm not doing it right, do it yourself. This is stupid," then no one is going to learn. Instead, each of you needs to put your ego aside, say "Thank you," and follow directions.

Sex is a skill. No one is automatically an expert. Each of you is responsible only for understanding your own response. Your partner's response you'll have to learn from the only living expert - your partner.

*Y*ou're going back to school this week.

Oh, don't worry; you won't have to crack a book or sharpen a pencil. You will *love* the final exam, however, and if you learn your lessons well, you'll graduate at the top of your class —

Magna cum *loudly!*

The class is Male Sexuality, and the object of your study is also your teacher. Remember what you learned in school — *it never hurts to flirt with the teacher.* So once he's completely relaxed and in the mood for a seduction, stroll into the room wearing your schoolgirl best...a little plaid pleated skirt and ankle socks, or if you can find one, that ultimate high-school fantasy — the cheerleader outfit! Wear glasses if you've got 'em, for that studious look.

When he asks what's going on, explain that you want him to teach you some things. Things they never showed you in school. Secret, erotic, naughty and slightly nasty things that only he can show you. For instance —

Do you like to be kissed like this? Brush your lips past his. *Or do you prefer this?* Firm, full-on-the-lips, and just slightly moist. *Do you like it when I suck your nipples like this...or is it better when I mmm...bite! And down here — should I just cup these in my hand, or do you like it when I give them a little squeeze?*

You already know where all his hot buttons are...but in this seduction, he's going to tell you exactly how he likes them pushed! Most important — don't ask if he enjoys your moves; of course he'll say he does. Instead, give him a choice each time. One style's good, but the other might be *ohmigodyesyesyes much* better. That's the one to memorize!

Teeth, or no? When you climax, should I stop...or go faster?

Once he's taught you how to give the very best orgasm in the world — reach into your nightstand and pull out your diploma. Make it simple or fancy; all it really needs is your name and the phrase "Ph.D in Se.X." So, professor — *did I earn it?*

If you've been a very good girl, you did. And if you've been bad, well — I guess you'll just have to stay after class for extra lessons! Hmm. Which do *you* like better?

Ingredients

1 Wise Teacher / 1 Eager Student / 1 Hand-Made Diploma

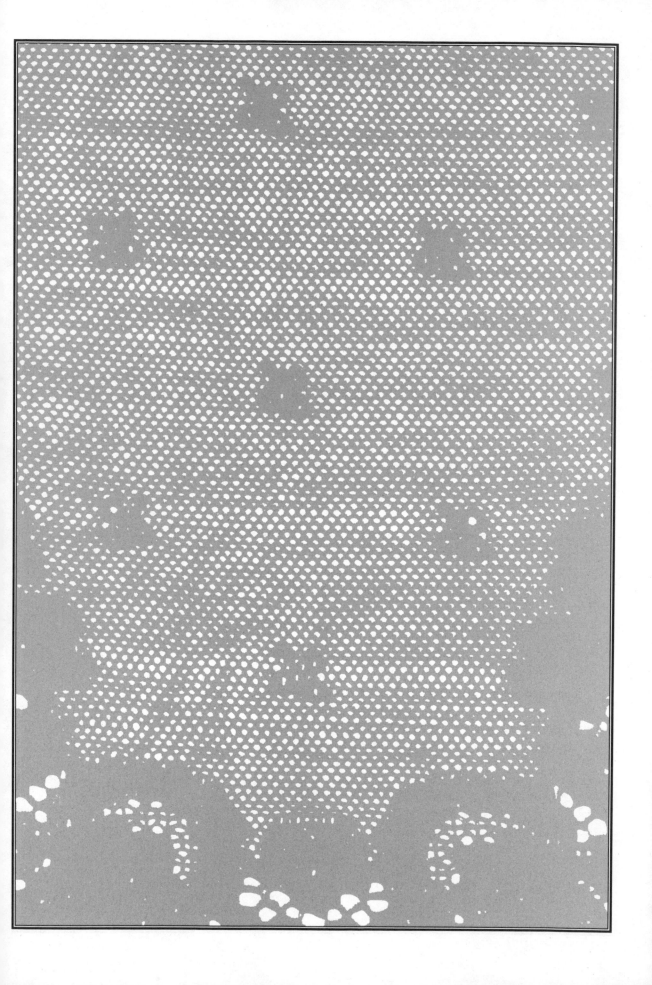

Nº 82

WINDOW OF OPPORTUNITY

For *Her* Eyes Only

DRIVE HIM WILD
Graham Masterton

To change and improve your sex life pronto, however, you can't wait for your man to make all the moves. With some men, you'll still be waiting when you're ninety. You'll have to show him that you're eager to put some zest into your lovemaking by coming on a little stronger than usual...suggesting sex in the middle of the afternoon, climbing into the shower with him, giving him "accidental" peeks as you dress and undress.

LIGHT HIS FIRE
Ellen Kreidman

A woman who knows that inside every man, no matter how old, how successful, or how powerful, there is a little boy who wants to be loved and to feel as if he's special, is a woman who knows a powerful secret. A man wants to know that he matters to you more than anyone else in the world.

*W*hat do you get when you mix a bit of fresh air, a *grrreat* view, a pinch of exhibitionism and a splash of secrecy with a special technique for G-spot stimulation? You get the window of opportunity...for an outrageous "quickie!"

A picture may be worth a thousand words, but today you're creating a scene that will leave him absolutely speechless. Put on your raciest high heels and a sexy full skirt. Call him into the bedroom by saying you need his help. As he approaches the door, lean out your open window and look back over your shoulder.

It's right over here by the window, honey.... Grab your skirt and pull it completely up over your derriere as he strolls in. *It's right over here by the window honey...*

Eeee-yow! What a picture! Your bare bottom, your wicked grin....You've got him hooked, and it sure won't take long to reel him in. In a blink he'll be there, touching and tasting, and fumbling with his zipper. When he finally drops his drawers and stands behind you, reach between your thighs and grab him. Stroke him. Massage his balls while you rub his penis against your clitoris and when its all so perfectly, deliciously wet slide him in. It's a sensation, and a vision, that will burn itself into his memory.

Now get your motor running! This time, *you* do the work. Buck your hips up and down, in and out. Big grinding circles are especially effective. And while it's been your task to seduce him today, guess what? Sex researchers say this particular angle is ideal for strong stimulation of your G-spot — so ride 'em, cowgirl! Enjoy the scenery, along with the sensual rush. And be sure to say hi to the neighbors if they pass by your window....*Yoo hoo!*

As a practical matter, you'll probably want to keep the drapes close by or the blinds partially drawn behind your torso. Then again, you can always play it safe and do it at night. And if there's any final piece of advice I can offer, it's this....

If you've been a bitch to him this week — you better nail your shoes to the floor!

Ingredients

1 Window / 1 Pair of ****-Me Shoes / 1 Sexy Full Skirt / 1 Bare Butt

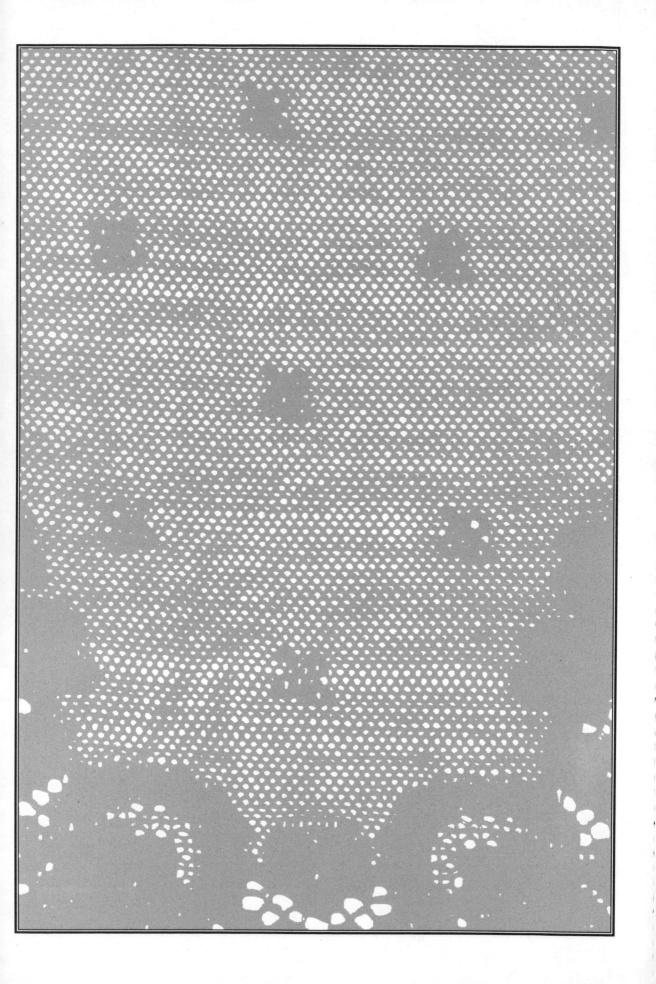

N.º 83

DEN OF INIQUITY

For *Her* Eyes Only

RED HOT MONOGAMY
Patrick T. Hunt M.D.

Make your lover feel special!!! It's the ultimate aphrodisiac. This is what women and men want more than anything. Everything that follows is, in one way or another, tied in to making the person you love feel wanted, needed, sexy, and desirable. How you make a person feel when they're around you is the key.

And at the end of the day, be enthusiastic about being reunited with your lover. Our bloodhound, Henry, jumps up and down, tail wagging, barking, licking, and drooling all over me. And he does this EVERY time I come home.

HOT MONOGAMY
Dr. Patricia Love and Jo Robinson

When people think about spicing up their love lives, they usually think about trying novel lovemaking positions or making love in unusual places. There's an even more basic way to add variety your lovemaking, and this is to vary the amount of time and effort you put into your sexual encounters. Most couples settle rather quickly into one style of lovemaking. Each time they make love, they spend about the same amount of time and energy.

Quickies have a definite place in a love relationship. They can satisfy the needs of the more highly sexed partner, relieve physical tension, and add more spontaneity - especially when the quickie is a stealthy encounter in an unusual place like the kitchen, a walk-in closet, or the backyard.

I firmly believe that the world would be a better place if people had fewer *skeletons* in their closets —

And more *orgasms!*

Well, this week's seduction is a start. And while it's a "quickie," it won't come as a total surprise to your soulmate. He'll have at least several minutes to realize that something really interesting is going on — several minutes of exquisite, delicious, erotic *anticipation* as he follows your trail of clues.

Your trail of footprints, to be more exact. Trace the outline of your shoes onto black construction paper and cut them out. You'll probably need a few dozen pair. Place them at the front door and mark out a path through several rooms. At one point, leave your shoes and continue with prints of your bare feet!

You can really get him crazy by leading him in circles, then up and down stairs. Make tracks outside, around the house, and then back inside again. The final pair of prints should lead right to your closet door.

Inside — it's you! Watch his face light up as he sees you laying on a soft blanket, propped up with lots of pillows, wearing a sexy lavender teddy and a come-hither smile. Grab him and pull him into your lair. Whisper that you've been planning this all day and you *just can't wait to feel him pressed against you....*

Unless you're one of the lucky few, even your biggest closet is a tight fit. This is not a problem — he can stand while you kneel before him and tug his Jockeys down. *Take him in your mouth...Mmmm...* and don't be surprised at the speed with which he responds. He's had sex on his mind since he walked through the door, and the sight of you in sheer lingerie, plus the slightly illicit feel of hiding in a tiny room, plus your brazen aggression equals one very hot and highly aroused man.

Oh, and don't go to too much trouble to clean the closet. Once you've got his attention — *and boy, do you have his attention!* — he'll be more than happy to clean it up for you later.

In fact, I think you might have cured your annual spring cleaning headache. You may not have to lift a finger — except to lay a track of footprints to the attic, the garage, the guest room....

Ingredients

Black Construction Paper, for shoeprints / 1 Sexy Teddy
Tan Construction Paper, for footprints / 1 Cozy Closet

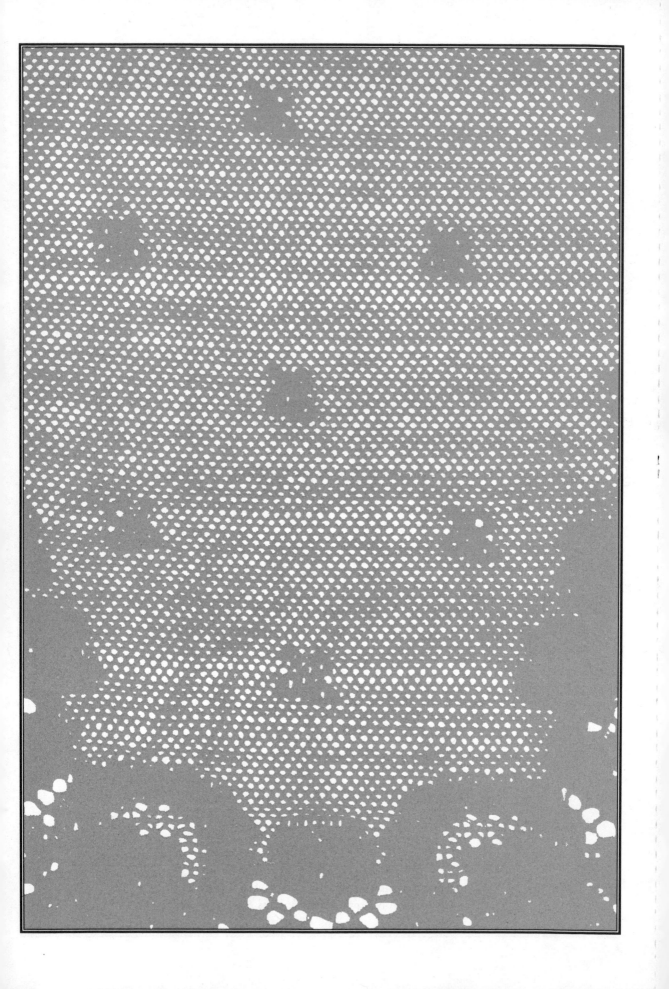

N° 84

EROTIC IMPULSE

For *His* Eyes Only

HOT AND BOTHERED
Wendy Dennis

What do women love in bed?

Well, no big surprises here. Women love a lover with a slow touch. First they a love titllating verbal seduction ("He has to fuck my head before he fucks me," one woman put it), and then they love a gradual physical seduction. What this means is that they love being undressed adoringly, and caressed from the top of their heads to the tips of their toes. On the other hand, sometimes they just love being bent over and plowed, so go figure.

HOT MONOGAMY
Dr. Patricia Love & Jo Robinson

Something that is unique to their relationship is the way that they deliberately use sex as a way to create intimacy. Typically, it works the other way around. Most couples establish a level of emotional intimacy that then leads spontaneously to lovemaking. Cara explained their opposite approach: "If we're not communicating, in a major way, if we're at odds about money, for example, which can be a major issue, then this chasm grows. We've found that we can use intercourse to forge a connection for us, sex can be the truest form of communication."

Thomas added, "To make love this way, you have to get rid of the mental idea that you have to feel a certain way, be turned on, feel close, in order to have sex. You don't. You can just decide to do it. For us, closeness can come as a result of having sex."

"We've invented a name for this kind of lovemaking," said Cara. "We call it a marital. It doesn't require that we have orgasm, and it's not necessarily very romantic. It can be almost mechanical. But it reestablishes that physical, sexual connection between us, which makes all our other problems seem more manageable."

*A*n unsolicited and spontaneous "quickie" can add spark to any relationship. This week, you're going to catch her completely by surprise, and add some extra excitement by *boinking against the clock!*

Of course, you don't want to just, um, come out of the blue, so to speak. So flirt with her throughout the day. Smile and tell her she's gorgeous. Brush up against her when you pass by. Fix her a drink, and deliver it with a kiss. She may not be thinking about sex, exactly, but she'll certainly be in a good mood when you spring your seductive surprise.

Tell her you have something in your eye and need help to get it out. Call her into the bathroom, close the door — and hold up a kitchen timer. Give her a wicked grin as you crank it up to five minutes, and explain that it's all the time you have for some fun and games.

You can sit her on the edge of the sink, lay down in the bathtub, or pile some towels on the floor. My personal favorite? Ask her to lean over the vanity, bare bottom exposed. Rear entry means you can't hug or kiss, but your fingers have easy access to her clitoris, and *golly gee*, that is one *grrreat* view in the mirror!

When the timer sounds off, all activity must cease. If an orgasm doesn't happen within that time limit, well, at least you'll be primed and ready for your lovemaking later in the evening.

And by the way — there's no rule that says *she* can't twist the knob on your timer.

On your mark.... Get set.... GO!

Ingredients

1 Kitchen Timer / 1 Hot Woman
1 Bathroom / 300 Hot Seconds

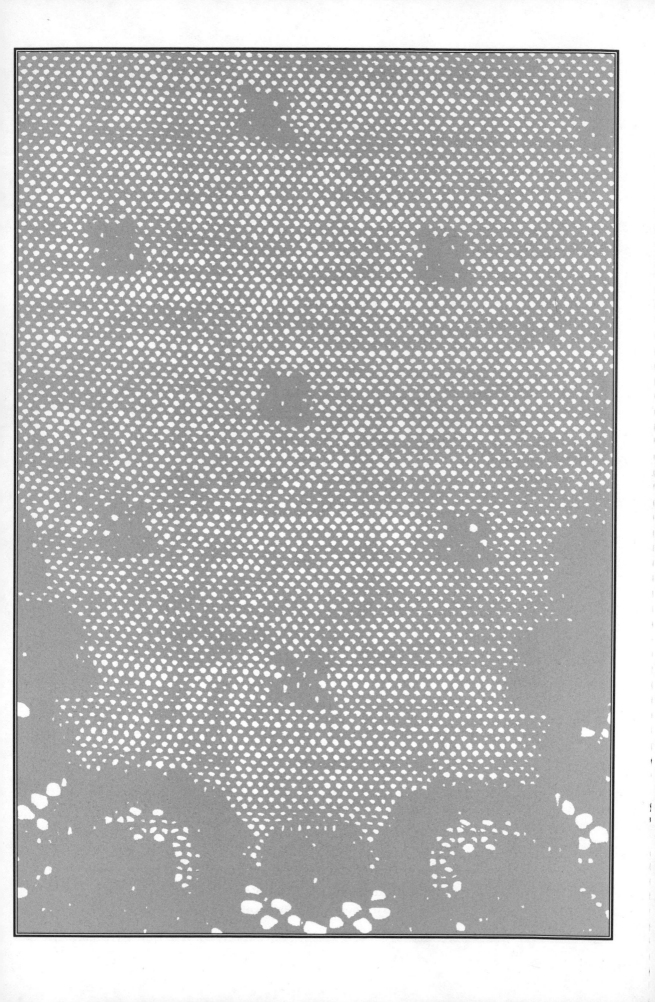

N° 85

HOT LUNCH

For *Her* Eyes Only

$$

HOT AND BOTHERED
Wendy Dennis

One of the best ways couples have found to inject a sexual thrill into long-term relationships is to treat the encounter as an affair. Here's my favorite success story. He had always dreamed of a nooner. For his fortieth birthday, she asked his secretary to clear his afternoon and she picked him up at the office at twelve. Then she drove him to a tacky motel, where she unpacked a little "whore's kit" of bubble bath, a couple of joints, and various jellies, unguents and motorized devices. After an extended bubble bath a' deux, they leapt on the waterbed and prepared to indulge, at which point he turned to her with a leering look and murmured sweetly, "Okay, honey, let's put whitecaps on this sucker!"

THE NEW MALE SEXUALITY
Bernie Zilbergeld, Ph.D.

Anticipating. This is related to romancing but not exactly the same. Some couples are very creative. They know how to use the mind to keep erotic feeling alive. I think of a number of couples who've told me when one of them gets turned on at work, that one will call the other one and make a date for later on. Usually both parties spend a lot of the rest of the day anticipating what will happen after work and getting themselves into a very sexy state of mind.

*B*reakfast may be the most important meal of the day, but after this seduction, it's lunch that will be the most eagerly anticipated!

Send him off to work with a *time-delay tease* — a small, gift wrapped package that he is not to open until one hour before lunch time. And tell him to plan for some extended time away from work today, if possible. You'll be taking him out to eat this afternoon.

Inside the package is a pair of your prettiest panties and a note:

I might need these later. Better keep them in your pocket.

He's starting to sizzle already! By the time you show up, he will definitely have an appetite. If you can snatch a second of privacy anywhere in his place of business, do it. A quick flip of your skirt will settle any doubts about the kind of lunch you have in mind. *Would you like to know what our specials are today, sir?*

Now it's out to the car and off to the hotel where you've rented a room for the afternoon. If he's not hungry yet, he will certainly need nourishment later, so pack a few sandwiches and drinks. But food comes later. Now — hugs and kisses! He will be unable to resist sliding his hand under your dress. Men are universally fascinated by the idea of a woman's bare bum, barely concealed. Let him touch you. Let him feel how wet you've become just thinking about his unique brand of room service. Pull his fingers to your lips and lick the sweet nectar away. And finally, when your temperature has risen several degrees, when the two of you are positively steaming....

Turn away from him and bend over the bed. Get into the ultimate "quickie" position — skirt up, backside unveiled, panties nowhere to be found. Remind him that he's on his lunch hour, so he better finish his dessert right away. Mmm, delicious! And no calories at all.

If he reminds you of the panties in his pocket, tell him to keep them as a souvenir. Oh, and since the room is already paid for, ask if he's interested in coming back after work.

You'd like to have him for dinner.

— *Ingredients* —

1 Pair of Panties, Gift Wrapped / 1 Private Room / 1 hour / A taste for, um, fast food

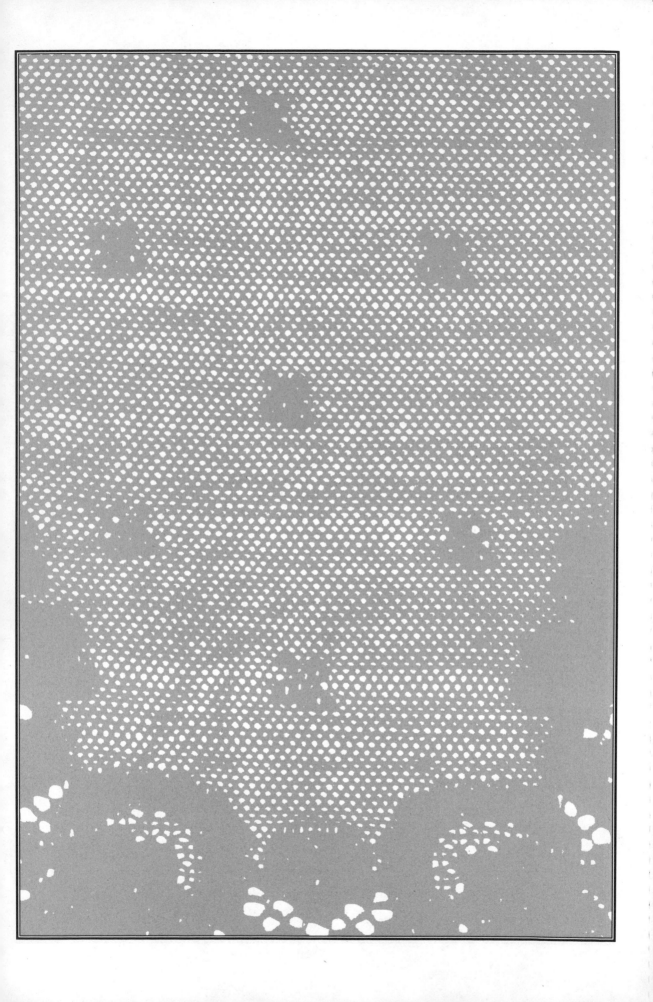

N° 86

FOR EVERY MAN WHO LOVES TO KISS

For *His* Eyes Only

DRIVE YOUR WOMAN WILD IN BED
Staci Keith

Remember high school? We kissed as though our lives depended on it: extra drool and lots of tongue. WILD tongue. In every orifice we could get to. Kissing is the first form of foreplay. Even by itself, it can be wildly exciting, terrifically sexy.

We used to administer "wet-willies" in high school too, remember? That was when you inserted your tongue into her ear in some weird kind of simulated intercourse. Wet-willies, while not always...er, tasteful?...are fun. The trick is, you don't cram your tongue in her ear, just delicately probe its folds. Breathe. It'll give her shivers and make her giggle.

As you're nibbling earlobes and ravishing nipples,
remember to savor the heady perfume of her flesh!

THE NEW JOY OF SEX
Alex Comfort, M.D. D.SC.

If you haven't at least kissed her mouth, shoulders, neck, breasts, armpits, fingers, palms, toes, soles, navel, genitals and earlobes, you haven't really kissed her.

"Jeffie and Maggie, sitting in a tree — K-I-S-S-I-N-G!!!"
The first thing women learn about relationships.

*D*o you know the single biggest complaint women have about sex? *Men rush them.* When a man suddenly leaps into action, with nothing but the Big Bang on his mind, a woman can feel, well…used. It's no wonder so many women lose interest in intercourse.

If you've fallen into that rut — shame on you! This week, you're going to startle her with your kindness and affection…and make her friends incredibly jealous!

Your seduction starts with a kiss. Tomorrow morning, when you might usually say goodbye with a quick peck — take her face in your hands, pull her lips to yours, and give her a long, lingering, full-on-the-mouth kiss. *"Wow! What was that for?!" "Mmm, I just sometimes forget how good you kiss."*

That evening, plant another one on her, the kind you gave her when you first fell in love. Do it the next day, and the next. Best of all — when you're surrounded by people at the mall or grocery store, wrap her in your arms and lay a big one on her. Deeelicious!

Sure, she may blush…but she'll feel like a million bucks. And you will never make a smoother move in your life if you can pull it off in front of a group of her friends. Bring along a small bag of gourmet chocolate-chip cookies. *Hi, sweetie, I got you something at the mall….I know you love these. Hey, take the whole bag; I got enough for everybody!* Another big kiss here — *Mmm, you are the BEST kisser!* — then make your exit. I guarantee you will be the topic of conversation for days to come. You may not be a perfect man, but you are now the most perfect man any of her friends know — and she has you!

The final night of your seduction is spent, you guessed it, kissing. Kiss her hair, her eyelids, her nose. Work all the way down her arms, out to her fingertips. Kiss the palm of her hand, her ribs, and her bellybutton. Soft, caressing kisses; hard, wet kisses. Nips and nibbles and kisses that leave marks. Tell her your plan is to shower her with nothing but kisses, if that's what she wants.

Oh, but she will want more. If "K" is for kissing, "F" is for…

Ingredients

100 Kisses / A Few Kind Words / A Bag of Cookies

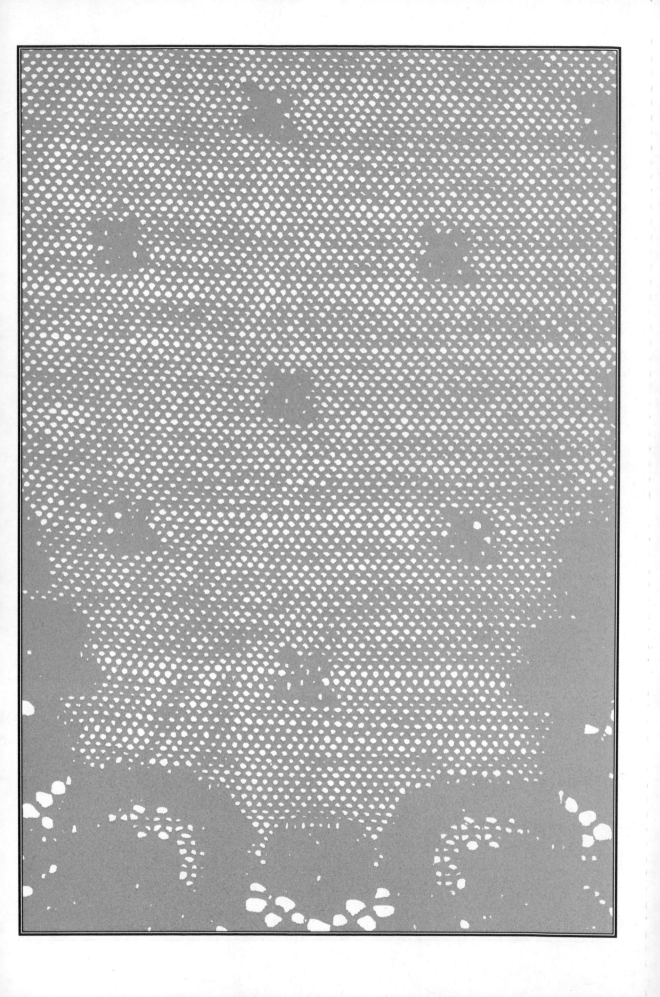

Nº 87

OUTRAGEOUS FOREPLAY

For *Her* Eyes Only

$

MY HOT TALK
Michelle Digiacomo

When the play-acting is creative, there are all manner of sensual experiences that can lead up to sexual intercourse. If you have the talent or inclination, you can make drawings of each other's genitals or bodies, or mold them. There are body paints for lovers, and paint tattoos and designs to try, as well as glitter lotion and body glitter.

Your sexual behavior is an expression of your humanness.

SECRETS OF A MISTRESS
Rose Smith

A common fantasy shared by many men is visualizing their women aggressively seeking their erotic pleasures from them. More than one man interviewed admitted that they enjoy their wives making the moves on them for some good loving. "When I know she wants me," says one man, "it makes sex better for me."

*W*ant to see his eyeballs pop out of his head? Come home one day and casually, accidentally flash a colorful, brand-new *tattoo,* peeking out from the top of your bra.

¡Ay Caramba! He'll be sputtering. He'll be shocked. And he'll be on the floor laughing when he finally realizes it's one of the temporary stick-on kind. *Had you going there, didn't I, sweetie?*

Your new decoration is just a hint of what's to come in this week's seduction. Because when you're both finally relaxed, behind closed doors and away from distractions — *when your private playtime finally arrives* — you're going to bring out a tray filled with stick-ons, big and small.

Here's how the game works. He gets to apply them to you, but he has to put them where he thinks your most, um, sensitive spots are! And to make it even more challenging, he first has to expose each erogenous area, without any help from you.

He's going to love his opportunity to slowly undress you. He'll get a thrill as he prepares your skin for it's artful addition. But here's the real surprise — the tattoos you picked out are the kind that come in a variety of flavors. *Mmmm! Dee-lish!* It may take him a while to figure out which places just make you giggle...and which make you *purr.*

Turnabout's fair play, of course, and so you get to slap a few on him, too. There's this one hitch, though. You're trying to create a work of art on a canvas that keeps *changing size!* Well, I'll leave it to you to work out that small, uh, growing, umm...I mean really big and hard problem.

Don't worry about cleaning up. Baby oil easily removes your temps, and considering their locations, getting them off is pretty much the same as getting you off. The real challenge, though, is finding a way to leave just one lovely and extremely feminine design — a butterfly, for instance — on his back where he can't see it. *Oh, no, honey, I washed them all off....*

Imagine what the guys at the gym will have to say about that!!

Ingredients

2 Bodies / 2 Dozen Temporary, Flavored Tattoos
1 Bottle of Baby Oil / 1 Sly Sense of Humor

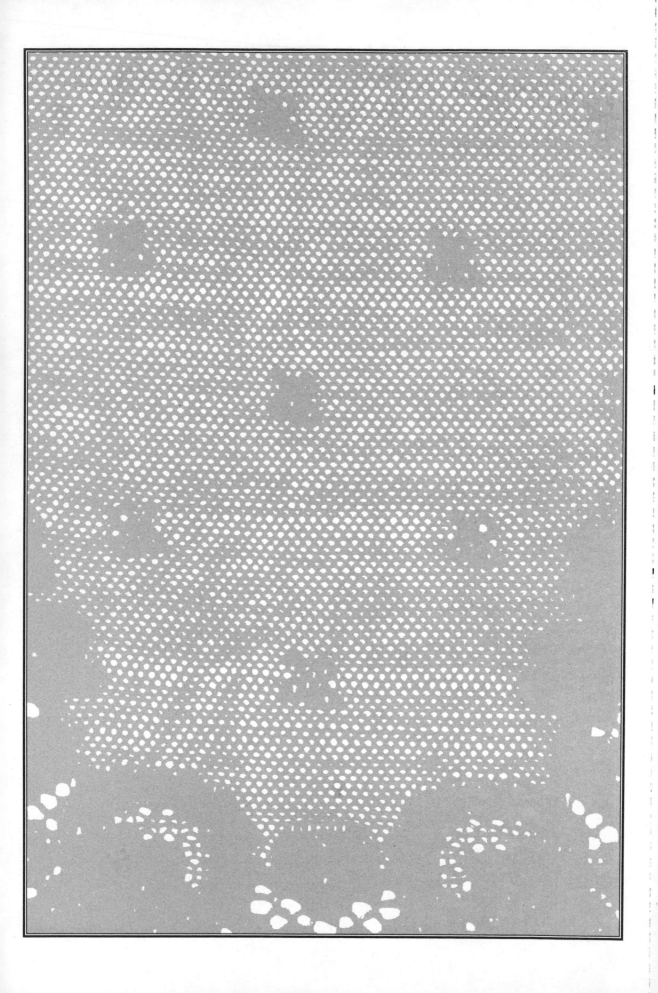

N.º 88

PANDORA'S BOX

For *Her* Eyes Only

WOMEN WHO LOVE SEX
Gina Ogden, Ph. D.

"What about being really creative about flooding the senses? If you're clever, you can eroticize just about anything you find in your bureau drawers, even your broom closet. Have you ever had a silk scarf dragged incredibly slowly across your abdomen or a feather duster flicked up and down your back and buttocks until you thought you'd die?"

Wonderful sex does more than melt both body and soul; it brings power, energy, and deep satisfaction to all aspects of our lives.

HOT MONOGAMY
Dr. Patricia Love and Jo Robinson

To restore the electricity to your sense of touch, you may need to be more experimental than you were years ago. Simply kissing your long-term partner may no longer push you over the edge when repetition and familiarity have dulled your senses. To re-experience that backseat-of-the-car eroticism, you may need to step outside your normal routine and introduce some unusual materials into your lovemaking, such as feathers, fur, silk, warm jets of water, whipped cream, warm towels, even ice.

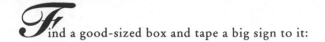ind a good-sized box and tape a big sign to it:

Touch — but don't look.

Actually, your favorite playmate can't do either, because your special box is sealed up for the few days it's on display. By the time your seduction rolls around, the only thing that'll be more aroused than his libido — is his curiosity!

Fill your box with a variety of *soft things* — items with a range of textures and compositions that will feel good against his bare skin. Gather as many of the following as you can: a silk scarf, a handful of cotton balls, a chiffon scarf, a feathered boa, a small stuffed furry animal, a swatch of velvet, a piece of lambs wool or fake fur, a nylon stocking, a baby diaper, a powder puff, a suede sash and a pair of satin panties.

Oh, wow! I'm getting goosebumps just thinking about it.

Tell him that his seduction starts with a hot shower. That'll help him unwind, and more importantly, it will soften up his skin and prepare him for the sensual rush ahead. Help him to dry off and seat him in a comfortable lounge chair, or let him relax against a mound of pillows on the bed. Take out the silk scarf first and caress his face with it. Trail it along the back of his neck, over his chest, and down his legs. Then tie the scarf loosely around his head, covering his eyes.

Ask him to concentrate on the feel of each item as you caress him with it. See how many he can identify without using his hands. Drag the boa down his chest to his toes. Have him open his legs and lightly dust his scrotum with the tips of the feathers. Wrap the nylon stocking around his penis, then slowly — *slowly!* — slide it off. Save the satin undies for the final touch. Pull them snug against his now-throbbing erection as you lightly glide your fingers up and down the length of his shaft. *What a fantasy. He spent his adolescence trying to get into women's panties — now he's getting off on them....*

He'll say you're driving him crazy with lust. But by the time you get to the bottom of Pandora's Box, that won't be much of a drive.

More like a short walk!

--- *Ingredients* ---

1 Box Full of Soft and Silky Items

WILD IN BED TOGETHER
Graham Masterton

I told a close friend of mine that I dressed up like a nurse to turn George on. I think she was pretty shocked, although she tried not to show it. She seemed to think that it was wrong to do something like that to please your husband. But I know for a fact how dull her sex life is; and I also know for a fact that I got just as much satisfaction out of dressing up like that as George did.

I still put on the uniform occasionally...maybe once a month, once every eight weeks. It's more exciting if you don't overdo it. And that's the only time I shave myself, too, so George always knows that he has something extra to look forward to, when I lift up that little short dress."

THE LOVING TOUCH
Dr.Andrew Stanway

Learning something as simple as a white coat can turn your lovemaking into an exciting gag of "doctors and nurses' or 'sex therapist an patient'.

*W*here did people ever get the notion that sex had to be serious all the time? We loved games as children. The best time we have as adults comes when we're playing. And yet some people never enjoy the sheer outrageous *fun* of turning sex into a game.

Tonight, you get to play doctor! You can pick up a little doctor's kit at any toy store; some supermarkets and all drug stores carry latex gloves and K-Y Jelly.

Of course, you can't have an office visit without an appointment. Type up a "reminder card" and mail it right to her office! *Please don't forget your appointment with Doctor Phielgood on _____ at _____ in his office at _____.*

She'll be startled until she realizes it's your handwriting...and your address!

Get a little silly when your patient arrives. Welcome her for her checkup, and make up as much "doctor talk" as you can. Ask her to undress and put on a gown (one of your old dress shirts — backwards & unbuttoned, of course), and make a big production out of snapping on your gloves and opening your medical bag.

On to the examining table...your bed, or a big reclining chair covered by a sheet. You'll find yourself drifting from comic relief into sexual anticipation as you start with a breast exam — one that concentrates on rolling her stiffening nipples between your rubber-encased fingers. Now smear some jelly on your gloves and tell her it's time for her pelvic. She'll know what position to adopt!

She's felt latex and lubricant before, but never with such an *erotic twist*...and when the probe begins, she'll respond like never before. Talk to her. Ask about her sexual response...strictly for professional reasons, of course. Does it feel better *here*...or does she find more stimulation over *there?*

Try to relax, miss; I'm going to push deeply right — now....

Oh, I see you enjoy that when I rub right here; yes, we men of science find that this treatment produces the most interesting reaction in our female patients...

Time to slip her the ol' thermometer, Doc!

Ingredients

1 Toy Doctor's Kit / Malpractice Insurance / 1 Pair of Latex Gloves
K-Y Jelly / A Lollipop — *if* she was a good patient!

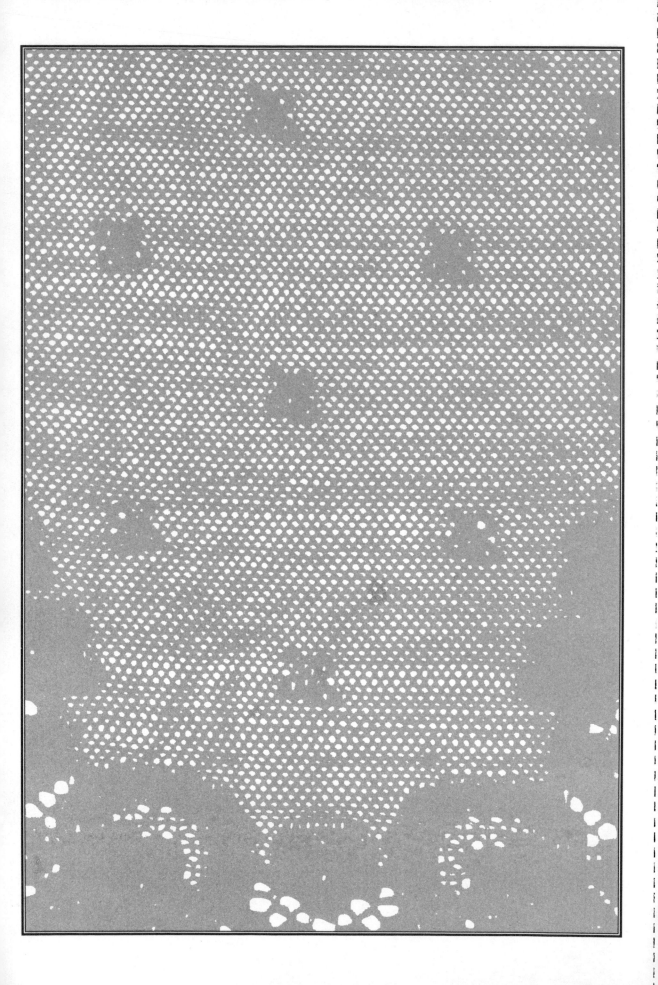

N.º

90

SPECIAL DELIVERY

For *His* Eyes Only

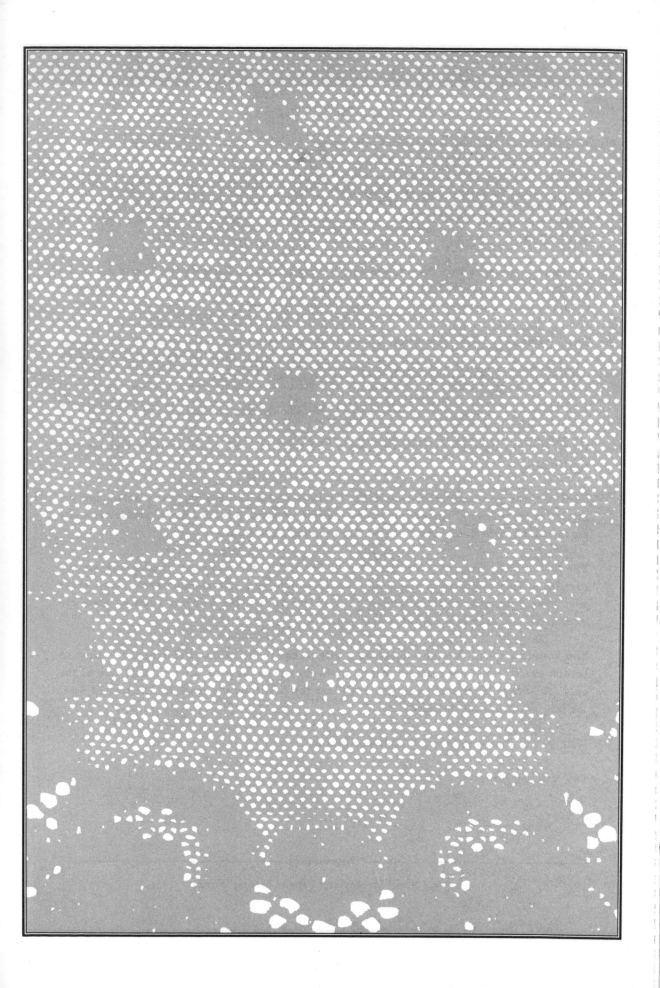

N^o *91*

THE BIG SCORE

For *His* Eyes Only

MAKING LOVE A MAN'S GUIDE
Whit Barry

More than foreplay, more than intercourse, more even than orgasm—when it comes to the ingredients that make up a pleasurable sexual experience, it's what comes afterward that counts the most. This was the conclusion reached by two psychologists who surveyed sex behavior in more than 250 cases, and published their findings in a book called Afterplay: A Key to Intimacy.

Moreover, they found, couples who can sustain intimacy after making love - instead of drifting off to sleep or into those "I've got to get some gas for the car tomorrow" thoughts - are much more likely to find significant emotional rewards in the experience of making love and in their relationships.

THE EROTIC IMPULSE
Edited by David Steinberg

EROTICISM IN WOMEN by Anais Nin

From my personal observation, I would say that woman has not made the separation between love and sensuality which man has made. The two usually are combined in woman; she needs either to love the man she gives herself to or to be loved by him. After lovemaking, she seems to need the assurance that it is love and that the act of sexual possession is part of an exchange which is dictated by love. Men complain that women demand reassurance or expressions of love. The Japanese recognized this need, and in ancient ties it was an absolute rule that after a night of lovemaking, the man had to produce a poem and have it delivered to his love before she awakened. What was this but the linking of lovemaking to love?

I believe women still mind a precipitated departure, a lack of acknowledgment of the ritual which has taken place; they still need the words, the telephone call, the letter, the gestures which make the sensual act a particular one, not anonymous and purely sexual.

*W*hy do men like romance? Well...mostly, it's because women *crave* it! Isn't she always more responsive after a bubble bath by candlelight? Don't you do everything in your power to romance her into a night of love? Well, foreplay doesn't *always* have to come first!

In fact, it's *afterplay* that really makes an evening special for a woman. Just as she needs flowers and sweet talk to get her in the mood, the same treatment can *sustain* the mood after a steamy, sensual encounter. You might want nothing more than a little shut-eye after working up a sweat between the sheets, but not this week! Tonight's seduction begins where most of them only end.

Buy her a rose, one that comes with a small glass water tube sealed over the end so you can hide it under the bed. When the peak of passion has passed — when she's still gasping for air after the shuddering climax you brought her to — don't turn your back on her. Instead, get up out of bed. Light a few candles. Bring her a glass of something cold and sweet to drink. Now climb back under the covers, but before you wrap your arms around her, reach under the bed...and present her with your living gift. *I saw this today and it reminded me of you, somehow. Perfect, and beautiful, and still blossoming into something even more amazing....*

Kiss her ears, her eyes, whisper those sweet nothings. Cuddle, snuggle, hold her and tell her how wonderful she made you feel. Regardless of your physical prowess in the bedroom, you have now made yourself into the greatest lover on earth — one who *nurtures the nurturer.* You're a man who does not take his bedmate for granted, who lets her know how much he appreciates her every move. You are every woman's dream.

Be forewarned, though. Giving up ten minutes of sleep this way may cost you — another hour or two of sleep! Something tells me that's a price you won't mind paying tonight....

Ingredients

1 Peck of Kisses / 1 Bushel of Hugs / 1 Basket of Sweet Talk / 1 Hidden Rose
1 Barrel of Stamina — the night is still young!

THE NEW MALE SEXUALITY
Bernie Zilbergeld, Ph.D.

In some circles, seduction and its synonyms such as lure and entice have bad reputations because it's thought that the woman is being tricked and will be harmed or wronged.

Most women enjoy sex and want to have it in the right circumstances. Interestingly , many of them complain that men know nothing about seduction and enticement. A woman in her twenties whom I interviewed had this to say:

To me, seduction is putting some thought into sex, doing something special and memorable for another. Maybe candles, special foods, bubble bath, or something like that. I like doing such things for a man and I sometimes do, but I haven't met a man yet who does them for me. To them, sex is more like let's get down to business.

Are these women saying they want to be lied to, bullied, and led into harm's way? Of course not. But they are saying they want, at least sometimes, to be led into sex. They want some convincing, some persuasion, some salesmanship. Not the salesmanship common in the selling of cars, but salesmanship of a sweeter, gentler kind.

HOT MONOGAMY
Dr. Patricia Love & Jo Robinson

Another way to indulge your sense of sight is to put more effort into the decoration of your bedroom. When you go to bed tonight, look around the room. Do the colors soothe or excite you? Is the bed welcoming? Do you have mood lightning? The right artwork can help create a romantic or erotic mood, and strategically placed mirrors can give you a whole new perspective on your lovemaking. Buying a new bedspread, sheets, or duvet can both enhance your sensual pleasure and declare your lovemaking a major priority in your life.

The course of true love ne'er did run smooth....

*W*ell, at least one part of your seduction will be as friction-free as possible — the part where she slides between your sheets! And if that's not the very best part, it's pretty darned close.

Every seduction requires a little effort, and for this one, that means doing something most men just hate. You're going to have to go *shopping....* Ugh! But I promise you, it'll be worth every excruciating minute. Why, the very first item on your list will have you visiting the most interesting stores....

You're looking for matching bra and panties in cool, sexy satin. Dig through her dresser if you're not sure of her size.

Next, you're searching for the sexual equivalent of WD-40, that notorious Teflon of the boudoir — *satin sheets.* Get them to match the lingerie, if you can. Sheets on the bed; undies in a gift box.

Ooooooh! Her body will love being kissed with that exquisite, silky touch. *Satin on satin....* It's cold, and slick, like blades on ice, like the Winter Olympics in your bedroom. *And the winner of the Gold Orgasm, representing the United States of America....*

Startle her with an even frostier feeling when you slide your tongue between her thighs. Pop a *mentholated cough drop* in your mouth before you draw her clitoris into your mouth. The vapors will chill her most sensitive skin, and when you pull back and blow a stream of air against her wetness, she'll positively shiver with anticipation. Between the slippery softness of satin and the erotic, icy coolness on your tongue, her climax will not be long delayed.

And if this remarkable trick starts to get widely known, take my advice. Buy stock in cough drops!

Can you imagine the advertising campaign?

It's the sexy, tingly, tasty, frosty, so-you-can-get-your-orgasm medicine!....

Ingredients

Satin Sheets / Satin Lingerie / 1 Mentholated Cough Drop

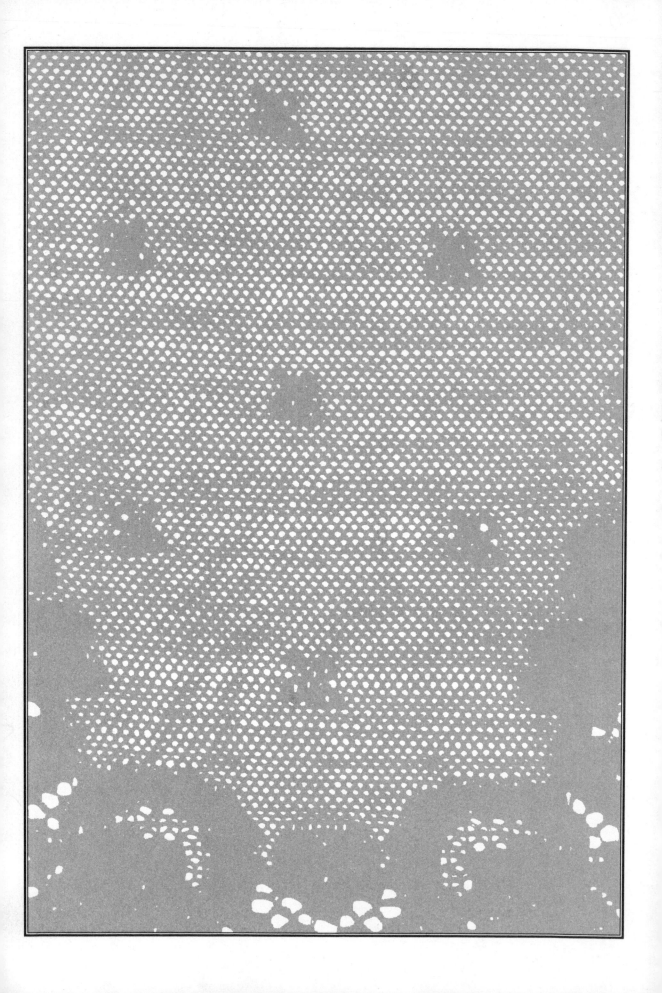

N.º

POINT OF NO RETURN

For *His* Eyes Only

TANTRIC SEX
E.J. Gold and Cybele Gold

"During the course of your ordinary sex, break contact before either of you is able to have an orgasm."

"Immediately withdraw physical contact, quietly get dressed, and do something else together. Anything but sex."

ONE HOUR ORGASM
Dr. Bob Schwartz, Ph.D.

"Peaking" is a technique that is designed to increase your ability to feel. As you are rubbing yourself and begin to feel the sexual pressure or tumescence build up in you, stop rubbing or slow down, or change direction. Especially do this when you are on the verge of an orgasm. As tumescence builds, bring yourself as close to the upper side of that feeling as is possible without going over the top...then let yourself down by stopping, slowing down, changing to a lighter pressure, or changing the direction you are rubbing.

*W*hat power. What discipline. *What an incredible orgasm!!* This is the complete opposite of the quickie. Does that make it a *slowie?* A *longie?* Whatever you choose to call it, the climax you achieve with this technique will be unlike any before.

Now, the timing of your seduction is fairly critical, so get an alarm clock and put it somewhere...unusual. Your sweetie's bound to notice if it's right in the middle of your living room! Set it for an appropriate time, and make sure it's *loud.*

Now you've been following the recipes in this book, so she won't be too surprised when you grab her late in the afternoon and kiss her. Flirt with her...get her into bed and play with her! Touch and stroke and nibble, but don't follow your instinct all the way to orgasm. Bring her to the edge, but before she comes... *why, there's that darned alarm going off!* Now, what could that mean?

It means it's time to get up and go out. *huh?!!* She may be a bit perplexed. Shoot, she may be gasping for air — but, hey, you've got a movie to catch! And your alarm has left you just enough time to get dressed and run to the theater for your feature.

Torture? No, not at all. What you're practicing is a *delayed orgasm.* Oh, your state of arousal doesn't quite go away. You're touching during the show, and when no one's looking, a quick squeeze here and there will be enough to remind her of the real purpose of your evening. More fondling as you get out to your car; by the time you get home you should both be at a slow boil. And here's where you discover the true power of this seduction....

You fooled around for, what, thirty minutes? Drove another thirty minutes; spent a couple of hours in the theater? *You've waited three hours for this.* And your bodies know it! Her hormones have been bubbling; adrenaline's been flooding through your veins. You're both primed and ready. Every cell is now screaming for sweet relief, and when it happens, you'll feel it in your hair. Your knees will come. Your toes will curl, your shoulders shake. You might forget to breath. You will never forget the awesome power of an orgasm postponed.

What movie? This *technique* gets two thumbs up!

───────────── *Ingredients* ─────────────

1 Alarm Clock / 2 Movie Tickets / A Whole Lotta Willpower

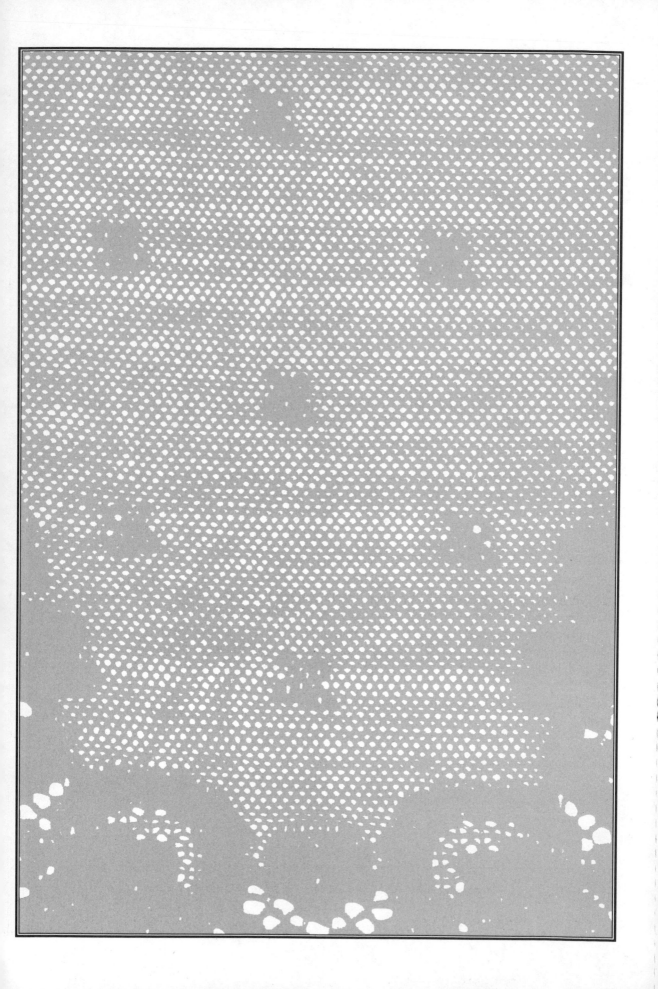

N^o **94**

STEAM HEAT

For *His* Eyes Only

SEX IS LIKE A HOT FUDGE SUNDAE
Pauline Falstrom, Ph. D.

"I want what I want, when I want it!" Don't we all. But even though we can't have everything we want when we want it, we can still have fun. We can take a moment and turn it into a pleasurable experience. We can have the hot fudge, the whipped cream, and the cherry on the top — just not every day. Would it be that good if we could? No, a treat like ice cream is much more satisfying when there is time to anticipate its delight. But once begun, it should be fully savored.

Have you ever watched a child eat an ice cream cone? Her tongue flicks, sucks and licks that ice cream without caring what anyone else thinks. Her eyes are bright and alert, cheeks are flushed and there is a grin between licks. Kind of like sex.

SECRETS OF SIZZLIN' SEX
Cricket Richmond & Ginny Valletti

Creating a Sensual Spa: Hardly anyone has a "House Beautiful" bathroom. Most of us make do with small stalls and tiny tubs which we can't even call our own. Don't, however, let this dampen your seaworthy spirit. With a sprinkling of imagination, transform your bathroom into a sensual spa of sorts. To make it a dreamy, steamy sanctuary, it's not necessary to have a whirlpool, pool man or pool all your resources.

*H*ere's a seduction that's totally hot. I mean really, *really* hot! You're giving your sweetie some sizzlin' sex in a steambath, and if you don't have your own personal sauna, keep reading — I'm going to to tell you how to *make* one!

You're going to need a little help with this seduction. Early in the week, ask her to pick up some ice cream and some cones to scoop it into at the grocery store. Please, no explanations just yet — just make sure it's her favorite flavor.

Come the weekend, get her out for a long, romantic walk or a bike ride. She may want a shower when you get back, but tell her to hold on. You've got something special in mind. She can go ahead and get undressed, maybe wrap herself in a towel — but she can't peek while you make your preparations.

First, create your sauna. Turn the shower to *hot* and keep the shower curtain open. Place several towels on the floor, and then shut the door. While the bathroom is filling up with steam, run to the kitchen and make a couple of ice cream cones. *Okay, hon, get ready! I've got a little surprise for you!*

Walk into the bedroom and present your treat with a flourish. Ask her to hold the cones while you quickly pull your clothes off. Lead her into your sensuous, steamy lovenest; lie down on your mountain of towels. Sure, your dessert's going to melt...and melt fast! Try to keep up by licking the rivulets of cream as they run down over your fingers. But be warned — the flicking of your tongues will only generate more heat!

Let some of your ice cream drop onto her breasts and lick it off. Take turns dripping it onto each other, and keep licking. Suck her sticky fingers; clean each other with your tongues. When you've slurped up the last sweet drops, press your hot, wet body against hers. Her breasts will stick to your chest and her thighs will seal themselves to yours. You've been lapping up cream like kittens, but now you're two cats in heat! Meeee-owww!

When you're passionate session is over, you've got one last thrill coming. Twist the faucet to *cold,* grab her hand and pull her under the stinging spray with you.

It doesn't take a weatherman to predict what'll happen next. Two hot bodies and one cold blast are all you need to make a sexual tornado!

Ingredients

2 Double Dip Ice Cream Cones
1 Bathroom with Steam Heat

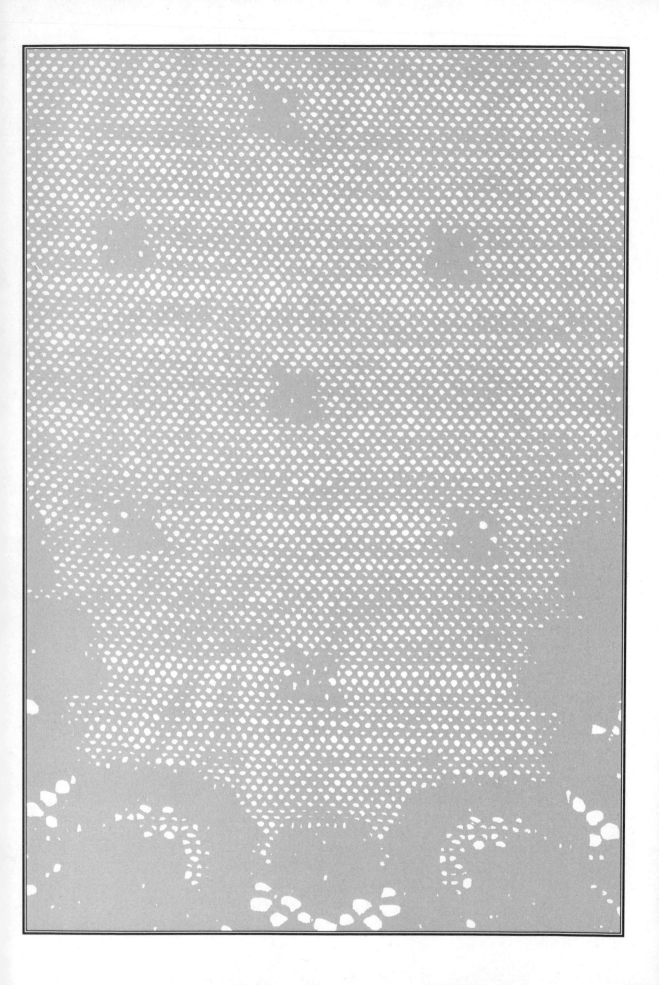

№ 95

THE SEXUAL LEXICON

For *Her* Eyes Only

$

HOT MONOGAMY
Dr. Patricia Love and Jo Robinson

Make room in your life for sex. Many people with low desire enjoy sex a great deal once they're aroused. The problem is that their low libidos don't provide them with much motivation to initiate sex. You may deliberately have to schedule time for lovemaking. Your partner is motivated by spontaneous desire; you may have to rely on mental incentive.

THE GOOD VIBRATIONS GUIDE TO SEX
Cathy Winks and Anne Semens

Most folks are intrigued by the idea of explicit sex talk, but don't know how to begin. Start with writing your own list of dirty words. If you need a little help developing a sexual vocabulary, track down something like The Dictionary of Sexual Slang. Read a variety of erotic material, from the explicit to the euphemistic. Watch an X-rated movie, paying special attention to the dialogue you find arousing. Take a look at which words hold a special sexual charge for you. You may find that you respond better to one type of language over another. For example "I crave the feel of your sweet lips on my ripe, juicy peach" might stir your lust more than "suck on my pussy until I explode." You may find you respond well to certain words or turns of phrase, or just a certain approach: "dirty talk right up close to my ear is the ultimate.

*Y*ou've heard of Strip Poker, of course. Well, get ready for Strip Scrabble™, the game where everybody comes in first place!

Dig up a Scrabble board and pull out enough tiles to spell a special message on his dresser. You've got kids in the house? Then make it something innocuous, along the lines of — *tonight at nine.* Privacy, though, means you can be a bit more risqué!

I wanna **** you.

Do you think that'll get his attention? Yeah, me too. When game time arrives, explain the rules. You each get two tile holders and fourteen tiles. The object is to spell out words relating to *sex* — legitimate or slang, nasty or not. If he makes a word on his turn, you will take off an article of clothing and he gets another turn. If he can't make a word, no one removes an item, but he gets to trade in some or all of his letters and then it's your turn. The prize is fifteen minutes of any erotic act you choose.

Let him go first. Poor thing, he has no idea that you came prepared to cheat. Hey, this is your seduction, after all! You've got twice the amount of clothing he has, but I don't imagine he'll mind all that much. It's such *interesting* clothing...a lacy teddy over a sheer bra and brief panties, stockings and garter, and a slinky slip, all hidden — at first, anyway — under a flowing skirt and blouse. And just in case he's thought of the same strategy, start with high heels and jewelry. Lots of jewelry!

Let the games begin...and let your ladylike manners go. In this game, you only get into trouble if you *don't* swear like a sailor! In seconds those words will lose their power to shock, and will just leave you giggling.

The loser is presumably the one who bares all first. That will be him, of course. But you're a gracious winner. Turn the tables by using your fifteen minutes to satisfy your man, and you'll be guaranteed to get a repeat match out of him.

Perhaps a different game next time. See my next book for rules to Naked Monopoly™ and Go Fish for Panties©. Or my favorite — Strip Clue™! (It was the butler in a G-string with a vibrator!)

Ingredients
---

1 Scrabble Game / 1 Slightly Overdressed Woman
2 Winning Attitudes / 2 bawdy vocabularies

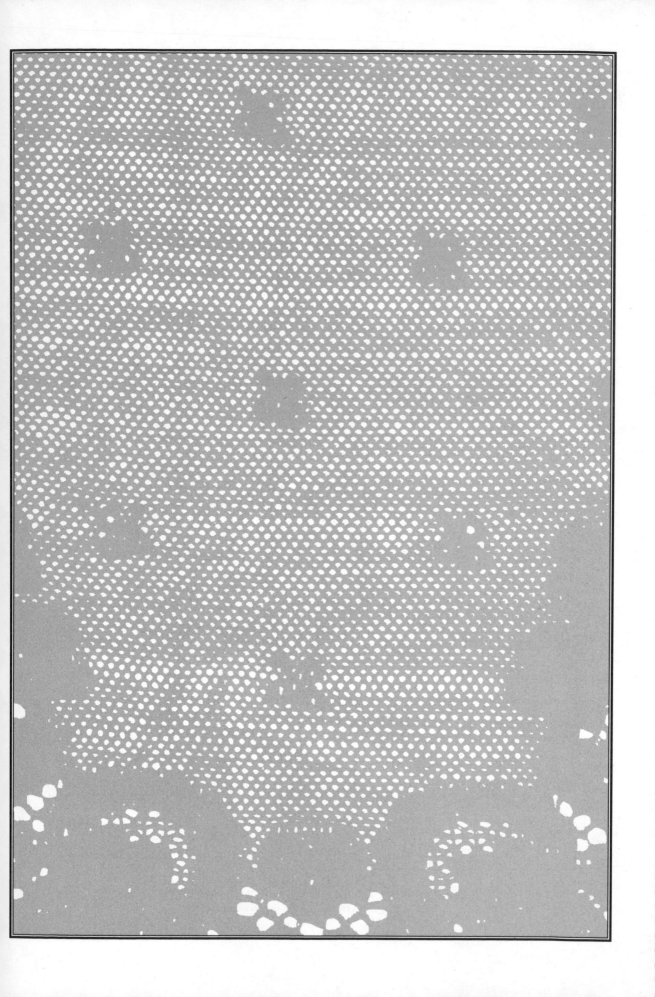

N.º *96*

JUST FOR THE FUN OF IT

For *Her* Eyes Only

$

SECRETS OF SIZZLIN' SEX
Cricket Richmond & Givvy Valletti

If you feel sensuous and believe you're a hot number, there's no doubt you'll portray that image. Sex therapist Judy Korenski aptly states, "Sex appeal comes from loving who you are." No matter how long you've been inside that body of yours, there are goodies galore to learn about having a fabulous, sexy self-image. Fall in love with yourself, then friends and lovers will beat a path to your door. Bernie Siegel, M.D., Wayne Dwyer Ph.D., Louise Hay and numerous renowned educators teach valuable self love lessons.

THE COUPLE'S COMFORT BOOK
Jennifer Louden

When you have spent a lot of time treasuring the unique wonder of your lover's body, turn to your materials. Move very slowly. Immerse your hands in the paint or clay. Rub it between your fingers. Contemplate how many times these same hands have touched your partner. Close your eyes. Lose yourself in the sensuous textures of your materials. Let your hands explore viscerally and non intellectually the link between the materials and your lover's body.

*W*heee! This seduction is *just plain fun!*

This week you're going to rediscover the Michaelangelo in you, the same way you figured it out as a kid — with fingerpaints!

Well, not exactly. *Body paint* is what you need, and you can find it in any adult boutique and even in the novelty shops at most malls. There's one other crucial item for this seduction — ask the man in your life to fetch a tarp....

Huh? A tarp, a big plastic sheet. Also called a painter's dropcloth.

Whaddaya need a tarp for? You'll find out soon enough, sweetie!

How come I gotta geddit? Because it's at the hardware store, silly, and I know how much you love going there. So look at your tools and gadgets and bring me back a tarp! *Well, okay!*

Wait for an evening when you're certain to be alone. Turn off the porch light and take the phone off the hook; you will NOT want to be receiving guests tonight! Spread your big plastic sheet across the bedroom floor, or around the bathroom if it's spacious enough. A single chair or stool — something washable, perhaps from the patio — completes the scene.

Lead your love into your studio, and blindfold him. He'll think he's getting a rubdown. *But don't mention that your "massage oil" is really brightly colored paint!* Strip him down and get creative with your living canvas. A few strokes in the, um, right places can turn your artwork into a *motion* picture! Finally, lead him to the bathroom mirror for the unveiling of your masterpiece.

Think he'll be shocked? You bet he will, and once you've stopped howling with laughter he will certainly want to take his turn at the palette. He may surprise you with his artistic skills. Or maybe not — heck, how often does he get to paint a naked woman?! This isn't high art, and the object isn't really all the touching and stroking and giggling that's going on.

It's the cleanup! What a *pretty* shower it will be. And what a grrreat excuse to take one together!

Ingredients

Body Paints
1 Large Plastic Sheet — Only a few dollars at any hardware store
1 Washable Chair (or one covered with more plastic)

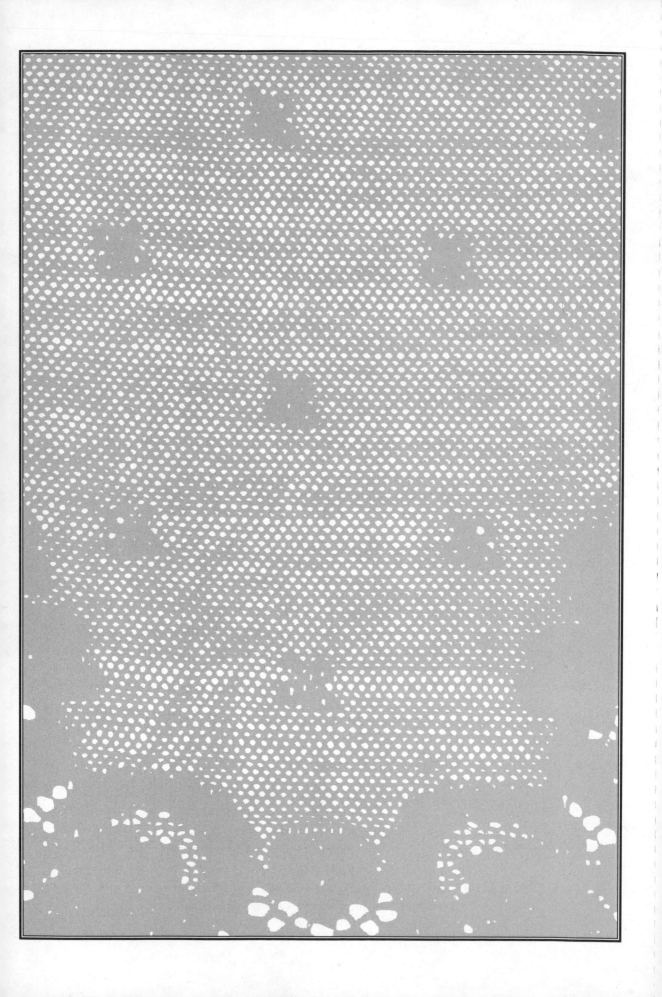

No. 97

THREE THUMBS UP!

For *Her* Eyes Only

$

HOW TO MAKE LOVE TO THE SAME PERSON
FOR THE REST OF YOUR LIVES
Dagmar O'Connor

"We were at a movie," one woman told me, "a ridiculous comedy that neither of us was particularly interested in. And we started to make out. What a wonderful term that is — 'making out.' I'd almost forgotten it. Well, we really went at it hot and heavy. My bra was undone, my hand was on his crotch. At one point we just looked at each other and rushed out to the car and made love right there in the parking lot. It was fantastic! But I guess it's a hard act to follow. We never have.

"Do it 'the first time' again," I told her and her husband. "Go to a movie — the more boring the better — and 'make out.' Go as far as you can. Break all the rules." It is an experiment we all could enjoy.

It is the secretiveness which makes these public games so exciting and which, in a way, can make us feel closer to one another. The secret is ours and no one else's. But, of course, we cannot enjoy the thrill of secretiveness in our own bedrooms at eleven o'clock — there is absolutely nothing "sneaky" about that.

*T*he movie "Basic Instinct" sure caused an uproar when it was released. What a potboiler! It featured evil bisexual murderers, attractive stars, lots of naked bodies — but what was everybody talking about when they left the theater?

The scene where Sharon Stone crossed her legs and showed the police, and the world, that she had neglected her mother's advice to wear clean underwear. Or any underwear! That one brief shot, those few milliseconds of public exposure, made her a household name...and made men across the country break into a sweat.

Yes, there's just something about a woman without bloomers that has universal appeal to the male of the species. I think it has something to do with the idea of *immediate access.*

Well, access is the name of the game in this seduction. You'll start by making a date with your sweetie to go to the movies. A *casual* date — in fact, so casual that he can wear the new sweatpants you'll present to him before the show. Whoops! His keys just fell straight through to the floor — must be a hole in his pocket. *Oh, I'm sorry, honey! I'll fix it when we get back....*

You, of course, craftily slit his pocket open on purpose, and sometime after you're seated — way in the back, naturally — you'll snuggle up close and slide your hand *right through the hole!*

You may not be able to see him blush with the lights out, but believe me, you have definitely caused blood to rush to his cheeks...and, um, other parts. Cup his testicles in your hand, and give them a gentle squeeze as you whisper in his ear. *Guess what? I'm not wearing anything under my skirt....*

Now prove it! Guide his hand under the loose folds of fabric in your lap. Mmm...you've been planning this for *days,* and I'll bet the anticipation has you just a bit wet before he even touches you. Arrange this right — a sweater across your lap, a jacket on his — and no one will ever notice as you stroke and fondle and play with each other through the show. He may not wait for the credits before he hustles you to the parking lot, and home.

I don't care what Siskel & Ebert had to say about it. This movie gets two thumbs up. *Three,* if you count the big one your fingers are wrapped around!

Now if you could only remember what the film was about....

Ingredients
---

1 Pair of Sweatpants with Custom Tailoring / 1 Dark Theater

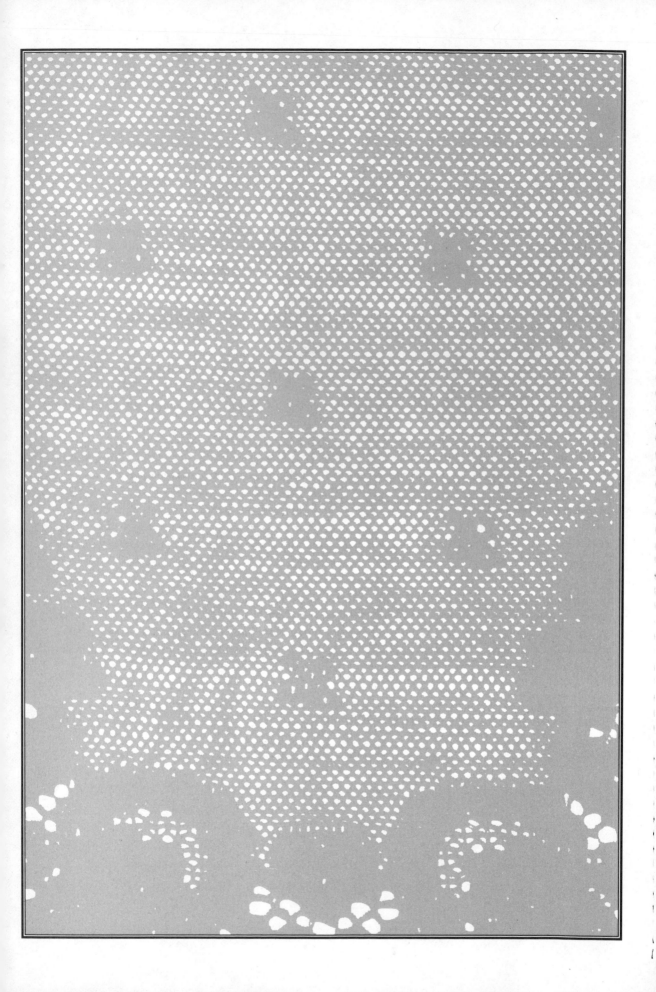

N.º 98

STANDING OVATION

For *His* Eyes Only

THE GOOD VIBRATIONS GUIDE TO SEX
Cathy Winks and Anne Semans

Whether you want to read alone to get yourself "in the mood," recite passages to your lover or re-enact scenes from what you're reading, the printed word has tremendous potential to inspire our sex lives. It can transform everyday sex into a euphoric communion or fuel our fantasies with people, places and positions we might never have dreamed up ourselves.

I recently picked up an Anais Nin erotica book and started to read some while I was alone. It got me rather hot and bothered and I KNEW that I must read this with my husband in bed. It proved to be very scintillating fodder.

THE LOVING TOUCH
Dr. Andrew Stanway

It is often said that men fall in love with their eyes while women fall in love with their ears. According to researchers, this difference between the sexes extends into their attitudes to pornography too.

Men are turned on by sexually explicit pictures, while women prefer the power of the written word. The huge sales of romantic novels, therefore, can easily be seen as the female equivalent of the market for men's girlie magazines.

*B*ookstores are loaded with romance novels. Scores of fresh titles come in every month — and I'll bet you've never looked at one of them. Trust me, the authors aren't offended by your lack of interest! These books cater to women, who are turned on by what they *imagine* as much as men are turned on by what they see.

Well, it's time for you to cross the line. This week, you're feeding her fantasies with steamy and seductive language, the kind that's guaranteed to get her temperature rising.

Look for books of erotic short stories, like "The Delta of Venus" by Anais Nin, or "Slow Hand," edited by Michele Slung. My personal favorites? I absolutely *melt* when I read "Women On Top" and "My Secret Garden," both by Nancy Friday. These are collections of fantasies written by women, for women, and are all available in your local bookstore. Pick one or two, have them gift wrapped, and present the package to your sweetheart early in the week...but tell her not to open it yet!

The night of your seduction, create a suggestive scene in your bedroom. Light some incense and pour some wine. Put on one of those mood tapes...ocean sounds are always a favorite. You'll need one small reading light on your side of the bed, but candles will add a more sensuous warmth to the room.

Now invite her to open her package — it's *storytime.* Start with a kiss, and snuggle close in bed. Pick a chapter and begin to read. Oh, it may take a few minutes, even a few stories before her imagination clicks, but you'll be helping her drift into her reverie. Cup her breast as you read. Gently roll her nipple between your fingers. A chapter or fantasy later, slip your hand between her legs to see if she's getting as hot as the story. No need to rush! Simply circle her clitoris with your fingertips, spreading her own juices as you do. The soft, constant stimulation will send her libido soaring with her imagination.

Follow the story. At the mention of penetration, *thrust* your finger into her; let her ride your hand. When our heroine takes a penis into her mouth, so will your love. The book gives the notes — but you're the musician playing a concert with her body.

And like any truly *grrreat* performer — you're going to find yourself taking requests from your fans all the time.

Encore!

Ingredients

1 Book of Erotica / 1 Tape of Nature Sounds / 1 Free Hand / Candles / Incense / Wine

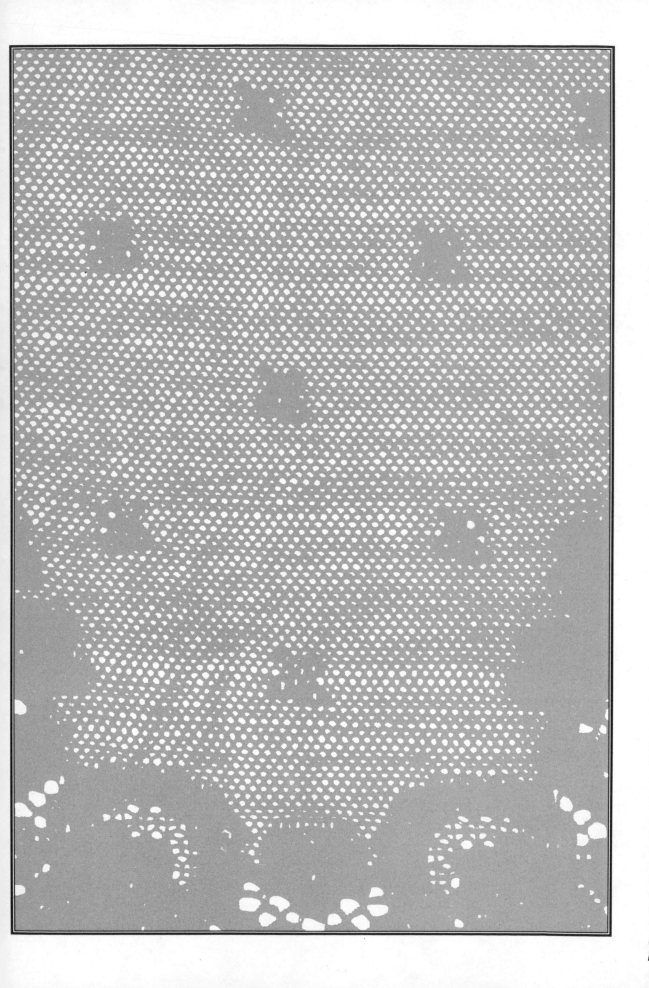

N<u>o</u>

BARELY LEGAL

For *His* Eyes Only

$$$

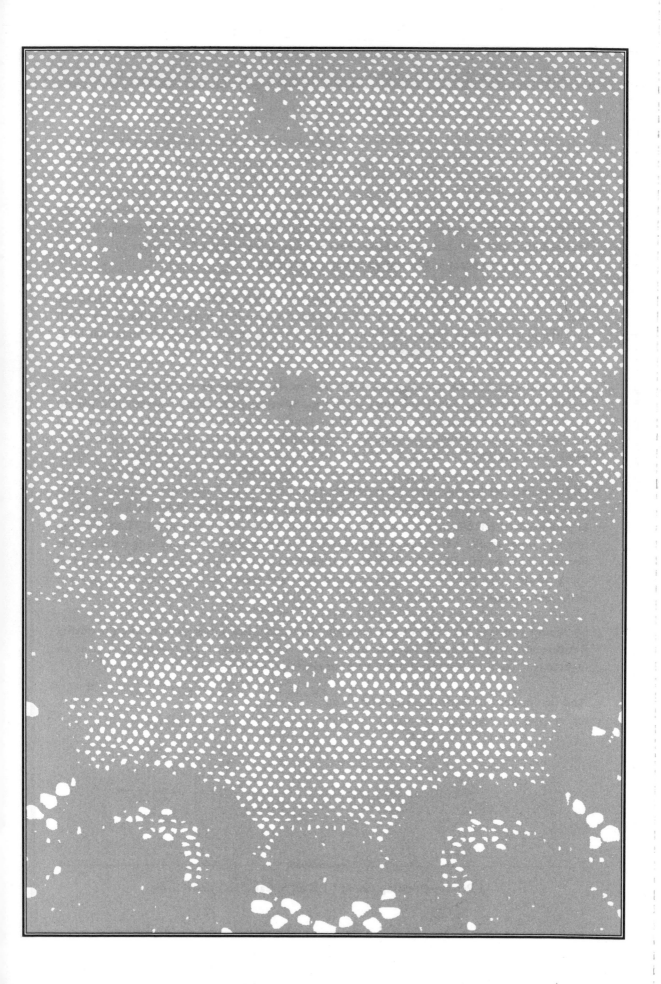

№ **100**

GATES OF HEAVEN

For *Her* Eyes Only

$

THE LITTLE BLACK BOOK OF ANSWERS
Laura Corn

What do you think about when you touch a woman's inner thigh?

"You're thinking about opening those gates, that's what you're thinking about. There's something incredibly erotic about that moment when a woman actually parts her legs for you, actually moves her knees apart. You know you've seduced, you've flirted, you've kissed, you've manipulated, you've touched, you've stroked and you've undressed and you get down to that one secret place that's always hidden. It's the last thing you see on a woman, it's the one thing that's completely hidden all the time, even when she's stark naked, if she's standing up, there's still one magic little spot that you can't get to. It's a trick of nature and you spend all your time trying to get there really, and when she finally, for whatever reason, leans back and pulls her legs up and parts her knees, pulls back the curtain as it were, you're looking on the holy of holies, you're looking on the sanctum sanctorum, it's heaven's gate."

THE NEW JOY OF SEX
Alex Comfort, M.D., D.SC.

Mirrors - These have always been an important part of sexual furniture in any bedroom not wholly devoted to sleeping. They turn love into a viewing occasion without loss of privacy and help the mise-au-point at a practical level. They also provide a turn-on by letting you see yourselves - he can see his own erection and movement without stopping. She may be turned on by seeing her own body, watching herself masturbate, seeing herself bound, or any of the other fantasies one can enact, so that both get viewer as well as participant pleasure.

If you have never made love in front of a big mirror, try it. You really need more than one to enable both to see clearly without having to shift around. The exercise is worth it, not only for voyeur effect but to show you how unridiculous you look making love.

*T*here may be no more magnificent sight in the world than two lovers, wrapped only in each other's arms. When we never make love without the sheets pulled up, it's easy to forget just how beautiful we look through the eyes of our soulmates.

This week, gather together all the mirrors you can find. One large full-length mirror completes the collection. Place them around your bedroom so that you can see your reflection no matter where you look. A few soft, flickering candles will provide all the light you need as you lead your lover into your hall of mirrors.

Move to your favorite music as you caress and kiss each other. You're inside a kaleidoscope of bare bodies; the whirling reflections around you are hypnotic — and erotic. When you move to the bed, make sure you can still see the mirrors! He'll be mesmerized by the sight of you groping and embracing and arousing one another. Once you've got his pulse racing, tell him it's time for the *floor show.*

Prop your mirror against the wall and ask him to sit in front of it. (He'll be more comfortable if he can lean back against the bed for support.) Now climb into his lap and face the mirror. Legs apart, knees up; you're going to show him the most intimate part of you...and you're going to show him what to do with it. Ask him if he likes the view as you start to stroke yourself. Show him what feels good; tell him you always love it when he touches you *right there.* Invite him to do it. And then reach down between your legs and do the same for him.

The picture you're creating is not just intensely erotic — it's empowering. You're in command of your own sexuality. You're becoming totally comfortable in your own skin, and at ease with his. It's an exquisite sensation of freedom. Make him grow firm, rub him against the Gates of Heaven, now parted and swollen, and then — slip him into you. *Watch* yourselves in the mirror as he disappears inside and then returns, gleaming and wet.

He won't last long, poor fella. The visual stimulation alone is overwhelming. And in the future, if you notice him staring dreamily into mirrors, don't worry. He's not getting vain.

He's reminiscing....

Ingredients

1 Large Mirror / Lots of Other Mirrors / Candles / Body oil

DRIVE YOUR WOMAN WILD IN BED
Staci Keith

The secret to being passionate is being completely in the moment. That means not judging what you did the moment before or planning what you should do the next moment. If you, too, want to join the ranks of the legendary lovers, you will open yourself up to the passion within you.

SECRETS OF SEDUCTION
Brenda Venus

Remember, a positive attitude creates more positive sexual energy in a relationship, whereas negative energy can destroy your sexual drive altogether. So if it's lost and you both want it found, work together, communicate and rekindle the romance with all the thoughtful "little things."

LIGHT HIS FIRE
Ellen Kreidman

Although there are many things in life over which we have no control, all of us are capable of creating memories. Remember, when we are old and gray, and all is said and done, we are left with only our memories. And what we remember best are those events that had special meaning - those crazy, out-of-character experiences.

*O*hmigosh — has it really been a year since you started following these recipes? You've had *one hundred* new erotic experiences?

I wonder how many of your friends can say that? Wow. It's kind of a shame you can't share the book with them, because now it's all ripped up! Well, you've had some fun and games, and learned quite a few new tricks along the way. I sincerely hope that all this practice has now become habit — that you've learned to *think* like creative, fun-loving, open-minded, caring, and highly skilled lovers. This week you can put that to the test, because now you get to design your own seductions for each other. Hope you saved all those torn pages! You might need them for reference.

Test day is this Saturday, or your next free day together. You're going to bring each other to a climax three times in three different ways. First thing in the morning, you'll each use your hands to get the other off. For lunch, you'll be, uh, eating at home, if you catch my drift. And at night, well, pick your own favorite variety of intercourse.

Remember your lessons! Mister, you need to *seduce her.* That means talk to her, compliment her, tell her what you like. If she doesn't get enough foreplay out of you by now, you just wasted your money and a year of study!

Madame, you have to *come on to him.* Show some interest. Flirt like crazy! By now, you've got a whole collection of interesting, sexy clothes, props and toys. Come up with three whole different outfits for your graduation exercises.

Oh, I'm just so excited I could pop! You can almost hear the strains of Pomp & Circumstances filling the air here at the Laura Corn Institute of the Erotic Arts. Imagine the emotional scene as we hand out diplomas to our two newest Masters of Seduction. Just picture yourselves standing there in black graduation robes.

Of course, after finishing this course, I'll bet you're both stark naked under those robes! Our graduation ceremonies tend to be a wee bit undignified here at the Institute.

Here's to another year of Grrreat Sex!

Ingredients

Anticipation / Massage Oil / Cake-Timer / Shoebox / String / Leather / Pizza / Passion
Lingerie / Tea / Technique / Straw / Strobelight / Mail / Music / Earjack Splitter
Paintbrush / Camera / VCR / Index-Cards / Movies / Vibrators / Candles / Golf Balls
Showers / Chairs / Steps / Gloves / Notes / Blindfolds / Toys / Maps / Invitations
Restaurants / Cars / And anything else you can think of — you're the experts now!

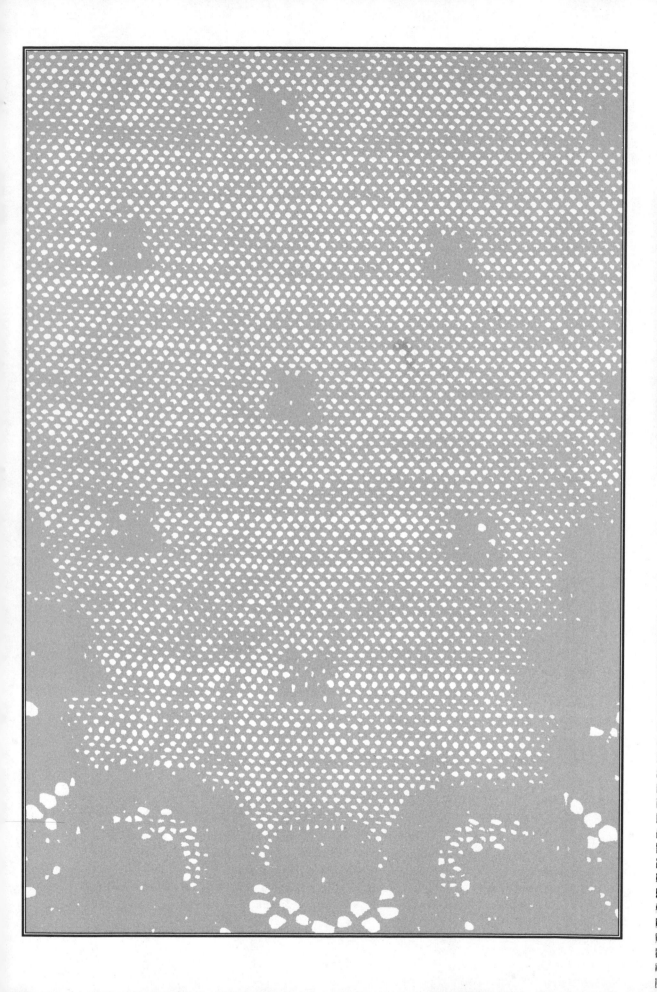

PERMISSIONS AND COPYRIGHT ACKNOWLEDGMENTS

S P E C I A L T Y   S H O P S

For extensive catalogs including many of the
products mentioned in this book,
write or call the following companies:

*For Adult Toys, Joys,
Videos, Books, Massage Oils, ETC:*

Good Vibrations
1210 Valencia Street
San Francisco, Ca. 94110
1-800-289-8423

Eve's Garden
119 W. 57th Street
Suite 420
New York, NY 10019
212-575-8651
1-800 8183837

For Flower Essences:

The Flower Essence Society
P.O. Box 459
Nevada City, Ca. 95959
916-265-9163 or 800-548-0075

For a Unique "Scent For You" and Aromatherapy:

The Carrington Lake House
115 Shoreview Ave.
Pacifica, Ca. 94044
415-330-5482

For Custom Blended Fragrance Oils:

Path of the Heart Fragrances
P.O. Box 3509
West Sedona, Az. 86340
602-282-9243